Navigating the Legal Ethics of Social Media and Technology

2014 Edition
Issued in June 2014

Stuart Teicher

For Customer Assistance Call 1-800-328-4880

© 2014 Thomson Reuters

This publication was created to provide you with accurate and authoritative information concerning the subject matter covered; however, this publication was not necessarily prepared by persons licensed to practice law in a particular jurisdiction. The publisher is not engaged in rendering legal or other professional advice and this publication is not a substitute for the advice of an attorney. If you require legal or other expert advice, you should seek the services of a competent attorney or other professional.

ISBN: 978–0–314–62144–3

Dedication

Dedicated to my wife, who always makes sure I'm headed toward *Tru North*. I love you.

About the Author

Stuart I. Teicher, Esq. is a professional legal educator who focuses on ethics law and writing instruction. A practicing attorney for over two decades, Stuart's career is now dedicated to helping fellow attorneys survive the practice of law and thrive in the profession. Mr. Teicher teaches seminars, provides in-house training to law firms and legal departments, and also gives keynote speeches at conventions and association meetings.

Mr. Teicher helps attorneys get better at what they do (and enjoy the process) through his entertaining and educational CLE seminars. His expertise is in "Technethics," a term Teicher coined that refers to the ethical issues in social networking and other technology. Teicher also speaks about "Practical Ethics"—those lessons hidden in the ethics rules that enhance a lawyer's practice.

Mr. Teicher is a Supreme Court appointee to the New Jersey District Ethics Committee where he investigates and prosecutes grievances filed against attorneys, an adjunct Professor of Law at Rutgers Law School in Camden, New Jersey where he teaches Professional Responsibility and an adjunct Professor at Rutgers University in New Brunswick where he teaches undergraduate writing courses.

Summary of Contents

Chapter 1. Introduction
Chapter 2. Our Fundamental Duties are Changing
Chapter 3. The Ethical Pitfalls in Social Media Use—Confidentiality and Privilege
Chapter 4. The Ethical Pitfalls of Social Media Use—Investigations
Chapter 5. The Ethical Pitfalls in Social Media Use—Advertising
Chapter 6. Solicitations
Chapter 7. The Hazards of Being Helpful
Chapter 8. Other Ethical Issues Created by Technology
Chapter 9. Guidence For The Future

Appendix

Appendix A. The Delaware Lawyers' Rules of Professional Conduct

Index

Table of Contents

CHAPTER 1. INTRODUCTION
§ 1:1 Introduction
§ 1:2 Sources of guidance
§ 1:3 Challenges
§ 1:4 Heightened state of awareness
§ 1:5 Breadth of Rule 8.4

CHAPTER 2. OUR FUNDAMENTAL DUTIES ARE CHANGING
§ 2:1 Introduction
§ 2:2 Rule 1.1 Competence demands that we understand
§ 2:3 Diligence Rule 1.3: Is an affirmative duty to "Check the Chatter" emerging?
§ 2:4 Supervision now encompasses understanding social media
§ 2:5 Professionalism issues

CHAPTER 3. THE ETHICAL PITFALLS IN SOCIAL MEDIA USE—CONFIDENTIALITY AND PRIVILEGE
§ 3:1 Introduction to Confidentiality
§ 3:2 Greater SM use, generally, makes problems for us in the practice
§ 3:3 Our duties are not changed: You post, you reveal, you breach: Commentary to Rule 1.6
§ 3:4 Postings never die
§ 3:5 Assistants and their duty to keep quiet: Rule 5.3
§ 3:6 Privilege

CHAPTER 4. THE ETHICAL PITFALLS OF SOCIAL MEDIA USE—INVESTIGATIONS
§ 4:1 Introduction to investigations
§ 4:2 The limits of a lawyer's ability to obtain social media information, generally
§ 4:3 The limits on investigations in jury situations

CHAPTER 5. THE ETHICAL PITFALLS IN SOCIAL MEDIA USE—ADVERTISING

§ 5:1 Introduction to advertising
§ 5:2 The reason we can advertise
§ 5:3 How the advertising rules are built
§ 5:4 What is an "Advertisement": Profiles
§ 5:5 What is an "Advertisement": Blogs
§ 5:6 Trends regarding other advertisements
§ 5:7 Texts as ads
§ 5:8 The touchy trend: The problem with posts
§ 5:9 The application of Rule 7.1 to advertising
§ 5:10 Other technicalities
§ 5:11 Controlling statements about you that are made by others, and "making" a communication
§ 5:12 Being aware of statements about you that are made by others and "making" a communication
§ 5:13 A specific problem with control and awareness: Lawyer rating sites
§ 5:14 Total lack of control: The inability to force conformance
§ 5:15 Copies of advertisements
§ 5:16 Advertising in the future

CHAPTER 6. SOLICITATIONS

§ 6:1 The theory behind the rule
§ 6:2 How the rule is built
§ 6:3 Direct messages as solicitation
§ 6:4 Texting as solicitation
§ 6:5 Daily-deal websites may also be off limits
§ 6:6 If technology changes, the application of the rule could change
§ 6:7 Beware of shortcuts: Hyperlink disclaimers are not always permitted
§ 6:8 Beware of shortcuts: The specific words in disclaimers matter
§ 6:9 When real-time electronic contact is not a prohibited solicitation

CHAPTER 7. THE HAZARDS OF BEING HELPFUL

§ 7:1 An introduction to being helpful
§ 7:2 Beware of assisting *that guy*
§ 7:3 Inadvertently establishing a lawyer-client relationship

TABLE OF CONTENTS

§ 7:4　Practicing outside our jurisdiction
§ 7:5　Unauthorized practice of law—Assisting laypeople
§ 7:6　Is there a duty to defriend?
§ 7:7　Ignoring the not-so-hidden, hazardous realities of the Internet

CHAPTER 8. OTHER ETHICAL ISSUES CREATED BY TECHNOLOGY

§ 8:1　Introduction to other technology
§ 8:2　Emails, yesterday and today
§ 8:3　Confidentiality and the cloud: The reasonable care standard
§ 8:4　Our fiduciary duty under Rule 1.15
§ 8:5　The extension of our duty to supervise
§ 8:6　The two facets of confidentiality
§ 8:7　The emerging affirmative duty to understand, anticipate, and act
§ 8:8　Is client consent required?
§ 8:9　Generally, no consent is probably required
§ 8:10　Exceptions exist, like sensitive information or express instruction
§ 8:11　Questions to ask
§ 8:12　Texting
§ 8:13　Mega issues with metadata
§ 8:14　What everyone's missing in the virtual law office debate
§ 8:15　The issues with wireless networks
§ 8:16　Implications for smart phones, iPads and other devices

CHAPTER 9. GUIDENCE FOR THE FUTURE

§ 9:1　Introduction
§ 9:2　Ability to assess the level of security afforded by the technology, including how the technology differs from other media use
§ 9:3　Ability to assess the level of security afforded by the technology, including whether reasonable restrictions may be taken when using the technology to increase the level of security
§ 9:4　Ability to assess the level of security afforded by the technology, including limitations on who is permitted to monitor the use of the technology to what extend and on what grounds
§ 9:5　Legal ramifications to third parties of intercepting the information

§ 9:6   The degree of sensitivity of the information
§ 9:7   Possible impact on the client of an inadvertent disclosure of privileged or confidential information or work product, including possible waiver of privileges.
§ 9:8   The urgency of the situation
§ 9:9   Client instructions and circumstances
§ 9:10 The takeaway on the technology permissibility factors

APPENDIX

Appendix A.   The Delaware Lawyers' Rules of Professional Conduct

Index

Chapter 1

Introduction

§ 1:1 Introduction
§ 1:2 Sources of guidance
§ 1:3 Challenges
§ 1:4 Heightened state of awareness
§ 1:5 Breadth of Rule 8.4

> KeyCite®: Cases and other legal materials listed in KeyCite Scope can be researched through the KeyCite service on Westlaw®. Use KeyCite to check citations for form, parallel references, prior and later history, and comprehensive citator information, including citations to other decisions and secondary materials.

§ 1:1 Introduction

Technology raises every lawyer's blood pressure. Some lawyers get excited, others get scared to death, but we all feel something. We all feel the same thing, however, when we think about technology and ethics. That feeling is uneasiness.

The ethical implications of using (or ignoring) technology are vast, and that makes all lawyers hot and bothered. I've spent the past several years identifying and evaluating the ethical issues that lawyers face when using social media[1] and other technologies, both in and out of the practice. Some of the problems are obvious, others should be obvious, and still others are far from obvious. Understanding all issues of "technethics," however, is critical.

§ 1:2 Sources of guidance

The primary source of ethical guidance comes from our jurisdiction's Rules of Professional Conduct, advisory opinions, and case law. Regarding the code, every jurisdic-

---

[Section 1:1]
[1]Sometimes referred to as "SM."

tion obviously has its own set of regulations. There are a lot of similarities among those codes because nearly every state in the Union has adopted some version of the American Bar Association (ABA) Model Rules of Professional Conduct (promulgated in 1983 and amended several times thereafter). It makes most sense, then, to refer to the ABA Model Rules throughout this book, but I can't. The ABA's Model Rules have copyright protection. However, the Delaware Rules of Professional Conduct are virtually identical to the ABA's code and they aren't subject to copyright protection. As a result, all references to "the rules" or quotations from code sections and references to the "ABA Rules," "Model Rules," "ABA-version" or other similar phrase are actually all taken from the Delaware Rules of Professional conduct (unless otherwise noted in a citation).

Another important resource is the commentary to the rules. Unfortunately, many lawyers don't understand the role of the comments and they ignore this rich source of guidance.

What's the difference between the code and commentary? Often the commentary elaborates upon the text of the rule. Also, there are lots of issues that the drafters want to address, but for whatever reason, it's not possible (or feasible) to include in the black letter rule. Sometimes the issue has too many variables and doesn't lend itself to a clear directive; other times there are policy considerations that dictate a more discretionary standard. In those situations the drafters often forgo writing a rule, and instead address the issue in the commentary. Thus, the comments contain insight into the grey area. That's important to note, because we're going to see that the social media lives in the grey area.

It's tough to craft specific standards for a medium that's changing on an almost daily basis. As a result, much of the direction the powers-that-be are providing is contained in the commentary. A short review of the ABA's proposed changes to the ethics rules from 2012 illustrate that perfectly. Much of the technology-related amendments aren't in the back letter rules.[1] For those of us trying to navigate our responsibilities, that presents a difficulty because the

---

[Section 1:2]

[1]Those amendments can be found at http://www.americanbar.org/content/dam/aba/administrative/ethics_2020/2012_hod_annual_meeting_105a_filed_may_2012.authcheckdam.pdf, last checked by the author on February 2, 2014.

commentary is not binding. The Preamble to the rules states in Comment [21] that, ". . . The Comments are intended as guides to interpretation, but the text of each rule is authoritative." That's just the first of several challenges that we'll face in this area of law.

§ 1:3 Challenges

Code can't keep up

When it comes to ethical guidance in the world of social media, the code and commentary are a lawyer's greatest source of guidance, but also the greatest source of heartburn. That's because it's tough for the code to keep up.

Consider how our ethics rules are developed. The ABA creates a panel to review an ethical concern and develop a corresponding rule. That process involves appointing lawyers, having meetings, drafting proposed rules, debating those rules, reviewing them at the committee level, sending them out for public comment, delivering them to the ABA governing body for consideration, then (hopefully) those rules get adopted. It's a necessary, but time consuming process. That's not it, of course, because the ABA's adoption has absolutely no effect on the individual states. In fact, each state needs to go through the same process for the rule to be binding in a jurisdiction. The problem is, by the time the procedure is complete and a rule is adopted, it's likely that the very technology it was designed to address has changed. The pace of technological advancements is far speedier than the rule adoption process. There are two resulting realities.

First, many of the rules end up being far less tailored than we'd like. The drafters can't address particular technologies specifically because it's highly likely that the technology will change and the rule will be irrelevant shortly after publication. As a result, the rules are more unclear than we'd prefer, and they provide guideline-style direction instead of specific permissions and restrictions. This means that we are forced to do a bit more individual interpretive analysis when evaluating ethical considerations in social media and technology use.

Advisory opinions not binding

The second reality is that we rely heavily on advisory opinions and court decisions. Advisory boards and courts aren't subject to the same time-consuming process as rule drafters, so they are able to be more responsive. As a result, we get a decent stream of guidance from across the country in the form of opinions and decisions. Granted, most of those decisions are from foreign jurisdictions, but it's important to understand them.[1] Most of the techethics cases (or hypothetical cases) presented to an advisory board for an opinion address issues of first impressions. They are usually about a topic that hasn't been addressed in many (if any) other jurisdictions. It is therefore likely that the members of the disciplinary board in your state will give considerable weight to those opinions from foreign jurisdictions. At the very least, they'll give serious thought to the analysis provided by the other jurisdiction's tribunal, thus affecting their decision. In fact, almost every opinion you read on the topic references/mentions/evaluates the opinions from other jurisdictions. Thus, it's critical to understand the decisions around the country, if you want to get an accurate sense for the thought process and trends in technethics.

Bear in mind, however, that the advisory opinions are limited in their usefulness. First, oftentimes they're not binding, even in the jurisdiction where they're written (hence the term "advisory" opinion). They're only written to help guide lawyers and they are considered to be persuasive, but they are not the letter of the law. Second, they frequently fail to address the toughest issues clearly. So much of what happens in the ethics world is fact-laden and it's even worse in the area of technethics. The variables are so numerous that it's almost impossible for an opinion to account for every nuance in a given situation. As a result, there are often a lot of gaps in the guidance provided by the advisory opinions.

<u>The buffer</u>

The other major challenge we confront with technethics is an issue that's common in every ethical matter. Consider what happens in the movies . . . and danger is lurking . . . an impending sense of doom. How do you realize, as a viewer, that the danger is actually on the horizon? The music. The dark, ominous music starts softly, then builds to a crescendo until—BAM! The bad thing happens. Well, there is no soundtrack in real life. In real life there aren't any signals that warn us when we're going down a dangerous path, and it's the same thing in the world of attorney ethics. There

---

[Section 1:3]

[1]And by "foreign," I mean states other than our own.

isn't a canary in a coal mine that drops dead when we start to behave in an ethically dangerous manner; rather we need to simply know when we're doing something wrong. We hope that our education and training sets off an internal alarm that causes us to step back when we enter ethically questionable territory. That's a tall order in ordinary situations and it's even more difficult when dealing with social media and other technology.

The danger is acute in the world of technethics because of the buffer. The buffer is that computer—that obstacle that sits between us, and everyone with whom we interact. The buffer desensitizes us from the dangers that lurk and it muffles the soundtrack that should be going off in our head. It causes otherwise ethically responsible lawyers to do some really stupid things.

§ 1:4 Heightened state of awareness

To confront these challenges, lawyers need to develop a heightened state of awareness. If you're a new lawyer, then this state of awareness might be something new. If you're a seasoned lawyer, you might have already developed this state of consciousness, but you probably need to learn how to apply it to the world of technethics. Regardless of the length of time you've been practicing, it's likely that you're already familiar with the relevant rules. In fact, much of what we discuss in this book isn't new material. Most of it is the application of familiar concepts; they're simply presented in a different context. That new context creates some wrinkles in existing rules for sure, but even those new ideas aren't terribly complicated. The tough part is noticing them. To some extent, you need to retrain your mind, just like you did in law school.

When most of us learned about ethical concepts in law school, we had an "aha" moment. I see it most often when I teach new students about conflicts. Learning the rules on conflicts isn't so difficult, but realizing when those rules come into play is a bit tough at first. The "hot spots" in fact patterns don't jump out at you when you're new to the topic, so we review lots of fact patterns. The students need to immerse themselves into various problematic fact patterns until they sensitize themselves to the dangers. After a while, it becomes second nature and they develop that heightened state of awareness.

If you're a seasoned practitioner, you've most likely al-

§ 1:4   NAVIGATING LEGAL ETHICS

ready developed that sense of awareness. But applying that to the world of technethics could be tough because the atmosphere is new. Thus, you'll probably have a bit of an "aha" moment at some point, most likely when you see how an obvious principle applies in a not-so-obvious context. Also, remember that you can't ever let your guard down. Ever.

That state of awareness needs to be active at all times, both in and out of the office. That's because there are ethical pitfalls whenever we use social media, whether professionally or personally. In fact, the very label for this platform—"social" media—is deceiving.

My definition of "social media" is broad and somewhat generic. I see social media as any Internet-based platform that allows users to engage in conversation and the exchange of information. Notice that I didn't refer to any particular type of platform. That's because they are too numerous to mention—a blog, a photo sharing site, and a restaurant review site, for instance—are all part of social media. I also provided a broad definition because the details of the category change constantly. In fact, the tag "social" media isn't relevant anymore, given that the category has been adopted (or should I say "co-opted") by the business world. That "intertwined" nature of social media use creates unique concerns for lawyers. The ethical dangers don't just arise from our use of social media and technology while in the office—they extend to our personal use as well.

§ 1:5 Breadth of Rule 8.4

That's why every lawyer must accept that what we do outside the office matters. I think that's good ethical direction, generally, but particularly in technethics. Our actions when using SM in a social context could give rise to disciplinary issues. I'll direct your attention to one of my favorite parts of the code, Rule 8.4.[1] I call Rule 8.4 "The Stupid Rule." Don't get me wrong, I don't think the rule itself is stupid. I just believe that if you don't know the things in Rule 8.4 are wrong, you're *stupid*. I mean, the rule is titled, "Misconduct." Need I say more? What most people don't realize about the rule, however, is the extent of its reach. Rule 8.4 has several

---

[Section 1:5]

[1]Del. Prof. Conduct R. 8.4.

8.4 http://courts.delaware.gov/rules/DLRPCFebruary2010.pdf, last checked by the author on August 13, 2013.

of the catch-all provisions that are used to prohibit a wide range of conduct, some of which might occur outside the office.

Since we'll refer to this rule several times in this book, let's take a look at it now. Here's the rule, and place close attention to subsections (c) and (d).

Rule 8.4. Misconduct

It is professional misconduct for a lawyer to:

(a) violate or attempt to violate the Rules of Professional Conduct, knowingly assist or induce another to do so or do so through the acts of another;

(b) commit a criminal act that reflects adversely on the lawyer's honesty, trustworthiness or fitness as a lawyer in other respects;

(c) engage in conduct involving dishonesty, fraud, deceit or misrepresentation;

(d) engage in conduct that is prejudicial to the administration of justice;

(e) state or imply an ability to influence improperly a government agency or official or to achieve results by means that violate the Rules of Professional Conduct or other law; or

(f) knowingly assist a judge or judicial officer in conduct that is a violation of applicable rules of judicial conduct or other law

To genuinely understand the rules, you need to review them with a proverbial fine-tooth comb. When the ABA created the Model Rules, every word in the code was carefully vetted. The drafters of the code were meticulous, paying special attention to things like states of mind and modifying words (reasonable, substantial, material, etc.). As we know, that entire process happened again at the state level in every jurisdiction. Sometimes the state officials adopted the Model Rules language, other times the rules were tweaked somewhat. What's certain in all instances, however, is that small details could have large consequences. A perfect illustration of that concept is seen in subsection 8.4(b).

Rule 8.4(b) tells lawyers that it's professional misconduct to, "commit a criminal act that reflects adversely on the lawyer's honesty . . ." Note the particular word chosen—"commit." The rule doesn't say that it's professional misconduct to be "arrested" for a criminal act; it doesn't say that

§ 1:5   NAVIGATING LEGAL ETHICS

you need to be indicted, or charged, or found guilty. Rather, it says that it's a violation of the code to simply commit the criminal act. Several jurisdictions have held that the act of committing the criminal act could give rise to an ethical violation, regardless of what happens in the criminal justice system.[2]

That makes logical sense and it's important for lawyers to understand the line of reasoning because it will help us decipher difficult issues in the world of technethics. The disciplinary system and criminal justice system have different goals. A criminal prosecutor may choose not to file charges against someone, drop charges against a defendant or upgrade/downgrade offenses based upon the goals that are advanced by the criminal justice system. Maybe they want to make a policy statement about criminal law, or take a tough stance to show that the state is serious about punishing offenders. None of that matters to the disciplinary authorities.

The ethics board cares about what the lawyer did, not what criminal punishment they receive (if any). The disciplinary system cares about protecting the public from unscrupulous lawyers.[3] Once the lawyer takes the unscrupulous action—once they commit the criminal act that reflects adversely on their fitness as a lawyer—then that lawyer has done something that conflicts with the with the goals of the disciplinary system.

Some jurisdictions aren't satisfied with the Model Rule's language. Several states have changed Rule 8.4(b) and made it misconduct to commit an "illegal act."[4] Those states appear to have a somewhat broader standard. You could imagine that far more types of conduct would be considered illegal, as opposed to just criminal. Now you can appreciate why it's critical to evaluate each word that's in the code. It's

---

[2]See, Matter of Rigolosi, 107 N.J. 192, 206 (1987), "[a]cquittal of a member of the bar following trial of a criminal indictment is not res judicata in a subsequent disciplinary proceeding based on substantially the same charge or conduct," citing, In re Pennica, 36 N.J. 401, 418 (1962).

[3]The Court website in New Jersey confirms that, "The primary purpose of attorney disciplinary proceedings is to protect the public . . . ." http://www.judiciary.state.nj.us/oae/atty_disc/atty_disc.htm, last checked by the author on February 2, 2014.

[4]See Ohio's Rule 8.4 at http://www.supremecourt.ohio.gov/LegalResources/Rules/ProfConduct/profConductRules.pdf, last checked by the author on January 17, 2014.

8

INTRODUCTION § 1:5

equally important, however, to consider the words that aren't there. For that, let's take a peek at Rule 8.4(c).

Notice that subsection (c) states that it's misconduct for a lawyer to "engage in conduct involving dishonesty, fraud, deceit or misrepresentation." There is no limiting language in that phrase—it doesn't say that we can't engage in those types of conduct "in the office," or "when working on behalf of a client." It states that we can't engage in the prohibited types of conduct, period. That includes our actions both inside and outside of the office and it illustrates the far-reaching nature of the rule. That's why you'll frequently hear me saying, "What we do outside the office matters." Rule 8.4(c) is one of the sections that make that concept a reality.

The far-reaching nature of the rule regarding misconduct is also evident in subsection (d). Rule 8.4(d) proscribes conduct that is "prejudicial to the administration of justice." Imagine how much activity could fit into that phrase. One could argue that such conduct might include anything from using foul language in the courtroom, to being excessively late to a deposition. Some states, like Alaska, realized how broad this section could be and they chose to delete that Model Rules section from their own state code. Take a look at your own code—you may be surprised what you find.

Some of you might find an additional section in Rule 8.4, one that's not in the Model Rules at all. Jurisdictions like Ohio have an additional catch-all type subsection in Rule 8.4 which states, "It is professional misconduct for a lawyer to . . .(h) engage in any other conduct that adversely reflects on the lawyer's fitness to practice law."[5] I guess the drafters were concerned that the Model Rules sections weren't broad enough, so they threw in the dreaded Rule 8.4(h). This section would catch other conduct that slips through the ethical cracks.

I'm a firm believer that these sections of the code are written broadly on purpose. I believe that the drafters want to catch as much bad conduct as possible. Don't get me wrong; I'm not opposed to that. If you do something that's unethical, I think you should get punished. But the breadth of these sections proves an adage that I mention at most of my seminars: If you do something repulsive, the disciplinary

---

[5]http://www.supremecourt.ohio.gov/LegalResources/Rules/ProfConduct/profConductRules.pdf, last checked by the author on August 13, 2013.

§ 1:5   Navigating Legal Ethics

board is going to find a way to get you. And Rule 8.4 is often the rule that they use to do so.

All of these concepts are in play when using social media. The Internet will not protect you from your bad conduct. The buffers won't shield you from ethical prosecution if you violate Rule 8.4, even if that conduct occurs on your own time. Permit me to float a few examples: Stalking is a crime in many states, whether explicitly or as part of a harassment statute. So if you harass that cute/handsome/intriguing paralegal that you met at your adversary's office during a deposition, you're going to have a problem. Well, cyber-stalking has also been criminalized by many states.[6] Thus, if you go after that paralegal on the Internet and you commit the cyber-staking crime, you could have a Rule 8.4(b) problem on your hands.

The same holds true for the other sections of Rule 8.4. If you're on Facebook, lying about who you are or holding yourself out to be something you're not, you might be engaging in a form of misrepresentation or deceit, thereby potentially causing a Rule 8.4(c) problem (we'll talk more about deception and untruths later). And notice, this type of misrepresentation may not be about your practice, but it still might violate the rule. It illustrates a concept that is not new, but has grown in importance with the increased use of social media. That is, there is no longer any distinction between your professional and your private life. Incidentally, you seldom see this in other professions. That's because as lawyers we are held to a higher standard. Our behavior is far more scrutinized than many of our professional peers. It's a time-honored reality about the practice of law, and if you don't like it . . . tough. As Hyman Roth said in the Godfather Part II, "This is the business we've chosen." The fact is, we are always "on."

---

    [6]http://www.ncsl.org/issues-research/telecom/cyberstalking-and-cyber harassment-laws.aspx, last checked by the author on August 13, 2013.

# Chapter 2

Our Fundamental Duties are Changing

§ 2:1 Introduction
§ 2:2 Rule 1.1 Competence demands that we understand
§ 2:3 Diligence Rule 1.3: Is an affirmative duty to "Check the Chatter" emerging?
§ 2:4 Supervision now encompasses understanding social media
§ 2:5 Professionalism issues

> **KeyCite[®]:** Cases and other legal materials listed in KeyCite Scope can be researched through the KeyCite service on Westlaw[®]. Use KeyCite to check citations for form, parallel references, prior and later history, and comprehensive citator information, including citations to other decisions and secondary materials.

§ 2:1 Introduction

I'm not going to spend time explaining the various social media platforms because that's something that most lawyers already understand. If you're not well versed with the topic, at least acquaint yourself with what I call "the big four—Facebook, LinkedIn, blogs and Twitter. There are lots of resources to consult. The key, however, is that you actually consult those resources. That's because the fundamental duty of competence demands that you understand social media.

§ 2:2 Rule 1.1 Competence demands that we understand

Facebook, Twitter, and the like are here to stay. They're not going to be dismantled any time soon and the reality is that they are growing. They have become an integral part of people's daily lives and they are infiltrating the practice as well. In fact, I speak with disciplinary counsel from various jurisdictions across the country and the one common refrain is that every lawyer must understand social media. Every

§ 2:2   NAVIGATING LEGAL ETHICS

ethics counsel I've spoken with agrees that you are not fulfilling your minimum duties of competence under Rule 1.1[1] if you don't understand social media. A reasonable case could be made that it's not just mandatory to understand social media, but technology in general.

Notice how I worded that sentence—I didn't say, it's important to understand "the law about technology." Rather, it's incumbent upon all lawyers to understand the underlying technology itself. That includes social media as well as other things like cloud computing, etc. That directive comes from Rule 1.1, "Competence," which states,

> A lawyer shall provide competent representation to a client. Competent representation requires the legal knowledge, skill, thoroughness and preparation reasonably necessary for the representation.

There are a few phrases in Rule 1.1 that could be used to demonstrate the case for competency. For example, exhibiting the requisite "thoroughness . . . necessary for the representation" means being aware of the platforms that your clients are using and how they can hurt your case. Also, one can't be appropriately "prepared" if they are not aware of the most revolutionary platforms that have transformed society as a whole. And isn't being "cutting edge" inherent in preparation? Finally, if we live in a world where social media is a part of our clients' daily lives and businesses, then I submit that the prevalence of social media has turned it into one of the mandatory "skills" that are reasonably necessary to effectively represent a client in today's world.

Given the infiltration that social media has had on both our lives and the lives of our clients, I think it's a waste of time to make those arguments further. They're a given. But if you need further proof that understanding SM is now mandatory for lawyers, consider one of the recent changes to the rule. In a group of amendments to the Model Rules, the ABA 20/20 Commission added the following critical language to the commentary for Rule 1.1:

> [6] To maintain the requisite knowledge and skill, a lawyer should keep abreast of changes in the law and its practice,

---

[Section 2:2]

[1]Del. Prof. Conduct R. 1.1.
    1.1 http://courts.delaware.gov/rules/DLRPCFebruary2010.pdf. Pages last checked by the author July 25, 2013.

including the benefits and risks associated with relevant technology, engage in continuing study and education and comply with all continuing legal education requirements to which the lawyer is subject (italics added).[2]

Logic dictates that the only way to understand the benefits and risks is to understand the technology itself. It's clear, then, that competence demands that we understand social media and other new technologies.

That doesn't mean that you need to make SM a centerpiece of your life. Heck, you don't even have to be an active participant. What's required, however, is that you have a sophisticated understanding of the medium. Our clients are using it, our associates are using it, and everyone else with whom we come into contact is probably using it as well. You need to be well versed in the systems that they're using. It doesn't even matter if you use social media in the actual practice or not—this isn't about *your* habits. It's about understanding the platforms that your clients are using so that you can provide adequate, relevant counsel.

I do, however, want to mention one way that SM is being used in the practice, because it impacts our ethical duties. Many lawyers are using SM to attract clients and they do so by becoming "brand builders."

Building a brand is Marketing 101—you want the public to associate your name with some word, or product, or service. When you hear "Hertz," you think of rental cars. When you hear "Apple," you think of shiny devices that all the cool kids use (at least that's what I think about). Lawyers are the same way. They want you to hear "personal injury in Minneapolis" and think of Bob Smith . . . they want you to hear "creditor's rights in Phoenix" and think of Mary Jones. They want the public to associate their name/firm with the area of law that they practice—that's building a brand. To reinforce these thoughts, these lawyers create an integrated social media presence.

An integrated social media presence is when a social media user has an active profile on various platforms and uses them in a synchronized way to get their message out to the public. So a lawyer might read a monumental new decision and write a blog post where she provides analysis. Then, she'll send a tweet to all of her followers where she lets them

---

[2]http://www.americanbar.org/content/dam/aba/administrative/ethics_2020/2012_hod_annual_meeting_105a_filed_may_2012.authcheckdam.pdf, last checked by the author February 2, 2014.

§ 2:2   NAVIGATING LEGAL ETHICS

know that she's just posted something on her blog. She might also attach a link to the court's official decision on her Facebook page. Whatever the combination, it's about using these various platforms in an integrated manner so she attracts as much attention as possible.

The brand builders are doing more than just attracting attention to themselves from a marketing perspective. The reputable ones are also providing important, timely information about the area of law they practice. Thus, their blog might not only be visited by potential clients, but also by other lawyers who want to stay up to date on the latest information in that particular practice area. This consistent use of SM by the brand builders, along with some other factors, is changing the game. Social media is morphing from something we might want to understand, to something that we are required to understand. As a result, it's transforming our fundamental duty of "diligence."

§ 2:3 Diligence Rule 1.3: Is an affirmative duty to "Check the Chatter" emerging?

Back in the day, lawyers learned about new case law and other developments in their practice area by checking the bar journal. Some of us seasoned guys and gals still get the actual paper via snail mail, but today many lawyers receive these updates via email. Regardless of the delivery method, some of us read those advance sheets the moment they arrive in the mail and others throw them into a Leaning Tower of Pisa-style stack in the corner of the office (or into the equivalent email folder where virtual dust gathers just as quickly). But even those of us who read the updates as soon as they're received might find ourselves violating the rules, given the realities of social media. Social media is changing the manner and speed that information moves through the practice, and it's redefining the fundamental duty of diligence in the process. Let's illustrate the point with a hypothetical:

> *The court issues an opinion containing a controversial major revision to a federal regulation that alters the tolling period for the statute of limitations for some relevant claim. Three weeks after the opinion is released, the issue arises in your practice-but you don't know about it because you didn't get the bar journal yet— and you blow the statute. Your client's claim is barred. A week later you see that the new regulation is the subject of a major article in the journal and you read the article diligently.*

OUR FUNDAMENTAL DUTIES ARE CHANGING § 2:3

Question: What will you argue at your (gulp) malpractice trial?

You're going to say, "Hey, as soon as I got that bar journal (or received that email), I read it! I fulfilled my duty to be diligent." The Rule appears to back you up. Rule 1.3[1] requires that a lawyer act, ". . . with reasonable diligence and promptness in representing a client," and reading an update notification only a week after its receipt certainly seems prompt. But given the way social media moves information, four weeks might not be considered reasonable anymore.

In fact, that's exactly what plaintiff's counsel is likely to say in response to your defense. "Four weeks?!" he will exclaim. "You didn't hear about that decision for a month after it was released? People were blogging about it and tweeting about it so much that they STOPPED talking about it by the time you read that article." And he's probably right—the brand builders of the world would have been talking about the revised regulation on social media for some time.

The day the new regulation was announced, some brand builder would have posted a link to the red-lined regulations. They would have followed up with a lengthy analysis of the new regulation, showing exactly how it differed from the old language, and what the new regulations meant in practice. That's what brand builders do—they get critical information out very quickly.

Furthermore, the chance of coming across that information has increased exponentially because of the "sharing" aspect of these platforms. As soon as something important is thrown out into the Internet, many users retweet it or otherwise share those posts with their followers. The more important the change, the greater frequency with which it's shared. The more sharing, the greater likelihood you'll see it.

Not only is the information available faster, it's also much easier to obtain. There are a variety of reputable outlets that make this information accessible. The news is replete with reports of how governmental agencies are permitting the distribution of information on social media platforms. For example, recently the SEC approved allowing companies to

---

[Section 2:3]

[1]Del. Prof. Conduct R. 1.3.

1.3 http://courts.delaware.gov/rules/DLRPCFebruary2010.pdf, pages 4–5. Last checked by the author July 25, 2013.

§ 2:3   NAVIGATING LEGAL ETHICS

release information to investors through social media.[2] Plus, there are numerous court systems that have formal Twitter presences.[3] Once the legitimate information disseminators get in the game, you know it's for real.

Going back to our hypothetical, it's likely that a court or bar association would have released something about the revised regulation through social media. Most lawyers know this is happening and they're seeking out the relevant information disseminators in the area of law they practice, and periodically checking what they have to say. It's actually quite easy. And therein lies the danger.

This ease of obtaining the information (and the ability to get it super-quick) is shortening the "lag-time." The lag-time is the amount of time that elapses between the occurrence of an important legal development and the time you're expected to know about that development. The availability of information on social media means that lawyers are expected to know about important changes sooner; thus, the lag-time has been decreased. How much time is a "reasonable" lag time? I don't know, but I feel comfortable saying that it's shorter than it was before social media existed. What concerns me most, however, is the affirmative duty that I believe is about to emerge.

If we know that the information is out there, then shouldn't we actually seek it out? That's what plaintiff's counsel will ultimately argue in the hypothetical above, won't they? "This information was low hanging fruit," he'll say. "It was out there on social media and, as a reasonably diligent lawyer, you should have gone to look for it." Not only should we have known sooner, but we should have made an active attempt to seek the information. Thus, what may be developing is an affirmative duty to check social media. I call it the, "duty to check the chatter."

I don't think it's a giant mental leap to make that argument, given the way social media is used in the practice today. It's one that's likely going to be made in malpractice actions (if it hasn't been already). What this means for lawyers is that the standard of diligence standard is being altered. The lawyer who wants to ensure that they comply

---

[2]http://www.bloomberg.com/news/2013-04-02/sec-approves-social-media-use-for-companies-material-disclosure.html, last checked by the author of August 15, 2013.

[3]The Illinois Court, for example, can be found here: https://twitter.com/illinoiscourts, last checked by the author on February 2, 2014.

16

with Rule 1.3 follows the key bloggers and tweeters in their practice area. The diligent lawyer frequently checks the reputable brand builders of the world and the legitimate information distributors. Lawyers can no longer sit back and wait for critical information to be delivered to us anymore. We need to go out and seek it.

This obligation hasn't been recognized in any jurisdiction of which I'm currently aware, but it's a logical extension of the existing duty. It is especially likely, given the similar development of an affirmative duty in the area of cloud computing and other technologies (to be discussed later).

§ 2:4 Supervision now encompasses understanding social media

I'm sure you now agree that competence and diligence demand that we understand this topic. But, despite what our mommies and daddies told us as children, it's not all about us. The ethics rules regarding supervision demand that we understand these platforms as well. Consider the two key rules: Rule 5.1,[1] which addresses the supervision of lawyers, and Rule 5.3,[2] which addresses the supervision of nonlawyer assistants. These rules mirror each other, but there are a few key differences to watch out for.

Rule 5.1. Responsibilities of partners, managers, and supervisory lawyers

(a) A partner in a law firm, and a lawyer who individually or together with other lawyers possesses comparable managerial authority in a law firm, shall make reasonable efforts to ensure that the firm has in effect measures giving reason-able assurance that all lawyers in the firm conform to the Rules of Professional Conduct.

(b) A lawyer having direct supervisory authority over another lawyer shall make reasonable efforts to ensure that the other lawyer conforms to the Rules of Professional Conduct.

[Section 2:4]

[1]Del. Prof. Conduct R. 5.1.

5.1 http://courts.delaware.gov/rules/DLRPCFebruary2010.pdf. Pages last checked by the author July 25, 2013.

[2]Del. Prof. Conduct R. 5.3.

5.3 http://courts.delaware.gov/rules/DLRPCFebruary2010.pdf. Pages last checked by the author July 25, 2013.

(c) A lawyer shall be responsible for another lawyer's violation of the Rules of Professional Conduct if:

(1) the lawyer orders or, with knowledge of the specific conduct, ratifies the conduct involved; or

(2) the lawyer is a partner or has comparable managerial authority in the law firm in which the other lawyer practices, or has direct supervisory authority over the other lawyer, and knows of the conduct at a time when its consequences can be avoided or mitigated but fails to take reasonable remedial action.

Rule 5.3. Responsibilities regarding non-lawyer assistants

With respect to a nonlawyer employed or retained by or associated with a lawyer:

(a) a partner in a law firm, and a lawyer who individually or together with other lawyers possesses comparable managerial authority in a law firm, shall make reasonable efforts to ensure that the firm has in effect measures giving reasonable assurance that the person's conduct is compatible with the professional obligations of the lawyer;

(b) a lawyer having direct supervisory authority over the nonlawyer shall make reasonable efforts to ensure that the person's conduct is compatible with the professional obligations of the lawyer; and

(c) a lawyer shall be responsible for conduct of such a person that would be a violation of the Rules of Professional Conduct if engaged in by a lawyer if:

(1) the lawyer orders or, with the knowledge of the specific conduct, ratifies the conduct involved; or

(2) the lawyer is a partner or has comparable managerial authority in the law firm in which the person is employed, or has direct supervisory authority over the person, and knows of the conduct at a time when its consequences can be avoided or mitigated but fails to take reasonable remedial action.

Subsection 5.1(a) basically requires that lawyers in a managerial role create appropriate policies that ensure that lawyers are confirming to the rules. The primary difference between this section and its counterpart in subsection 5.3(a) is that nonlawyer assistants don't need to conform to the ethics rules because they're not lawyers. As a result, you can see at the end of subsection 5.3(a) that the slightly different language. Instead of requiring that lawyers conform to the "Rules of Professional Conduct," Rule 5.3(a) insists that the nonlawyer's conduct be, "compatible with the professional obligations of the lawyer." One could argue that such language may actually create a more difficult situation since "professional standards" is more vague and amorphous than "Rules of Professional Conduct." Regardless, there are similar obligations in both instances.

Subsection (b) of both rules imposes duties on lawyers who have direct supervisory responsibilities over other lawyers and nonlawyer personnel. It imposes a direct responsibility for supervision upon lawyers with such authority. However, the subsection that puts a lump in many a lawyer's throat is subsection (c). In both Rules, subsection (c) addresses when we may have vicarious liability for the actions of another lawyer or assistant.

We all know that our associates and nonlawyer assistants are using social media. Some of them are only using it on their own time and yet others are using it in firm-sanctioned blogs or even marketing efforts. Yet some of us remain ignorant, lazy, or otherwise unmotivated to stay abreast of the topic. Well, if we know that they are using the platforms and we know that there are ethical concerns with their use (as you'll see shortly), then how can we claim to be exercising proper supervision if we don't understand the very platforms that these lawyers are using? The answer is, of course, we can't. Thus, just like competence and diligence, the rules on supervision demand that all lawyers understand SM.

Let's hammer this point home with some illustrations. What are you going to say if someone approaches you in the courthouse and says,

> **Colleague**: "Hey Jim, I'm so sorry to hear about that problem you're having with that new paralegal you hired last month."
> **You**: "What problem with that new paralegal?"
> **Colleague**: "Wow, you didn't see that Twitpic he posted with that Judge while they were out at a club last weekend? It's been retweeted a thousand times!"
> **You**: "Ummmm . . . what's a Twitpic?"

Or maybe you'll be the victim of this go-around:

> **Client**: "Hey Lauren, how are you dealing with your partner's blog post?"

§ 2:4   NAVIGATING LEGAL ETHICS

You: "What blog post, what do you mean?"
Client: "You didn't read that racist rant that your associate threw down on his blog, 'This Week in New Jersey Criminal Law?' You don't subscribe to his RSS feed?"
You: "Ummmm . . . what's an RSS feed?"

Right now I know what some of you are thinking. You're thinking, "Ummmm . . . what's an RSS feed?"[3] The bottom line is that you need to understand the platforms that your associates and nonlaw staff are using if you want to be providing adequate supervision.

§ 2:5 Professionalism issues

The fundamentals of ethics aren't only located in the code. The duty to maintain a sense of professionalism has long been considered to be a critical part of proper lawyer behavior, even though those tenets aren't located in the rules. For me, this is a sore spot. That's because—I'll admit it—social media turns me into a teenager. Maybe it's because I find myself interacting with old high school friends, maybe it's because there's so much juvenile humor in the social media world, or maybe it's the buffers that desensitize me and permit my personality to slip back a couple of decades. Or maybe it's a little bit of all of that. Whatever the motivation, the fact remains that I make some bad jokes and I post some dumb comments when I use social media.

There isn't necessarily anything wrong with that. Besides, there are people out there watching me to make sure I don't cross the line. Facebook, for instance, monitors profanity in posts and nudity in photographs. So to a certain extent there is self-policing in the industry. On the other hand, sites like http://www.Tumblr.com allow plenty of inappropriate conduct to be posted on line. The question for lawyers, however, isn't whether your juvenile or risqué posts will be permitted by the social media platform, it's whether they're permitted by the ethics rules and our concepts of professionalism.

Did you notice that added element? I said ethics *and* professionalism. Until now we've talked about the ethics rules and the limits they impose on a lawyer's behavior on social media. But there are concepts of professionalism that apply as well. Nearly every state has a creed, pledge, or a statement issued by a committee on professionalism of some

---
[3]I'm not going to tell you. Go look it up.

sort. Very often those documents consist of aspirational goals— things lawyers should strive to achieve, rather than the restrictive type of regulation found in the ethics rules. Our ethical and professional mandates are different—the text of both vary greatly, as does the impact of failing to comply. Compare the following two items. First, the ethics rule I call "the Stupid Rule," Rule 8.4[1] entitled Misconduct, which states:

> It is professional misconduct for a lawyer to: (c) engage in conduct involving dishonesty, fraud, deceit or misrepresentation . . .

That's pretty restrictive when you consider the fact that there is no language in the rule that limits its application to your professional life. It doesn't say that the offending conduct is not permitted in the course of the practice of law. It says that a layer can't engage in dishonesty, fraud, deceit or misrepresentation *period.* Thus, what we do outside the office matters. Now compare Rule 8.4 to the language in a statement on professionalism. Here is a portion of The Washington State Bar Association Creed of Professionalism[2]

> As an officer of the court, as an advocate and as a lawyer, I will uphold the honor and dignity of the court and of the profession of law. I will strive always to instill and encourage a respectful attitude toward the courts, the litigation process and the legal profession.

The difference in the quality of language is apparent— the ethical rule is more foreboding and more restrictive. The professionalism statement, on the other hand, sounds more duty-bound, loftier. But, similar to Rule 8.4, the professionalism concepts are also telling lawyers that what we do outside the office matters. The statement, "I will uphold the honor and dignity of the . . . profession of law" is not restricted to our actions in our practice. It applies to our entire life, including our social media life.

Thus, just like in our actual life, we need to maintain

[Section 2:5]

[1]Del. Prof. Conduct R. 8.4.
8.4 http://courts.delaware.gov/rules/DLRPCFebruary2010.pdf. Pages last checked by the author July 25, 2013.

[2]http://www.wsba.org/News-and-Events/~/media/Files/Legal%20Community/Committees_Boards_Panels/Professionalism%20Committee/Creed%20of%20Professionalism.ashx, last checked by the author on January 16, 2014.

§ 2:5   Navigating Legal Ethics

professional presence in our virtual lives. The concepts of professionalism demand it. This sounds like an easy task, in theory, but I know that I'm not the only one who reverts to teenage (or otherwise stupid) behavior when using social media. The buffers desensitize us all and we need to remain on guard. We must remember that maintaining the dignity of the profession includes how individual lawyers behave in the courtroom, in the supermarket, and on social media.

Putting this into action in your life isn't very difficult; it just means giving some attention to the matter. Thus, make sure you're careful about the statements you post (avoid profanity), don't post risqué pictures, screen what others say about you—things like that. And if you're a student or a younger lawyer, maintain a professional on line presence. Do that now. I tell my law students that it's never too early to start cleaning up your Facebook page.

Chapter 3

The Ethical Pitfalls in Social Media Use—Confidentiality and Privilege

§ 3:1 Introduction to Confidentiality
§ 3:2 Greater SM use, generally, makes problems for us in the practice
§ 3:3 Our duties are not changed: You post, you reveal, you breach: Commentary to Rule 1.6
§ 3:4 Postings never die
§ 3:5 Assistants and their duty to keep quiet: Rule 5.3
§ 3:6 Privilege

> **KeyCite®:** Cases and other legal materials listed in KeyCite Scope can be researched through the KeyCite service on Westlaw®. Use KeyCite to check citations for form, parallel references, prior and later history, and comprehensive citator information, including citations to other decisions and secondary materials.

§ 3:1 Introduction to Confidentiality

Earlier we discussed how the computer acts as a buffer. It sits between us and everyone with whom we interact. As a result, it desensitizes lawyers from the dangers that exist in social media use. Nowhere is this more implicated than in confidentiality matters. Of course, every time I discuss the issue of confidentiality and social media use in a group, I get eye rolls. "How dumb do you think we are?" attorneys complain. "Don't you think we KNOW to keep our mouths shut?" The answer is yes . . . but. *Yes*, I think lawyers know about confidentiality. *But,* we consistently violate our obligations. Mostly, it's because of the buffers, but it's also because we just don't appreciate some of the dangers. Remember the mantra, "Don't be stupid?" It applies to the issue of confidentiality in a big way.

§ 3:2 Greater SM use, generally, makes problems for us in the practice

Social media as become a fixture in many of our lives. It's

infiltrated every aspect of society and the content that gets posted is all-encompassing. People reveal anything and everything about their lives and work and they post that information constantly. Posting on social media has become such an impulse that a smart therapist could build a practice centered on Facebook addiction. This is a relatively new phenomenon and it's a remarkable societal change.

There was a day when people intensely guarded their privacy. My grandmother was reluctant to reveal anything, even to her closest neighbor (or relatives, but if you knew some of my cousins you'd find that understandable). But the current generation of social media users takes a different approach. The very nature of the medium encourages the exchange of information. In fact, that's the crux of a successful business oriented social media presence—to become a person who provides valuable information to their audience. That's exactly what those brand builders we discussed earlier are all about. As a result, we've become increasingly comfortable with revealing information when using SM platforms.

We're also far more tolerant of other people revealing information about us. Being "tagged" in a photo or having a comment "retweeted" sometimes feels like a badge of honor. In fact, if you're using social media for business purposes, that type of publicity is coveted. There are plenty of companies who get paid big bucks to increase the amount of exposure you get on SM platforms and that type of third-party sharing is one of the metrics they use to determine their success.

Acceptance of social media in our daily lives is also evident in the manner in which we reach out and touch others. For many, SM platforms are becoming the primary and preferred method of communication. Direct messages on Twitter and Facebook are a common way for friends to communicate. Even in the business world, one frequently receives direct messages from a LinkedIn connection instead of an email. Platforms like Facebook are trying to become your communication hub by creating software like "Facebook Home."[1] That software makes Facebook a far more prominent ap-

---

[Section 3:2]

[1]Information about Facebook Home can be retrieved here, https://www.facebook.com/help/402916809804734, last checked July 25, 2013 by the author.

plication on your phone, thus making it more likely that you'll utilize the platform as the primary mode of communication with your contacts.

All of these factors—the prominent role SM plays in our lives, the frequency that users post, the inclination to reveal information about ourselves, the acceptance of information being revealed by others, the use of SM as a primary method of communication—when taken as a whole, is indicative of a paradigm shift regarding one's expectation of privacy. The reality is that we are developing a lower expectation of privacy, society-wide. That's spilling into the practice of law because of the "commingling effect."

Many lawyers are commingling their social media use. One moment a lawyer might post a comment on Facebook about how cute her nephew looks in his baseball uniform, and a few seconds later she'll post a comment on a blog criticizing a recent court ruling (respectfully, of course) and display a link to that comment on her personal Facebook page. This intertwined use of SM is blurring the lines between our personal and professional lives. As a result, the habits we develop in our personal SM use are spilling over into our law practice oriented use. That includes the decreased expectation of privacy and its wreaking havoc for lawyers.

§ 3:3 Our duties are not changed: You post, you reveal, you breach: Commentary to Rule 1.6

Blatant disclosures of client names and information are clear confidentiality violations. While that's easy to understand in theory, problems occur when we consider how things play out in practice. The decreased overall expectation of privacy is warping our ability to (1) notice when we make inappropriate disclosures, and (2) judge whether our purposeful revelations actually constitute a violation of confidentiality. The soundtrack that should be playing loudly in our head is muffled, or even on mute. Throw in the fact that most lawyers only have a basic understanding of Rule 1.6[1] to begin with, and even fewer are familiar with the commentary to the rule, and you can see a bad situation brewing.

[Section 3:3]

[1]Del. Prof. Conduct R. 1.6.

1.6 http://courts.delaware.gov/rules/DLRPCFebruary2010.pdf. Pages last checked by the author July 25, 2013.

The practice is littered with anecdotes of lawyers who've made statements on social media that blatantly violate confidentiality rules. Maybe they tell a story about a client in a blog, or they tweet a picture of a funny piece of evidence that the client dropped off at the office (both of which I've seen firsthand). In many of those situations a review of the rule isn't even necessary because it's a violation of the most basic of confidentiality principles. Why do they do it? When asked afterwards, many of those lawyers simply throw their palms in the air and say sheepishly, "I just wasn't thinking," or "It simply didn't occur to me." But that's not the motivation for all lawyers. It's worth considering the motivation behind some attorneys who purposefully post client information, lest we find ourselves in the same place.

The Activist Lawyer

There are plenty of lawyers who want to use their position to affect some societal change. Some want to advance a social agenda, others want to see a wrong be made right—there is no limit on the activist intentions that might be ascribed to members of the bar. Lawyers who pursue any such cause frequently use social media to spread the word about their issue of choice. That's all well and good, until it violates the ethics rules.

There are a variety of disciplinary cases that consist of lawyers acting as a sort of as web-based vigilante. They don't just advocate their case in a formal court, rather they advocate the case in the court of public opinion by writing lengthy blog posts. In some cases the blog posts are well reasoned, researched tomes which make a sophisticated case for some change to the system. Others are unsupported rants which are motivated by palpable anger. Regardless of the character of the post, the one thing that all activist lawyers need to remember is that they can not reveal confidential information.

I had intended to give some specific examples of these vigilante lawyers in action. They problem is that I'm only able to find the complaints that were filed against these lawyers, not the actual decisions. As a result, I'm forgoing providing the actual names of the (allegedly) offending lawyers, lest I get accused of presenting a skewed version of the facts. What we must acknowledge, however, is that when we become a member of the bar, we accept a curtailed right of free speech.

Rule 1.6 restricts what we can say about our clients and

their cases, even if those revelations are motivated by the most noble of intentions. Of course, in every disciplinary matter where an activist lawyer is being raked through the coals, the offending lawyer's response normally challenges that free speech restriction. More often than not, the ability of the practice to enforce Rule 1.6 is upheld. Vigilantes be warned.

The Defensive Blogger

Some clients get angry at their lawyer (a shock to you, I'm sure). It's common for the most offended among them to run to social media to vent their frustrations. It's almost human nature to want to defend ourselves and some lawyers have done just that on social media sites. The problem is that lawyers who take to the net to defend themselves run the risk of revealing confidential information in the process. A lawyer in Illinois took such steps and found herself on the receiving end of a disciplinary complaint which alleged a violation of Rule 1.6.

Apparently, a client posted a review of the lawyer's services on a legal referral website where he discussed his dissatisfaction with the lawyer's services.[2] The lawyer contacted the client by email and requested that he remove the posting, but the client refused.[3] Sometime after that the website removed the posting from the online client reviews of that lawyer.[4] The client then posted a second negative review.[5] According to the Illinois Attorney Registration and Disciplinary Commission, the lawyer replied to the client's post and revealed confidential information about the case.[6] The ARDC held that the lawyer's reply contained information relating to her representation of the client and exceeded what was necessary to respond to the client's accusations.[7]

These are the dangers of defending ourselves on social media. It doesn't even matter whether the comments we

---

[2] Decision from disciplinary reports and decisions search before the hearing board of the Illinois Attorney Registration and Disciplinary Commission, In the Matter of Betty Tsamis, Commission No. 2013PR00095, at 3 http://www.iardc.org/rd_database/rulesdecisions.html, last checked by the author on January 27, 2014.

[3] Tsamis at 3–4.

[4] Tsamis at 4.

[5] Tsamis at 4.

[6] Tsamis at 4.

[7] Tsamis at 4.

§ 3:3   NAVIGATING LEGAL ETHICS

post are true or not—if they are protected by Rule 1.6, we can't divulge that information.

The Therapy Blogger

The Internet is a place where many people can vent in an effort to get some sense of relief. To a certain extent, that release can be therapeutic. It's a technique that's available to anyone in the social media universe, but it presents problems for lawyers. This was a matter that we see addressed in Illinois once again.

A disciplinary complaint against a lawyer alleged that the lawyer posted derogatory comments about judges.[8] The complaint also alleged that she posted information about her clients in her blog, which information was confidential and would be "embarrassing or detrimental to" the client.[9] The complaint further alleged that even though the lawyer used aliases in the posts, the blog post contained sufficient identifying information such that the lawyer's co-workers would determine the identities of the clients and the judges to which the lawyer referred.[10] The Illinois Supreme Court suspended the lawyer's license and the Supreme Court of Wisconsin imposed reciprocal discipline.[11]

The Wisconsin Court noted that the lawyer blogged for therapeutic reasons. The lawyer claimed that she "began the blog about her thoughts and experiences to help her deal with her stressful situation," but discipline was, nonetheless, imposed.[12] Thus, lawyers need to be careful—even if we are using the Internet for reasons that might ultimately be personally healing—the duty to maintain confidences is not abated.

The Buffers

Yet another reason that sophisticated and otherwise ethically conscious attorneys are making bonehead moves on social media is because of the buffers. They fail to notice

---

[8]Complaint Before the Hearing Board of the Illinois Attorney Registration and Disciplinary Commission, In the Matter of: Kristine Ann Peshek, Commission No. 09CH89, Filed August 25, 2009, at par. 9, 10, 11.

[9]Peshek Complaint at par. 9.

[10]Peshek Complaint at par. 12.

[11]Supreme Court of Wisconsin, In the Matter of Disciplinary Proceedings against Kristine A. Peshek, Case No. 2011AP909-D, Opinion Filed June 24, 2011, at 1.

[12]Wisconsin Peshek Decision at 1 and at 4.

when they make an inappropriate disclosure because the computer desensitizes us to the danger. We don't see the audience, so we don't necessarily realize that there are actual people who will hear our words. When we're in public, with people in our faces, our training kicks in and alarm bells go off in our heads. We make the connection between statements and confidentiality and we are more careful about what we say. But the different atmosphere and context of social media catches many of us off guard. Plus, the atmosphere is enticing.

We read the snarky, cute, attention-getting comments being made by our friends and we want to get in on the action. Our eagerness to join the party dominates our mind and ethical restrictions don't even get considered.

The more difficult situations are those where we are conscious of confidentiality concerns and we make a post that we don't think constitutes a confidentiality problem.

Toward that end, consider the following Facebook posting:[13]

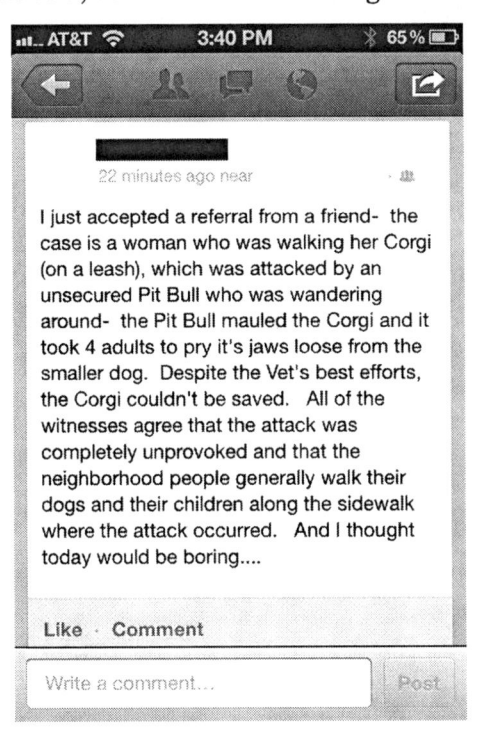

>
> 22 minutes ago near
>
> I just accepted a referral from a friend- the case is a woman who was walking her Corgi (on a leash), which was attacked by an unsecured Pit Bull who was wandering around- the Pit Bull mauled the Corgi and it took 4 adults to pry it's jaws loose from the smaller dog. Despite the Vet's best efforts, the Corgi couldn't be saved. All of the witnesses agree that the attack was completely unprovoked and that the neighborhood people generally walk their dogs and their children along the sidewalk where the attack occurred. And I thought today would be boring....
>
> Like · Comment

---

[13]The screenshot is from my personal phone, sometime in 2012 and 2013.

§ 3:3   NAVIGATING LEGAL ETHICS

The reason for the post is clear; it's a not-so-thinly veiled marketing ploy. There are probably two motivations: The lawyer wants his Facebook audience to know that he has a thriving practice and, more to the point, he does dog bite/personal injury cases. But did he violate the rule? The relevant rule states:

Rule 1.6. Confidentiality of information[14]

(a) A lawyer shall not reveal information relating to the representation of a client unless the client gives informed consent, the disclosure is impliedly authorized in order to carry out the representation, or the disclosure is permitted by paragraph (b).

(b) A lawyer may reveal information relating to the representation of a client to the extent the lawyer reasonably believes necessary:

(1) to prevent reasonably certain death or substantial bodily harm;

(2) to prevent the client from committing a crime or fraud that is reasonably certain to result in substantial injury to the financial interests or property of another and in furtherance of which the client has used or is using the lawyer's ser-vices;

(3) to prevent, mitigate, or rectify substantial injury to the financial interests or property of another that is reasonably certain to result or has resulted from the client's commission of a crime or fraud in furtherance of which the client has used the lawyer's services;

(4) to secure legal advice about the lawyer's compliance with these Rules;

(5) to establish a claim or defense on behalf of the lawyer in a controversy between the lawyer and the client, to establish a defense to a criminal charge or civil claim against the lawyer based upon conduct in which the client was involved, or to respond to allegations in any proceeding concerning the lawyer's representation of the client; or

(6) to comply with other law or a court order.

Rule 1.6(a) prohibits revealing information "relating to the representation of a client." In many jurisdictions, that

---

[14]See Appendix A.

includes revealing the very existence of the lawyer-client relationship itself. When we evaluate the lawyer's comment from the screenshot, however, we need to ask whether the rule was violated. After all, the client wasn't named. But did this lawyer (let's call him Chad, since it sounds nothing like his real name and I'm a child of the 80's, a time when Chad was a cool name) break the rule? The black letter law doesn't give us much direction, but the commentary is key. Comment [4] to Rule 1.6 states,

> Paragraph (a) prohibits a lawyer from revealing information relating to the representation of a client. This prohibition also applies to disclosures by a lawyer that do not in themselves reveal protected information but could reasonably lead to the discovery of such information by a third person. A lawyer's use of a hypothetical to discuss issues relating to the representation is permissible so long as there is no reasonable likelihood that the listener will be able to ascertain the identity of the client or the situation involved.[15]

In order to see if Chad ran afoul of the second sentence in the comment, we must determine whether he revealed enough details such that a reasonable person would be able to figure out who he was talking about. Let's evaluate.

Like most ethics matters, context and the particular facts of the case are key. Here we have a relatively juicy news story—*pit bull-bites-dog* is the type of story that always makes the papers because of the controversy surrounding that breed of dog. Of course, the attractiveness of the story alone isn't dispositive. However, Chad was located in a moderately sized Midwestern city, a locale with a closely-knit legal community and relatively few media outlets. It's the type of place where everyone knows everyone else (or pretty close to it). The reality is that it's far more likely that a reasonable person could determine who Chad was talking about in a smaller media market. Had this occurred in New York City, Chicago, or some other large city maybe we'd feel differently, but context is key. Thus, Chad's actions are quite close to a rule violation.

I used Chad as an example of someone who knowingly posted something on social media and may have made an

---

[15]This commentary is identical to the ABA comment, but it is taken from the Arkansas Rules of Professional Conduct, retrieved from https://courts.arkansas.gov/rules-and-administrative-orders/%5Bcurrent%5D-arkansas-rules-of-professional-conduct, last checked by the author on July 26, 2013.

§ 3:3   NAVIGATING LEGAL ETHICS

ethical gaffe because they were unaware of the nuances of the rules and commentary. Of course, he could have just as easily fallen into the first category—he could have failed to appreciate that he was running into a confidentiality concern at all. The lessons are the same, regardless of how we found ourselves in the confidentiality quandary. Make sure you understand the rules and develop a heightened state of awareness.

§ 3:4 Postings never die

The issue of confidentiality is certainly impacted by the information that we reveal. But it is compounded by the permanence of the medium. Consider the long-term significance of the comments we make on social media. The things we say are memorialized forever. Postings never die. I present the following bits of evidence in support of that assertion.

First, consider the website, http://www.icerocket.com. A review of the site as it exists today reveals that it's a search engine for posts made on various social media sties. Throw in a name, topic, or other keyword that you want to search and it will return links to blogs, Twitter and Facebook where your search term is mentioned. The site encourages you to, "explore billions of social conversations."[1] Seems harmless enough. However, I stumbled upon this site several years ago, when its stated mission was quite different.

When the site first came out, it purported to be creating a history of the Internet. I searched my own name (doesn't everyone?) and that search yielded far more detailed and disturbing results. Prior comments that I made on various social media outlets were produced. Things that I thought were long gone were, in fact, quite easy to gather. Regardless of the site's stated business mission today, the fact remains that the capability of the site to access that type of information appears to exist. In fact, regardless of how they program the search results to be revealed to the user, the site appears to continue to collect a truckload of information from the Internet. It may seem like a benign search engine, but it actually appears to be a massive information depot. And my gut tells me that a short Internet search would reveal other platforms with similar capabilities.

[Section 3:4]

[1] http://www.meltwater.com, which appears to be the website for the company that owns the icerocket website, last checked by the author on September 4, 2013.

It's possible that the icerockets of the world don't give you cause for much concern. If that's the case, then permit me to discuss the next bit of evidence that will prove that "postings never die."

In 2010, the Library of Congress announced that they acquired the Twitter archives.[2] The purpose for doing so is to make the archive accessible to researchers.[3] A review of the Library of Congress updates for this project show that they are quite proud of the deal they struck with Twitter because it will enable them to maintain an ongoing relationship where they can continue to archive the site's content going forward.

Admittedly, that would probably have been seen as a far bigger deal before the whole Edward Snowden information release occurred, but it's still pretty significant. And there's a big reason for run-of-the-mill lawyers to be more concerned about the Library of Congress than the governmental intelligence gathering operations.

The Snowden-revealed governmental data collection is likely to be used in a national security context. Sure, there are potential leak issues and there is the ability for them to use the information for whatever they want. But their general mindset appears to be to keep the information close to the vest. The Library of Congress, however, has a completely different approach. They are purposefully setting the archive up so that it could be used as a research tool by the general population.

The fact that a lawyer's statements on social media will be memorialized forever should concern us for several reasons. For the most part, it's because it greatly increases the chances that our mistakes will be held against us.[4] In the past, poorly worded oral statements were subject to interpretation. People had to remember exactly what was said and that's tough sometimes. The more time passed, the

---

[2]http://blogs.loc.gov/loc/2010/04/how-tweet-it-is-library-acquires-entire-twitter-archive/, last checked by the author on August 27, 2013.

[3]http://blogs.loc.gov/loc/2013/01/update-on-the-twitter-archive-at-the-library-of-congress/, last checked by the author on August 27, 2013.

[4]Disclaimer: The purpose of pointing out these types of things is to present a complete explanation of the ethical realities of these platforms. When I make statements like this I'm always worried that someone will misread it and think that I'm in favor of lawyers getting away with acting badly. I'm not. I believe that lawyers need to be held accountable for their misdeeds.

less reliable a person's memory becomes. As a result, their credibility decreased somewhat. However, preserving our social media statements means that all of our problematic posts are preserved in perfect form. That makes great evidence in a disciplinary matter or malpractice case.

Our clients may also suffer unfortunate consequences from the permanence of social media posts. Errant breaches of confidentiality will exist forever. A damaging comment might not be so damaging at the time it's made, or a problematic post might go unseen for some time. But as time passes, things change. New claims arise, people start to troll the Internet to find damning evidence, and the Library of Congress and icerocket-type search engines are making sure to keep alive those poorly chosen words that our clients might utter.

And don't think you're safe if you simply delete a post. It's great if you or your client realize the error of your ways and go back to eliminate the post. But if another person had already seen the bad statement, they can take a screenshot and save it/share it on their own. You don't think that's likely? Take another look at the pit bull example above—that's a screen shot of my friend's post that I took with my iPhone.

§ 3:5 Assistants and their duty to keep quiet: Rule 5.3

It's not just the lawyers who need to worry about revealing confidential information; it's our staff as well. Consider the following hypothetical:

> A celebrity CEO stops by your office. Handsome, beautiful, charismatic, gracious . . . he/she makes a heck of an impression on your secretary. The question is . . . who will your secretary tell that evening?

The answer could be, "a spouse," or, "their best friend." But the real answer is, they'll tell EVERYBODY. They're going to run right to Facebook, or Twitter, or whatever the latest social media outlet happens to be, and they're going to shout from the cyber-rooftop, "I met so-and-so CEO today when they stopped by at my boss's office and did you know that they're, like, soooo good looking I was, like, OMG, they're really nice, but did you know that, LOL, they're much shorter in real life?" And what if your secretary is connected with someone who sees that post and says to themselves, *Wow, if that CEO is in that lawyer's office, it can only mean one thing—the merger is going to happen / white collar criminal charges are true / bankruptcy is imminent,* or some other variation.

It's not just we and our lawyers who need to be educated on the issue of confidentiality when using social media, it's our staff as well. And they need to be taught that, just like lawyers, what they do outside the office matters. The genesis of that concept comes straight from Rule 5.3,[1] in particular subsection (b), which states, "a lawyer having direct supervisory authority over the nonlawyer shall make reasonable efforts to ensure that the person's conduct is compatible with the professional obligations of the lawyer . . ."[2] It is without question that conduct "compatible with the professional obligations of the lawyer" includes concepts of confidentiality.

§ 3:6 Privilege

As we all know, "confidentiality" is an ethics rule. If you violate it, the disciplinary authorities will be coming after you. But beware of the semi-related issue of privilege as well. Privilege is an evidence rule. Basically, it holds that we can't be forced to reveal the advice we give to our clients. Our communications with our clients are privileged, provided that we jump through the right hoops. One of those hoops is confidentiality— we are only entitled to claim privilege protection if the conversations we have with our client are kept confidential. Of course, there are more requirements, but confidentiality is the one we care about right now.

Consider the following disastrous situation: A lawyer has a young-ish client. The parties are called to court for a mandatory mediation. They meet behind closed doors, but nothing is resolved. That evening, the client goes home, hits Facebook and says, "I had the worst day in court today. The judge told us that we had to meet and try to find some way to settle the case. We didn't settle and I have a great case. But my lawyer told me that as long as I don't say anything

---

[Section 3:5]

[1] Del. Prof. Conduct R. 5.3.

5.3 http://courts.delaware.gov/rules/DLRPCFebruary2010.pdf. Pages last checked by the author July 25, 2013.

[2] Del. Prof. Conduct R. 5.3(b).

5.3(b) http://courts.delaware.gov/rules/DLRPCFebruary2010.pdf. Pages last checked by the author July 25, 2013.

about that other doctor's report we have, we're gonna be fine,"

Just. Blew. Privilege.

Sure, it was an inadvertent statement, but it was still voluntary and broadcasting it to third parties probably amounts to a waiver of privilege. We need to make sure that we remind our clients that they need to keep their big laptops shut!

The danger of this type of action and the frequency with which it appears to occur makes me believe that the confidentiality/social media question is something lawyers should add to their initial client meeting checklist. We need to make sure that we warn our clients about this potential gaffe because doing so could prevent them from hurting their case. But I also believe it's a potential malpractice-avoidance technique. Consider what will happen if you don't warn a client about this pitfall and they end up blowing privilege because they revealed something on social media. They're going to blame you for not warning them. Thus, it seems wise to specifically warn our clients about this issue as a matter of course.

Chapter 4

The Ethical Pitfalls of Social Media Use—Investigations

§ 4:1 Introduction to investigations
§ 4:2 The limits of a lawyer's ability to obtain social media information, generally
§ 4:3 The limits on investigations in jury situations

> **KeyCite®:** Cases and other legal materials listed in KeyCite Scope can be researched through the KeyCite service on Westlaw®. Use KeyCite to check citations for form, parallel references, prior and later history, and comprehensive citator information, including citations to other decisions and secondary materials.

§ 4:1 Introduction to investigations

The first lawyer to realize that we could find valuable information for our client matters on the Internet must have felt like they struck gold. I can see their facial expression in my mind's eye, reflecting a combination of revelation, shock, and opportunity. Their eyes most likely grew even wider when they found the treasure trove of information that exists on people's social media accounts. But for a certain time only the most technologically savvy lawyers availed themselves of this tool. Some didn't understand the new medium and others, even if they were familiar with the technology, weren't quite sure about the permissibility of trolling Facebook (and the Internet in general) in search of information to be used in the course of the practice. And there was good reason, because for some time the matter was unresolved.

For that reason, I used to tell lawyers at my CLE seminars that social media searches were not a substitution for legitimate discovery techniques. But times have changed. Today, Internet and social media searches *are* legitimate discovery techniques. It is almost commonplace these days to receive interrogatories where the opposing party asks for information regarding at least some aspect of your client's social

§ 4:1   Navigating Legal Ethics

media behavior. They might also include statements made on social media in the definition of "statements" in the instruction section of the regulations. Your individual jurisdiction will likely have an entire progeny of cases that addresses whether, and to what extent, lawyers are permitted to ask about a party's social media use, account information, etc. I'd expect that this issue is among the most hotly debated pre-trial motions that lawyers are seeing these days. I'm not going to spend time evaluating that issue because it's a question of evidence law and it's likely going to be governed by the particular decisions in your jurisdiction. What I care about is the ethical angle. Is it ethically permissible to investigate other people/parties/witnesses by using social media?

§ 4:2   The limits of a lawyer's ability to obtain social media information, generally

Information that is put out into the public domain for the entire world to see is fair game. If there are no restrictions, no barrier that must be overcome in order to see the information, if it is freely available to the entire world, then there cannot be any expectation of privacy and no lawyer will have an ethical problem viewing and using that information. The matter is so basic and well established that I submit it doesn't even need an opinion or rule to establish its credibility.

But what about searching for and using information that is not posted for public consumption? We need to consider the information posted by a person who intends for those postings to be seen only by their network of friends/contacts and whose privacy settings are consistent with that intention. Can we search for that data? There's a decent argument to be made for allowing us to try to get at that information. One could argue that, to a certain extent, there is an assumption of risk on the part of the poster.

Users of social media acknowledge that there is no such thing as *complete* privacy. The share button, the retweet, these are all functions that allow our handpicked network to deliver our pictures and comments to those people outside of our circle of friends. Users know that these facets of the platforms exist, yet they use the programs anyway. In fact, this vulnerability is exploited all the time. People who want to find out information for personal reasons or business purposes can get pretty crafty in doing social media searches and many of us both understand that and accept some element of risk in that regard. Everyone from a prospective suitor to a prospective employer checks up on people by perusing social media platforms. But the person seeking your information may not be that cute guy or gal you met at the movies last week. It could be a lawyer searching for information to be used against you in a legal matter. And those lawyers don't just want the publicly available information. That's not always so helpful. The real goodies lay behind the curtain— in your protected social media pages. The question is whether lawyers can use manipulation to get access to those social media pages.

There are a few tactics available to lawyers to gain access to those restricted pages. For instance, lawyers could break in. Of course, we know that hacking into someone's profile would be criminal and, therefore, a violation of the rule prohibiting Misconduct, Rule 8.4(b).[1] But what about using some other assertive tactic that's short of criminal behavior? To explore that, consider the following hypothetical:

> *You represent someone who is involved in a dispute. You think your adversary will be filing a complaint soon, so you're getting prepared for the apparent litigation. You know that you will need to call Susan as a witness in that litigation, but you don't know much about her. Before you commence litigation you ask your client, Andrew, to "friend" Susan on Facebook. You tell Andrew, "just try to be social and let's gather information we could use against her in litigation."*

When I present that example to people face-to-face, I get a lot of furled brows and pursed lips. "That doesn't smell right," they say. One person from the Midwest hit the nail on the head when he said, "That's just dirty pool." Both reactions reveal two things: the behavior doesn't feel right, yet it's hard to articulate the exact problem.

The conduct isn't an outright lie because neither the lawyer nor its agent is actually making an improper misrepresentation. If it were, the statement(s) might violate one of the rules on misrepresentation in the disciplinary code. Instead, this action appears to be some sort of manipulative conduct through an omission of sorts, which

---

[Section 4:2]

[1]Del. Prof. Conduct R. 8.4(b).

8.4(b) http://courts.delaware.gov/rules/DLRPCFebruary2010.pdf. Pages last checked by the author August 13, 2013.

§ 4:2 NAVIGATING LEGAL ETHICS

makes it a bit more difficult to assess. And not every lawyer would find it objectionable. After all, much of what we do in the adversary system has some manipulative flavor to it.

This fact pattern isn't one that I came up with on my own—it's a question that was raised to the Philadelphia Bar Association Professional Guidance Committee. In March of 2009 the Committee released Opinion 2009-02 that addressed the topic. An inquirer asked the Committee to determine if it was reasonable for a lawyer to use a third person to gain access to someone's social media page in order to gather information that might be used against that person. The third person wouldn't be instructed to speak any untruths, only to remain silent about their true motives. The Committee opined that the behavior would be improper.

The Committee stated that "the proposed course of conduct contemplated by the inquirer would violate Rule 8.4(c)[2] because the planned communication by the third party with the witness is deceptive."[3] You might recall that Rule 8.4(c) is a critical part of the rule on Misconduct (or as I've referred to it elsewhere in this text, "the Stupid Rule"). That section states that it is professional misconduct for a lawyer, "to engage in conduct involving dishonesty, fraud, deceit or misrepresentation . . ." The opinion further explained that the conduct was problematic because "it omits a highly material fact, namely, that the third party who asks to be allowed access to the witness's pages is doing so only because he or she is intent on obtaining information and sharing it with a lawyer for use in a lawsuit to impeach the testimony of the witness."[4] Thus, it isn't an affirmative misrepresentation that triggers the ethical violation; rather it's the omission of a material fact that constitutes deception.

The Committee made that clear when they stated,[5] "The omission would purposefully conceal that fact from the witness for the purpose of inducing the witness to allow access when she may not do so if she knew the third person was associated with the inquirer and the true purpose of the access

---

[2] Del. Prof. Conduct R. 8.4(c).
8.4(c) http://courts.delaware.gov/rules/DLRPCFebruary2010.pdf. Pages last checked by the author August 13, 2013.
[3] Philadelphia Opinion 2009-02 at 3.
[4] Philadelphia Opinion 2009-02 at 3.
[5] Philadelphia Opinion 2009-02 at 3.

was to obtain information for the purpose of impeaching her testimony."[6]

The Philadelphia Committee opinion about social media friending was an extension of the anti-deception approach that is common throughout the country. In that case, there was no overt lie; rather, the lawyer omitted some material information and that omission constituted deception. It seems a logical extension, given the tendency of the ethics authorities to hold a high standard for lawyers when dealing with Misconduct and Rule 8.4(c). However, not every jurisdiction agrees.

The Association of the Bar of the City of New York, Committee on Professional and Judicial Ethics issued Formal Opinion 2010-2 regarding obtaining information from social networking websites. In a somewhat curious opinion, the Association came to a different decision from the Philadelphia Committee. The New York City Bar addressed, "the narrow question of whether a lawyer, acting either alone or through an agent such as a private investigator, may resort to trickery via the internet to gain access to an otherwise secure social networking page and the potentially helpful information it holds. In particular, we focus on an attorney's direct or indirect use of an affirmatively 'deceptive' behavior to 'friend' potential witnesses." It appears they used quotation marks because they weren't convinced that the word deception applies to the situation.

The New York City Bar acknowledged that the City had a somewhat assertive approach to discovery. It stated that it would be inconsistent with that policy to, "flatly prohibit lawyers from engaging in any and all contact with users of social networking sites."[7] They concluded that a lawyer, or her agent, "may use her real name and profile to send a "friend request" to obtain information from an unrepresented

---

[6]It should be noted that the opinion doesn't only state that the omission is deception. The Committee mentioned very briefly that they believed that the conduct also constituted the making of a false statement of material fact to the witness and would therefore be a misrepresentation that violates Rule 4.1. Unfortunately, the opinion says absolutely nothing else about the apparent 4.1 violation, so it's unclear how they arrive at that conclusion.

[7]New York City Bar Association Opinion 2010-2 at 1.

§ 4:2 NAVIGATING LEGAL ETHICS

person's social networking website without also disclosing the reasons for making the request."[8]

The New York City Bar was clear that deception is not permitted; they just had a different view of what deception actually entailed. They agreed that creating a false persona to obtain information or other such tactics were a violation of the rules. But the Association considered the truthful friending of unrepresented parties to be a permissible informal discovery.[9] The opinion stated that "while there are ethical boundaries to such 'friending,' in our view they are not crossed when an attorney or investigator uses only truthful information to obtain access to a website, subject to compliance with all other ethical requirements."[10]

Thus, in the Philadelphia and New York City opinions, we have two decisions that could yield conflicting results. For instance, if a lawyer (or agent of the lawyer) uses truthful information to initiate the social media connection, that disclosure satisfies the NYC authorities. However, that disclosure alone might not reveal the purpose for the connection request. Thus, even though the disclosure of the person's identity satisfies the NYC opinion, it still seems lik it runs afoul of the Philadelphia opinion because, despite using a truthful identifier, the information exchange "... omits a highly material fact, namely that the third part who asks to be allowed access to the witness's page is doing so only because he or she is intent on obtaining information and sharing it with a lawyer for use in a lawsuit to impeach the testimony of the witness."[11]

I would be wary of that New York City decision for a few reasons. First, it doesn't seem consistent with the litany of preceding opinions. If anything, the trend across the country is to ratchet up the pressure on lawyers. Courts and advisory boards seem to be more stringent about what constitutes deception, rather than less.

The second reason is that the decision left what I call an "escape clause." At the very end of the decision the New York City Bar made it clear that the friending would be permitted, subject to compliance with "all other ethical requirements." That phrase gives the Association a lot of

---

[8] New York City Bar Association Opinion 2010-2 at 1.
[9] New York City Bar Association Opinion 2010-2 at 2.
[10] New York City Bar Association Opinion 2010-2 at 1.
[11] Philidelphia Opinion 2009–02 at 3.

wiggle room. Rarely is any disciplinary matter cut-and-dry. There are often some other facts that muddy the waters. Every disciplinary matter is fact sensitive and, therefore, easily distinguishable. It wouldn't take much for a tribunal to find some facts that don't comply with "all other ethical requirements."

Third, it's not clear that the New York City Bar opinion would even be honored in its own state. The New York State Bar Association Committee on Professional Ethics rendered Opinion #843 which, admittedly, dealt with a different question. However, in the course of its discussion it referenced the Philadelphia opinion and didn't disagree with the Philadelphia rationale.

Finally, and most significantly, the New York City opinion isn't grounded in the same logic as the other opinions regarding deception. This, to me, is a critical consideration.

All of the previous decisions on deception in investigation focus on the point of view of the target.[12] They all hold that the attorney's actions take advantage of a vulnerable layperson and the Philadelphia opinion is written from that point of view as well. That's important because the very purpose of the ethics rules is to protect the public from unscrupulous attorneys. The rationale in the New York City opinion, on the other hand, is grounded in the lawyer's pseudo-right to utilize a certain form of informal discovery. Thus, in Philadelphia, the decision is motivated by protecting the public, whereas the New York City the decision is motivated by protecting the lawyer. My gut tells me that most states would adopt the former rationale, because it's more consistent with the underlying goals of the ethics rules.

§ 4:3 The limits on investigations in jury situations

Investigating other parties is only one facet of the ethical dilemma faced by lawyers who use social media for research. The problems extend into the jury box as well. Ex parte communications with prospective jurors and members of a sit-

---

[12]Philadelphia isn't the only jurisdiction that opined on the topic. So did the New Hampshire Bar Association (Opinion 2012-13/05), the San Diego County Bar Association (Opinion 2011-2) and others.

§ 4:3   NAVIGATING LEGAL ETHICS

ting jury have long been prohibited.[1] That's been well established by the ethics rules, in particular note Rule 3.5(b):[2]

Rule 3.5. Impartiality and decorum of the tribunal
A lawyer shall not:

(a) seek to influence a judge, juror, prospective juror or other official by means prohibited by law;

(b) communicate or cause another to communicate ex parte with such a person or members of such person's family during the proceeding unless authorized to do so by law or court order; or

(c) communicate with a juror or prospective juror after discharge of the jury unless the communication is permitted by court rule;

(d) engage in conduct intended to disrupt a tribunal or engage in undignified or discourteous conduct that is de-grading to a tribunal.

But the advent of social media has created a difficult wrinkle because lawyers are using social media to research both prospective and sitting jurors. That isn't frowned upon, per se. In fact, the New York City Bar Association recognized that this type of research is consistent with a lawyer's fundamental duties. It noted that, ". . . standards of competence and diligence may require doing everything reasonably possible to learn about the jurors who will sit in judgment on a case."[3]

The problem is that part of the lawyer's investigation process through social media could include communicating with the jurors, thereby violating Rule 3.5(b). There could be friending, exchanges of messages, or a lawyer might just observe a juror's social media page (which might be problematic as we will see). The issue is trying to figure out which of those actions actually constitutes a "communication" that violates the Rule. The authorities are concerned because "social media . . . can blur the line between independent,

---

[Section 4:3]
    [1]New York City Bar Association, Formal Opinion 2012-2 at 1.
    [2]Del. Prof. Conduct R. 3.5(b).
    3.5(b) http://courts.delaware.gov/rules/DLRPCFebruary2010.pdf. Pages last checked by the author August 13, 2013.
    [3]New York City Opinion 2012-2 at 2.

§ 4:3

private research and interactive, interpersonal 'communication.'"[4]

The New York City Bar didn't make many waves when it opined that "friending" a juror constituted a prohibited communication.[5] That's pretty much a no-brainer. It shook things up slightly, however, when it stated that simply *researching* a juror's social media page could constitute a communication.

The Bar was concerned about situations where a lawyer researched the juror's page and the website sends message to the juror letting them know that the lawyer had viewed the juror's page.[6] The New York City Bar stated that the key factor was the effect that such knowledge would have on the receiver (in this case, the juror).[7]

The New York City Bar stated that "it is the 'transmission of,' 'exchange of' or 'process of bringing' information or ideas from one person to another that defines a communication"[8] and that in the world of social media, "this focus on the transmission of information or knowledge is critical."[9] In a situation where a juror was notified that a lawyer was viewing the juror's social media page ". . . the researcher imparted to the person being researched the knowledge that he or she is being investigated."[10] The New York City Bar believed that "The transmission of the information that the attorney viewed the juror's page is a communication that may be attributable to the lawyer and even such minimal contact raises the specter of the improper influence and/or intimidation that the Rules are intended to prevent."[11]

Thus, the key question is whether the juror would have learned of the lawyer's research.[12] In addition to being

---

[4]New York City Opinion 2012-2 at 2.

[5]New York City Opinion 2012-2 at 3.

[6]Examples of how that could happen include if LinkedIn tells a user who has viewed their profile recently, or if Twitter lets a user know the identity of a new follower, perhaps.

[7]New York City Opinion 2012-2 at 4.

[8]New York City Opinion 2012-2 at 4.

[9]New York City Opinion 2012-2 at 4.

[10]New York City Opinion 2012-2 at 4.

[11]New York City Opinion 2012-2 at 5.

[12]New York City Opinion 2012-2 at 3.

§ 4:3   NAVIGATING LEGAL ETHICS

intimidating, the knowledge of that research might "tend to influence the juror's conduct with respect to the trial."[13]

This view of what constitutes a "communication" probably wasn't anticipated by many readers. However, I'm sure you've seen throughout this publication that the trend is to interpret the definition of a "communication" more broadly, and this decision is certainly in line with that sentiment. Clearly, that could have a significant impact on a lawyer's use of social media in jury situations. Beware . . .

---

[13]This quote actually comes from a different opinion out of New York City. NYCLE Committee on Professional Ethics, Formal Opinion No. 743, Issued May 18, 2011 at 3.

Chapter 5

The Ethical Pitfalls in Social Media Use—Advertising

§ 5:1 Introduction to advertising
§ 5:2 The reason we can advertise
§ 5:3 How the advertising rules are built
§ 5:4 What is an "Advertisement": Profiles
§ 5:5 What is an "Advertisement": Blogs
§ 5:6 Trends regarding other advertisements
§ 5:7 Texts as ads
§ 5:8 The touchy trend: The problem with posts
§ 5:9 The application of Rule 7.1 to advertising
§ 5:10 Other technicalities
§ 5:11 Controlling statements about you that are made by others, and "making" a communication
§ 5:12 Being aware of statements about you that are made by others and "making" a communication
§ 5:13 A specific problem with control and awareness: Lawyer rating sites
§ 5:14 Total lack of control: The inability to force conformance
§ 5:15 Copies of advertisements
§ 5:16 Advertising in the future

> **KeyCite®:** Cases and other legal materials listed in KeyCite Scope can be researched through the KeyCite service on Westlaw®. Use KeyCite to check citations for form, parallel references, prior and later history, and comprehensive citator information, including citations to other decisions and secondary materials.

§ 5:1 Introduction to advertising

Advertising issues give me a stomachache. There are a variety of reasons that it causes me to feel that way: some of the new features in social media technologies don't quite fit into existing definitions, it's tough to know when one is engaging in behavior that's covered by the rules, and the code is struggling to keep up. Plus, much of the direction

§ 5:1

we've received has been reactive in nature—usually it's in the form of an advisory board opinion that's given in response to a question posed by a member of the bar. And, as you can imagine, not all states look at a question the same way. In fact, sometimes there can be a difference of opinion within a state itself, like those cases where a city bar association decision conflicts with the decision of the state bar. Unfortunately, the result has been piecemeal guidance, at best.

Furthermore, the idea of calling this section "advertising" might be a mistake all together. That term hearkens back to an age where Madison Avenue-types created display ads for print publications or copy for radio spots that a local DJ would read between segments. The beginning of the Internet age didn't upset the applecart too much. The initial, primitive websites were passive and largely static, which made them quite similar to traditional forms of advertising. It wasn't such a mental leap for advisory boards and the ABA to say, *websites are advertising . . . . apply the same rules.* But as social media came on the scene, all of that changed.

The biggest change was in the interactive nature of the platforms. A host of new issues arose once we were able to engage in active conversation with the advertising target. Also, we are now presented with a variety of communications. We've gone way beyond direct mail, display ads, and television commercials. Now we have tweets that get disseminated to unknown viewers in foreign jurisdictions and thinly veiled self-promotional posts sent out from our personal Facebook accounts. Which of these communications are permitted? Which of these statements actually constitutes a "communication" that triggers the rules? It's these types of questions that give me a stomachache.

Several opinions from across the country shed light on these questions. But the objective is not to simply understand the existing opinions. The ultimate goal is for you to have some ability to navigate social media use in the future. In fact, the chances are high that you're going to have to address issues with platforms that might not even exist at the time of this writing. To get proper guidance we need to quickly review some fundamentals about the ethics rules because it's those concepts that will guide you going forward.

§ 5:2 The reason we can advertise

Lawyers weren't permitted to advertise our services for

most of modern history. Self-promotion was beneath us and not worthy of our distinguished profession. A review of the code reveals that the powers-that-be didn't appear to have an overt reversal in their philosophy. Of course, one never knows what was percolating beneath the surface, but the given reason for finally permitting lawyers to advertise was not to allow lawyers to increase their business prospects. Advertising was permitted because disseminating information about our services helped the public in obtaining legal services.[1] It's all about "the public's need to know about legal services." In particular, the need to get such information into the hands of "persons of moderate means."[2] The drafters were conscious that they were bucking convention, but they apparently felt that it was the right thing to do. They stated in the commentary, "The interest in expanding public information about legal services ought to prevail over considerations of tradition."[3]

Notice, again, that it's all about the client. That's a theme that you've likely seen elsewhere in this book because it's a seminal concept in the rules. The ethics code is all about creating a system and a code of behavior that serves the needs of the client and protects the client and the public interest. There are other goals as well (protecting the integrity of the profession, advancing the rule of law), but we must remember that the disciplinary code is client-centric.

Understanding this background is not just an academic exercise. This philosophy must inform our decisions about social media use and advertising. After all, there are many places where the guidance from the rules and bar committees is incomplete or seemingly irreconcilable. We'll need to determine what behavior is appropriate in those situations and the only way we can ensure that our choices are consistent with the spirit of the rules is if we understand these underlying concepts.

[Section 5:2]

[1] Del. Prof. Conduct R. 7.2, Comment [1].
[2] Del. Prof. Conduct R. 7.2, Comment [1].
[3] Del. Prof. Conduct R. 7.2, Comment [1].

§ 5:3 How the advertising rules are built

The advertising rules are located in section 7 and it's easiest to start with Rule 7.2.[1] The beginning of that rule tells us that we're permitted to advertise and where those advertisements may occur. It states that, "a lawyer may advertise services through written, recorded or electronic communication, including public media."[2] Keep an eye on that word "communication" because it's going to be a big factor in this conversation. When, exactly, does a statement rise to the level of a "communication" such that the advertising rules are triggered? More on that later.

While Rule 7.2 gives us the right to advertise and informs us where those advertisements might be placed, the preceding rule governs the content of those ads. Our ads can't be false or misleading, as provided in Rule 7.1:[3]

Rule 7.1. Communications concerning a lawyer's services

A lawyer shall not make a false or misleading communication about the lawyer or the lawyer's services. A communication is false or misleading if it contains a material misrepresentation of fact or law, or omits a fact necessary to make the statement considered as a whole not materially misleading.

It's important to appreciate the breadth of this rule. Read it again and concentrate on the words that *aren't* there. Notice that the rule doesn't actually tell us that we can't make misleading communications in "advertisements." It's not that specific. The rule doesn't refer to the language of our newspaper display ads, nor does it tell us that we should avoid making false communications in the content of our television ads. It's far more broad than that—it states that lawyers can't make false or misleading communications

---

[Section 5:3]

[1] Del. Prof. Conduct R. 7.2.
    7.2 http://courts.delaware.gov/rules/DLRPCFebruary2010.pdf. Pages last checked by the author August 13, 2013.

[2] Del. Prof. Conduct R. 7.2(a).
    7.2(a) http://courts.delaware.gov/rules/DLRPCFebruary2010.pdf. Pages last checked by the author August 13, 2013.

[3] Del. Prof. Conduct R. 7.1.
    7.1 http://courts.delaware.gov/rules/DLRPCFebruary2010.pdf. Pages last checked by the author August 13, 2013.

ADVERTISING § 5:3

about ourselves or our services, *period*. Thus, Rule 7.1 is going to apply anytime we make a self-promotional statement.

There are several states in the country that get a little deeper into the regulation of the content of advertisements. Some jurisdictions want to ensure that lawyers' ads remain relevant to the practice of law. Thus, every once in a while you'll see text similar to this, which is found in New Jersey:

> No advertisement shall rely in any way on techniques to obtain attention that depend upon absurdity and that demonstrate a clear and intentional lack of relevance to the selection of counsel; included in this category are all advertisements that contain any extreme portrayal of counsel exhibiting characteristics clearly unrelated to legal competence.[4]

The final building blocks in the advertising rules that are pertinent to our discussion are found in the balance of Rule 7.2 and also in Rules 7.3[5] and 7.4.[6] These rules address certain "technicalities" in advertising and marketing, each of which has been the subject of considerable Technethics debate.

Rule 7.2 doesn't just only grant permission to market our services as discussed above, it also imposes limitations on those ads. Note that when reading all of the details in the upcoming rules, keep in mind that these rules were created during a time where it was easy to determine whether something was an ad.

Rule 7.2 (cont'd)

> (b) Except as permitted by Rule 1.5(e), a lawyer shall not give anything of value to a person for recommending the lawyer's services except that a lawyer may
> (1) pay the reasonable costs of advertisements or communications permitted by this Rule;
> (2) pay the usual charges of a legal service plan or a not-for-profit or qualified lawyer referral service. A qualified lawyer referral service is a lawyer referral service that has been approved by an appropriate regulatory authority; and
> (3) pay for a law practice in accordance with Rule 1.17.

---

[4]N.J. RPC 7.2(a), http://www.judiciary.state.nj.us/rules/apprpc.htm#x7dot2, last checked by the author November 13, 2013.

[5]Del. Prof. Conduct R. 7.3.
   7.3 http://courts.delaware.gov/rules/DLRPCFebruary2010.pdf. Pages last checked by the author August 13, 2013.

[6]Del. Prof. Conduct R. 7.4.
   7.4 http://courts.delaware.gov/rules/DLRPCFebruary2010.pdf. Pages last checked by the author August 13, 2013.

(c) Any communication made pursuant to this rule shall include the name and office address of at least one lawyer or law firm responsible for its content.

Some states have a key additional technical mandate. A common feature in codes across the country is the requirement that lawyers keep copies of advertisements. Frequently it sounds like this excerpt from the Missouri code:

> Rule 4-7.2 (b)[7] A copy or recording of an advertisement or written communication shall be kept for two years after its last dissemination along with a record of when and where it was used. The record shall include the name of at least one lawyer responsible for its content unless the advertisement or written communication itself contains the name of at least one lawyer responsible for its content.[8]

Other jurisdictions require another important detail—the need to file copies of all advertisements that a lawyer uses in their practice. Texas has a rather comprehensive rule in that regard:

Rule 7.07. Filing Requirements for Public Advertisements and Written Solicitations

(a) Except as provided in paragraph (d) of this Rule, a lawyer shall file with the Lawyer Advertisement and Solicitation Review Committee of the State Bar of Texas, either before or concurrently with the mailing or sending of a written solicitation communication:

(1) a copy of the written solicitation communication being sent or to be sent to one or more prospective clients for the purpose of obtaining professional employment, together with a representative sample of the envelopes in which the communications are enclosed; and

(2) a check or money order payable to the State Bar of Texas for the fee set by the Board of Directors. Such fee shall be for the sole purpose of defraying the expense of enforcing the rules related to such solicitations.

(b) Except as provided in paragraph (d) of this Rule, a lawyer shall file with the Lawyer Advertisement and Solicitation Review Committee of the State Bar of Texas, ei-

---

[7]Notice that the rule designations (the numbers) vary slightly when incorporated into the individual state codification systems.

[8]http://www.courts.mo.gov/courts/ClerkHandbooksP2RulesOnly.nsf/c0c6ffa99df4993f86256ba50057dcb8/9ec523dc894bc66d86256ca60052120f?OpenDocument, last checked by the author November 13, 2013.

ther before or concurrently with the first dissemination of an advertisement in the public media, a copy of that advertisement. The filing shall include:

(1) a copy of the advertisement in the form in which it appears or is or will be disseminated, such as a videotape, an audiotape, a print copy, or a photograph or outdoor advertising,

(2) a production script of the advertisement setting forth all words used and describing in detail the actions, events, scenes, and background sounds used in such advertisement together with a listing of the names and addresses of persons portrayed or heard to speak, if the advertisement is in or will be in a form in which the advertised message is not fully revealed by a print copy or photograph;

(3) a statement of when and where the advertisement has been, is, or will be used; and

(4) a check or money order payable to the State Bar of Texas for the fee set by the Board of Directors. Such fee shall be for the sole purpose of defraying the expense of enforcing the rules related to such advertisements.[9]

Remember the reasons for having these requirements because these principles are going to guide us in the next section when we apply this to social media. And don't forget—these rules aren't here to make it easier for us to get clients, they're here to advance the purpose of the rule. The purpose of attorney advertising is to allow the public to get information about the legal services that are available to them. But the flip side of allowing lawyers to publicize those services is that they might denigrate the profession, mislead the public, etc. Thus, the rules are engaging in a balancing act— they are trying to give lawyers the opportunity to advertise, while keeping an eye on the content and otherwise regulating the promotional effort.

§ 5:4 What is an "Advertisement": Profiles

The advent of the Internet didn't pose much of a problem and the powers-that-be were able to apply the rules to the first web-based self-promotional efforts pretty easily. Origi-

---

[9]http://www.law.uh.edu/libraries/ethics/trpc/7.07.html, last checked by the author on November 13, 2013.

§ 5:4   NAVIGATING LEGAL ETHICS

nal websites weren't very different from passive display ads. But the reality of modern social media presents a variety of new ways for lawyers to engage the public. Take our profile pages on certain social media platforms, for instance. Those profiles aren't our personal websites—or are they?

Consider the items that are found on a person's LinkedIn profile page: Your name, office address and other contact information, information about your education, a resume listing of places you've worked, maybe a roster of notable clients, things like that. When you consider those items, you realize that it's the same information that you'd put on a personal website if I'd asked you to create it from scratch. This deeper look into the content of that profile reveals that it's the functional equivalent of a personal website. In fact, it's so much like a personal website that people often include a link to their LinkedIn public profile in their email signatures.

If your LinkedIn profile is the equivalent of a personal business website, and it's established that websites are considered an advertisement for attorney ethics purposes, then doesn't it follow that your LinkedIn profile is also an "advertisement"? It sure seems so. In fact, the State Bar of Texas obviously agreed with this interpretation. In its Interpretive Comments to the Texas ethics rules the Bar stated, "Landing pages such as those on Facebook, Twitter, LinkedIn, etc where the landing page is generally available to the public are advertisements."[1] That means that the attorney ethics rules regarding advertising need to be applied to your profiles and the content restrictions of Rule 7.1 would apply. Lawyers must, therefore, make sure that they don't make false or misleading statements on their profiles that could run afoul of the rule. We have to self-police our online presence.

The idea of keeping an eye on our profile content is an important consideration, but compliance might not be that difficult. After all, many profiles are simply overblown CVs. They're not so much avenues for self-promotion as they are resumes on steroids. The content restriction has far greater impact on another popular social media presence. Blogs.

§ 5:5 What is an "Advertisement": Blogs

Blogging is a popular activity among lawyers and there

[Section 5:4]

[1]Texas Interpretive Statement 17(C).

are several motivations. Some lawyers want to spread their knowledge of the law and they offer the information as a public service. Others are passionate about some cause and want to spread the word about that cause or otherwise state their opinion on some state of affairs. Still others have a promotional motivation—they blog so they could attract clients, or encourage other lawyers to refer work. Blog posts often contain analyses of case law or statutes, a lawyer's personal opinion about a court decision, or some other detailed examination of a legal topic. Of course, these motivations could (and often do) overlap. For instance, lawyers who blog about hot topics in the law are also probably seeking marketing exposure in the process. So they're clearly self-promoting—but does that make them "advertising"?

A review of Rule 7.2(a)[1] can lead one to believe that some blogs are ads. They are "written," they are located on the Internet which is a "public media" and they are a form of "electronic communication" (these are all catchphrases in Rule 7.2). Plus, the layout of blogs these days bear an incredible resemblance to websites. One could use the free blogging platform WordPress and download a template that makes the blog almost indistinguishable from a "website." I'm actually starting to wonder if those terms are merging—often, they could be used interchangeably. Proof can be found in my own blog.

I blog about hot topics in attorney ethics. This means, of course, that no one reads my blog. But the few audience members I've had over the years would see that I eliminated my conventional website and my blog serves as my primary web presence. The screen shot below shows how I have a navigation bar on top, blog posts on the left and various columns/panels/plugins on the rest of the page.

[Section 5:5]

[1]Del. Prof. Conduct R. 7.2(a).

7.2(a) http://courts.delaware.gov/rules/DLRPCFebruary2010.pdf. Pages last checked by the author August 13, 2013.

§ 5:5

Blogs can be programmed to look and feel like a website, and the opposite is true as well. Current websites could be programmed to disseminate information like a blog, they could have blogging platforms embedded into the site, etc. They could also invite the exchange of information through comments or otherwise. It's the interactive nature of the modern website that likely prompted the American Bar Association Standing Committee on Ethics and Professional Responsibility to issue Opinion 10-457 in 2010. In that opinion they confirmed that they consider the information included in a lawyer's website to be "communication about the lawyer or the lawyer's services" and is subject to Rule 7.1.

It seems like a no brainer . . . blogs have become very similar to websites, so they are advertising. But it's not quite that simple. If both the lawyer and the disciplinary authorities agree that the blog is promotional in nature, then it's clear. But there are many instances where a lawyer claims that their blog is not advertising, rather it's constitutionally protected speech. Such was the case with Horace Hunter, Esq., in Virginia.

Horace Hunter is a lawyer in Richmond, Virginia and he maintained a blog called, "This Week in Richmond Criminal Defense."[2] The Virginia State Bar had a variety of problems with the blog. They considered the blog to be an advertising vehicle and, among other things, they argued that it contained misleading content and it lacked the requisite disclaimers. (The Virginia disciplinary rules have a quirk that you don't see in many other jurisdictions. They require disclaimers in certain attorney advertising.)[3] Hunter put up a variety of defenses including the assertion that the blog was not an ad; rather, it was constitutionally protected speech.

The Court looked closely at how the blog was built and also what the content consisted of. The court noted that the blog was not interactive, meaning that it didn't permit for comments and the exchange of information. It was passive, more like a traditional website. They noted that the majority of the posts were entries about cases where Hunter obtained

---

[2] http://www.hunterlipton.com/news.php, last checked by the author on November 13, 2013.

[3] Horace Frazier Hunter v. Virginia State Bar, Record No. 121472, Circuit Court of the City of Richmond, February 28, 2013 at 2.

favorable results for his own clients.[4] The court even confirmed that some clients were upset about their cases being listed on Hunter's blog.[5] Regarding the motivation for the blog, the Court confirmed that Hunter himself had testified at his hearing that marketing was one reason for having written the blog.[6]

Hunter didn't fare so well in the decision. The Court upheld the constitutionality of Virginia's advertising rules and, after analyzing Hunter's speech in this case, determined that Hunter's posts constituted advertisements.[7] The Court stated that Hunter's speech was "self-promotional" in nature and that he, "chose to commingle sporadic political statements within his self-promoting blog posts in an attempt to camouflage the true commercial nature of his blog.[8] The court held that "the blog posts are potentially misleading commercial speech that the [Virginia State Bar] may regulate."[9]

For reasons we'll discuss below, it's important to note that there was a dissent. The dissenting Justices saw Hunter's posts as constitutionally protected political speech. The dissent had a more noble view of Hunter's blog posts. They believed that Hunter's posts discussed flaws in the criminal justice system and the Justices insinuated that the blog is something akin to a public service.[10] "Even if marketing was Hunter's sole motivation," the dissent states, "economic motivation cannot be the basis for determining whether otherwise political speech is protected."[11] The dissenting Justices believed that as political speech Hunter's posts would be subject to a heightened scrutiny test and after applying that test, Hunter should not be forced to insert the advertising disclaimer mandated by Virginia's Rule 7.2.[12]

The Horace Hunter opinion obviously isn't binding in other jurisdictions, but it gives us some valuable lessons when it comes to blogs. Notice a couple of key items. First, the Court evaluated the content of the posts themselves. They could

---

[4]Hunter at 2.
[5]Hunter at 3.
[6]Hunter at 4.
[7]Hunter at 11.
[8]Hunter at 13.
[9]Hunter at 23.
[10]Hunter at 26.
[11]Hunter at 29.
[12]Hunter at 31.

§ 5:5

have blanketed the overall blog platform or genre as an advertising vehicle, but they didn't do that. Instead they considered the content of the speech in each post. They considered what was being said, about whom, and how often the statements about each type of matter were actually made. Thus, what you say in your blog posts appears to be important in determining whether the blog is considered an ad.

That concept has been confirmed elsewhere, besides just Virginia. Other states have stated that some blogs might not be subject to advertising regulations. In Texas, for example, the ethics authorities told lawyers that, "blogs . . . considered to be educational or informational in nature" are not treated like advertisements.[13] But what the Texas authorities giveth, they also taketh away because in the very next sentence they warn that, ". . . attorneys should be careful to ensure that such postings do not meet the definition of an advertisement . . ." In other words, the content matters.

The second lesson from the Horace Hunter matter is that there was more than just content at issue. The court also evaluated the details of the social media platform. It was important, for instance, that the blog wasn't interactive and that it was accessible from his law firm's website.[14] Thus, the details of how your platform is actually built is important in determining whether the blog is considered an ad.

Third, the fact that there was a dissent means something. This decision could have easily gone the other way— and that might be the case in your jurisdiction.

Many blogs are just like Horace Hunter's. Lots of lawyers who blog are up front about doing it for marketing purposes. Content-wise, oodles of lawyer blogs talk about their client success stories.[15] One can even find a variety of blog platforms that are set up the same way as Hunter's— it's common for law firms to embed their blog in the firm website or provide a link from one to the other. Plus, lots of firms disable the commenting feature in their blogs. Many sophisticated firms want to get information out to the public and prove they're a thought leader, but they're concerned about

---

[13]See the Texas Disciplinary Rules of Professional Conduct (TDRPC), Revised Interpretive Comment 17(D).

[14]Hunter at 1.

[15]See the conversation about the resulting confidentiality issue elsewhere in this publication.

giving the crazies of the world an opportunity to go to town on the firm blog.

So, are blogs advertising? My answer is, "most likely." The majority decision in the Hunter case is a reasonable one and it's plausible that your jurisdiction would share the court's sentiment. Thus, given all of the foregoing, it's reasonable to assume that most attorney blogs could very likely be considered advertisements. Of course, to a certain extent, one could say that "it depends." We learn from *Hunter* that simply calling it a "blog" isn't necessarily definitive; rather, it's the attendant circumstances and the content that will likely govern. But, given the reasonableness of the opinion, the fact that many lawyer blogs are similar to the Hunter blog, it's my opinion that the majority opinion in the Hunter case will be the majority opinion in the rest of the country.

Consider the impact of the rules if you maintain a blog that is considered to be advertising. It means that the content restrictions of Rule 7.1 apply to your blog content. You can't make false or misleading statements about yourself or your services. That can be a big deal, depending upon the type of things you blog about. You need to choose your words carefully if you're talking about cases you've worked on, or what type of abilities/experience you might have. A post containing a boastful, self-serving, exaggerated statement that might be considered harmless "puffery" when uttered by a non-lawyer, might cause you to violate Rule 7.1.

If your blog is advertising it also means that you need to comply with the technicalities of Rule 7.2. Your name and office address might be required per subsection 7.2(b). You might need to post appropriate disclaimers if you live in a state that has a requirement like we saw in Virginia. You might need to keep copies of the blog posts if the rule in your jurisdiction requires same. None of this might be that complex, but it's another burden to add onto the heap of things we need to do in our practice.

§ 5:6 Trends regarding other advertisements

The position that blogs are likely to be considered advertising is bolstered when you consider the trends throughout the country. Many disciplinary committees have opined on whether different types of communications are considered advertising and the trend is toward a broad view. More and more self-promotional communications are considered to be covered by the advertising rules. A great example is Opinion

§ 5:6   Navigating Legal Ethics

964 from the New York State Bar Association Committee on Professional Ethics.[1]

Opinion 964 considered whether business cards are advertisements. Technically, the opinion examined a specific facet of the rules: when does an exchange of information constitute a "communication" that triggers the advertising rules? It's an interesting question—business cards convey information about a lawyer, so they're certainly a form of communication. But are they the type of communication covered by the advertising rules?

The opinion acknowledged that not all communications made by lawyers are advertising (There's that "communication" term again. It's a key consideration).[2] The opinion further acknowledged that some business cards might not be considered an ad. It states, "When a business or professional card or letterhead is used in the ordinary course of professional practice or social intercourse without primary intent to secure retention—e.g., simply to identify the lawyer—it does not constitute advertising."[3] However, the opinion notes that, "If such cards or letterhead were given or sent to someone other than an existing client or another lawyer, and primarily in furtherance of an effort to secure retention of the lawyer or law firm, then the card or letterhead would constitute advertising."[4]

Thus, even business cards could be seen as an advertisement. The implications are similar to that of blogs and other communications we've discussed. It means that Rule 7.1 applies to business cards, so you need to be careful not to use any misleading language, or you'll be in ethical hot water. It also means that the technicalities of Rule 7.2(b) apply to those business cards, so you'll need to make sure that you have your office address on there, that you keep copies of the cards, etc.[5]

The message being sent to the practice is that disciplinary

[Section 5:6]

[1]New York State Bar Association Opinion #942 (4/4/2013).

[2]Op. 964 at par. 10.

[3]Op. 964 at par. 11.

[4]Op. 964 at par. 13.

[5]Of course, you only have to comply with the rules on the business cards that you'll hand out to potential clients because only that set is considered an advertisement. Let's face it, though, no one is going to have two sets of business cards.

§ 5:7 Texts as ads

Communicating by text message is an accepted part of everyday life. In fact, my unofficial research shows that it's the preferred method of communication by the 15-25 year old demographic. I don't think there's a soul that would refute that finding! However, despite its adoption in the general public, texting isn't quite so popular in the practice of law.

According to the informal polls I take at my live seminars, many lawyers are reluctant to use text messaging to communicate with clients. For those who do use the medium, it's often the clients that are pushing the issue—they are requesting that the lawyer communicate via texts. There doesn't appear to be any consistent pattern in the legal world, but there is one universal truth: texting is being used in the practice of law, though it's being adopted at a far slower rate than in the rest of society.

While there may be a general resistance among lawyers to use texting for communication, there appears to be a strong push for some attorneys to use texting for promotional purposes. That was the issue that confronted the Supreme Court of Ohio's Board of Commissioners on Grievances and Discipline. In its Opinion 2013-2,[1] the Board tackled "Direct Contact with Prospective Clients: Text Messages." In that opinion the Board laid out the scenario for how texting is being used to solicit professional employment. Lawyers get the cell numbers of prospective clients from accident or police reports. They then text a solicitation for professional employment to the cell number they find in the report. The message usually only has general information about the lawyer and often it has a link to their website that contains additional advertising material.[2]

The Board addressed whether this type of communication was covered by the advertising rules, and they decided in the affirmative. As you recall from our discussion above,

---

[Section 5:7]

[1]Ohio BCGD Opinion 2013-2 (issued April 5, 2013).

[2]Ohio BCGD Opinion 2013-2 at 2.

§ 5:7   NAVIGATING LEGAL ETHICS

Rule 7.2(a)[3] permits advertising through "written, recorded, or electronic communication." The opinion held that texting constitutes "electronic communication" when it stated,

> 'Electronic communication' is not defined in the Rules of Professional Conduct . . . but it is generally understood to include text messages *[citations omitted]*. . . A text message could also be a "written communication" for purposes of Prof.Cond.R. 7.2 as " 'written' denotes a tangible or electronic record of a communication or representation, including handwriting, typewriting, printing, photostating, photocopy, audio or video recording and e-mail." Prof.Cond.R. 1.0(p). The comments to Prof.Cond.R. 7.2 fail to reference text messages, but demonstrate that the Rules were drafted to take into account new or non-conventional advertising methods.[4]

Not only are texts considered ads, but the opinion also confirmed that lawyers are permitted to use text messages to advertise their services.[5] However, the analysis didn't end there. The opinion noted that if texts are indeed used for advertising purposes, then Rule 7.1[6] would govern their content. That means that a text which is sent as a promotional message is considered to be an advertising "communication" and is subject to the prohibition against false and misleading statements.[7] In Ohio the commentary to the rules gives examples of statements that might violate Rule 7.2,[8] such as characterizing fees such as "cut-rate," "lowest" or making unsubstantiated comparisons with other lawyers.[9]

The point is that when texting is used in a promotional manner, it's considered an advertising communication in states like Ohio and others that adopt this view. The rules are being extended to cover all types of new electronic communications. And while texting is a permitted form of

---

[3]Del. Prof. Conduct R. 7.2(a).
   7.2(a) http://courts.delaware.gov/rules/DLRPCFebruary2010.pdf. Pages last checked by the author August 13, 2013.
[4]Ohio BCGD Opinion 2013-2 at 2–3.
[5]Ohio BCGD Opinion 2013-2 at 3.
[6]Del. Prof. Conduct R. 7.1.
   7.1 http://courts.delaware.gov/rules/DLRPCFebruary2010.pdf. Pages last checked by the author August 13, 2013.
[7]Ohio BCGD Opinion 2013-2 at 4.
[8]Del. Prof. Conduct R. 7.2.
   7.2 http://courts.delaware.gov/rules/DLRPCFebruary2010.pdf. Pages last checked by the author August 13, 2013.
[9]Ohio BCGD Opinion 2013-2 at 4.

advertising, the content of those texts must pass muster under Rule 7.1, just like any other similar communication.

§ 5:8 The touchy trend: The problem with posts

As we've seen in the foregoing analysis of websites, blogs, and even business cards, ethics authorities throughout the country are finding self-promotional communications to be considered "advertising" with increasing frequency. The authorities evaluate the content of the speech a lawyer or law firm uses, along with other attendant circumstances, and they determine that the particular vehicle is an advertisement. In each case, the ultimate decision is made about the vehicle itself: The website is an ad, the blog entry is an ad, the business card is an ad. But social media has introduced a new opportunity to make statements that aren't attached to any particular vehicle. The post.

A social media "post" is a short statement that stands on its own. Unlike an email, text, or direct message, the post is a statement that's made to your entire network of followers. In some platforms it's even made to a far bigger audience—anyone who's listening to what you're saying or reading what you're writing.

The social media post is found on almost every platform in some form or another. The home page of LinkedIn allows you to "Share an Update," Facebook encourages you to tell everyone "What's on Your Mind," and Twitter urges you to tell the masses, "What's Happening" (but only in 140 characters or less). Nearly every social media platform you could think of provides for the status update in one form or another, whether it's through a comment attached to a photo in Instagram or a text post on Reddit.

Posts are a unique animal, the likes of which we haven't seen before. The only pre-social media equivalent I could think of is standing on a street corner and making a declaration to anyone who is within earshot. In the past, any time a lawyer made a statement it was tied to some more formal vehicle like a newsletter or an article in a professional journal. Sure, there was the errant radio commentary or statement made to the media, but those were infrequent. Social media posts, on the other hand, are spit out in rapid-fire style to everyone who is listening (both now and later). This causes some unique problems for lawyers.

§ 5:8

Imagine that a lawyer posts the following statement from their personal[1] Facebook page:

> I just successfully appealed my property taxes & saved myself a ton of $$. 'Bout time I used my lawyerly powers to help myself!

Why did the lawyer make that post? For the same reason that the lawyer made the post we discussed in the confidentiality section. And for the same reason that untold numbers of other lawyers make posts every moment of every day—to promote themselves. It's a not-so thinly veiled attempt to tell the world that they have an active practice and that "you too can be a client." In this case, the lawyer is creating the illusion that he's only announcing the savings he got for himself. He might argue that he's just bragging. But the bragging has a purpose—it's to remind his social network that he does tax appeals and that he's available to do them for you too. You might argue that it wasn't the motive, but you'd be wrong. That's because I was the one who wrote that post.

That might have not been the post verbatim. I posted the comment a few years ago and I didn't save the text. But that was exactly my thinking. I wanted all of my friends to know that I did a good job in appealing my own taxes and that I could do it for them as well (for a fee, of course). It was a self-promoting statement made from my personal Facebook page, but it was still a subtle form of advertising. That begs the question whether it's a communication that is subject to the advertising rules. Very few states have opined on that, but Kentucky considered some drastic action.

In 2010, the Kentucky Bar proposed an amendment to their advertising rules that would require lawyers who use social media for marketing purposes to pay a filing fee and permit regulation of their profile by the bar's Advertising

---

[Section 5:8]

[1] You'll notice that the entire analysis presumes that the postings are coming from a lawyer's personal social media account. An account that is maintained by the firm would almost certainly be seen as an advertisement and any statement made would likely be considered to be subject to the attorney ethics rules.

Commission.[2] According to the ABA Journal article which reported this potential rule change, the new rules would have provided that communications that are of a non-legal nature would not be considered advertisements, but those that are of a legal nature would be subject to the advertising rules. But how do you determine whether a social media post is of a "legal nature"? Take my post above as an example. Even a mediocre lawyer could make a realistic argument for both positions, that the statement was either a legal or nonlegal post. It could be advertising, or just bragging. That's probably true for most self-serving posts made by lawyers on a daily basis.

To the best of my knowledge, the Kentucky rules were not amended to reflect these changes. I checked with various sources over the years to follow up and I wasn't able to speak with anyone who could explain why the amendments were abandoned. My completely unsupported opinion is that it's because the proposed rule changes would be too difficult to enforce. First, you're opening up a Pandora's Box. Once you start sifting through the posts, you need to actually come up with some standards, and that is likely going to be a Herculean effort. Second, there's a practical aspect to consider. What bar has the resources to administer such an extraordinary undertaking? I would expect that most bar associations or disciplinary authorities are stretched quite thin and I doubt that they would be able to devote the number of personnel that's actually needed to pull off the amount of inspections that would be necessary to enforce these rules.

The State Bar of Texas has also chimed in on the issue of social media posts in the interpretive statements to its ethics rules. The Bar stated that if a status update is, "considered to be educational or informational in nature," it's not to be treated as an advertisement.[3] However, just like we discussed in the blog section, the Texas Bar also notes that lawyers "should be careful to ensure that such postings do not meet the definition of an advertisement." Thus, the Texas language doesn't give us much substantive guidance. So where does that leave us? Luckily there are a few places to look for some guiding principles.

---

[2]http://www.abajournal.com/news/article/seeking_clients_via_facebook_in_ky._bar_may_regulate_social_media_comments, last checked by the author, November 16, 2013.

[3]See the Texas Disciplinary Rules of Professional Conduct (TDRPC), Revised Interpretive Comment 17(D).

§ 5:8

The State Bar of California Standing Committee on Professional Responsibility and Conduct issued Formal Opinion No. 2012-186 in which they specifically addressed under what circumstances an attorney's postings on social media would be subject to attorney advertising rules.[4] California hasn't adopted the ABA version of the ethics rules, but their analysis is helpful nonetheless.

Even though California doesn't have the same rules, the issue turned on the same word we've discussed at length, "communication." The committee needed to decide whether the posts were "communications" that triggered the advertising rules. It's the same concern that ABA states have because their version of the rule states that, "a lawyer may advertise services through written, recorded or electronic communication, including public media."[5]

The opinion notes that the California rules defines "communications" as, "any message or offer made by or on behalf of a member *concerning the availability for professional employment* of a member or a law firm directed to any former, present, or protective client . . ."[6] The ABA-style codes don't have the same definition; however, Rule 7.2 Comment [2] gives some solid direction. It states:

> [2] This Rule permits public dissemination of information concerning a lawyer's name or firm name, address and telephone number; the kinds of services the lawyer will undertake; the basis on which the lawyer's fees are determined, including prices for specific services and payment and credit arrangements; a lawyer's foreign language ability; names of references and, with their consent, names of clients regularly represented; and other *information that might invite the attention of those seeking legal assistance. [Emphasis added]*[7]

The California Committee posed four hypothetical postings and evaluated whether the text of each post was, "concerning the availability of professional employment." Let's evaluate them and then apply the ABA-style standard to see how it all pans out. We'll see that the first three are easy. One, however, is a problem . . . a potentially big problem.

---

[4]http://ethics.calbar.ca.gov/portals/9/documents/opinions/cal%202012-186%20(12-21-12).pdf, last checked by the author November 16, 2013.

[5]Delaware Rule 7.2(a).

[6]California Opinion 2012-186 at 3.

[7]Of course, this is the commentary, not the black letter law, but it's all we have.

ADVERTISING § 5:8

Three of the hypothetical posts found in the opinion were:

Won a million dollar verdict. Tell your friends to check out my website.
Won another personal injury case. Call me for a free consultation.
Another great victory in court today! My client is delighted. Who wants to be next?

The committee believed that the words "tell your friends to check out my website," conveys a message or offer concerning professional employment."[8] Likewise in the next statement, the directive to "call me for a free consultation" was problematic. The Committee believed that an offer for a consultation (even if it's free) is a step toward securing potential employment and indicates that the lawyer is available to be hired.[9] The final post was also a cause for concern for the committee because the phrase "who wants to be next" suggested the availability for professional employment. Since the posts were considered "communications," those statements would be subject to the advertising rules.

How would these three examples fare under the ABA-style code? If we consider the language set forth in Rule 7.2 Comment [2] to be the standard, we probably get the same result. Do these three posts "invite the attention of those seeking legal assistance?" It appears that they do. The three clauses that concerned California in these examples were "Tell your friends to check out my website," "Call me . . .," and "Who wants to be next?" Each of them sounds like the lawyer is encouraging someone to act in a way that will further the forming of a potential lawyer-client relationship. I'd say that such statement would qualify as, "inviting the attention of those seeking legal assistance."[10]

On to that troubling hypothetical post that California considered in the opinion. Here it is:

Case finally over. Unanimous verdict! Celebrating tonight.

The California Committee did not find this post problematic. They stated that "this statement, standing alone, is not a communication" under the rule.[11] The committee held that "Attorney status postings that simply announce

---
[8]California Opinion 2012-186 at 5.
[9]California Opinion 2012-186 at 5–6.
[10]Del. Rule 7.2[2].
[11]Cal Op. 2012-186 at 4.

§ 5:8   NAVIGATING LEGAL ETHICS

recent victories without an accompanying offer about the availability for professional employment generally will not qualify as a communication."[12] It's important to note that the Committee evaluated the text of the statement and considered whether that text, standing alone, was concerning the availability of professional employment, regardless of that attorney's subjective notice for sending it.[13] They reviewed the text and ignored the motive. To use language from our law school days, they stayed within the four corners of the post.

But would we have the same result in an ABA-style state? Here is where I think there's cause for concern. According to the ABA-commentary, we need to ask whether the post "invite[s] the attention of those seeking legal assistance." I submit that that's a far broader standard. Look at how the operative ABA-language compares to its California counterpart:

> making an offer/stating you're available (California)

> vs.

> inviting attention (ABA-style)

In California they're asking whether the lawyer has made an offer or statement of availability. Asking the question in that manner allows California to ignore the lawyer's motivation and stay within the four corners of the post. The ABA's "inviting attention" language, however, seems to incorporate motive.

The ABA standard is not asking whether the post was inviting *employment*, it's asking whether the post was inviting *attention*. If the attorney's motive was self-promotion, then you could reasonably argue that the post was made to invite the attention of those seeking legal assistance. Consider that last California example, "Case finally over. Unanimous Verdict. Celebrating tonight!" There clearly isn't any offer for legal services, but one could see how the reason for making that statement would be to invite the attention of potential clients. After all, it's a bit of bragging, isn't it? The lawyer may only be stating overtly *look at me, I'm a winner,* but the unwritten part of the statement is, *and I can win for you too!*

---

[12] Cal Op. 2012-186 at 4.
[13] Cal Op. 2012-186 at 4.

ADVERTISING § 5:8

Let's go back to my tax appeal post and evaluate it under the California and ABA-style standards. Remember that I posted:

> I just successfully appealed my property taxes & saved myself a ton of $$. 'Bout time I used my lawyerly powers to help myself!

It's similar to that California post, maybe even a little less problematic on its face. My tax appeal post clearly doesn't invite someone to hire me. It's not offering my services, nor is it discussing my availability as a lawyer. In fact, it isn't even bragging about the success I had for a client—it's about my success in representing myself. Under the California standard I'd almost certainly be okay. The big question, of course, is whether I'm "inviting the attention" of those seeking legal assistance according to the ABA-style standard. Looking within the four corners of the post, maybe not. But if you evaluate my motive, then the answer is yes. That much I can say for sure, because I'm telling you that's EXACTLY what I was doing. I was trying to find a way to subtly advertise my services without being "in your face" about making such a statement. I was being mildly discreet because that's the way you need to do it on social media.

The reason for being somewhat coy in your posts is cultural. The social media world doesn't always like blatant self-promotion. They don't like their "friends" jamming advertisements down their throat. That type of behavior is greeted with getting unfollowed or blocked. Everyone who uses the platform with the hopes of getting some self-promotion knows that the only way to get your message out there without offending (and ultimately losing) your followers, is to do it in a subtle way. Understated self-promotion, even if poorly disguised, is accepted on these platforms. It might be reluctantly accepted by some users, but it's accepted nonetheless. If you acknowledge that culture, then you can see why disciplinary authorities would consider thinly veiled self-promoting statements to be "inviting the attention" of those seeking legal assistance.[14]

I understand that taking this argument to its logical conclusion is troubling. If we accept the foregoing statement

---

[14]One other note: I realize that I'm putting a lot of emphasis on the phrase "invite the attention" and some might find that problematic. After all, it's a short phrase that's buried in the commentary. However, these analyses are cases of first impression and when the authorities consider these issues they are likely to evaluate every element of the code. I believe

§ 5:8   NAVIGATING LEGAL ETHICS

about online culture as reality, then one could justifiably argue that in a social media context any statement, regardless of its content, can be considered as having been made to invite attention. Then, under the ABA-style code, all of our posts about our practice would be subject to the advertising rules. That's exactly where I'm going with this. Any statement about a lawyer's services that is made from that lawyer's personal social media account has a high probability that it will be considered to be a "communication" that is subject to the advertising rules. There are exceptions, but I believe that they only exist in theory.

Take, for example, a lawyer who doesn't make any posts about their practice at all. Then, one time in the entire history of their social media existence they make a statement like the tax appeal post above. In that case, I think they're in the clear. What if they make a self-promoting post only once a year? Again, they're probably in the clear. A solitary post is most likely not a problem. But most lawyers don't make solitary posts.

More often than not, lawyers commingle content. Even if they maintain a separate presence for their firm, most lawyers who are active on social media make frequent posts about their professional services on their personal page. That's just the way it happens. The one thing you can count on is inconsistency and overlap.

Sometimes a lawyer will make a post that is an indisputable invitation for attention, then sometime thereafter they'll make a seemingly harmless mention of their practice. They may go quite some time without logging onto their social media account at all, then they'll spend a day online making multiple posts about their practice in quick succession. Still other lawyers might make more frequent posts about their professional life, but the quality of those self-promoting statements will be only subtly promotional in nature. Note the various factors at play: frequency between posts, quantity of posts, quality of the content of those posts, etc. The potential combinations of those factors are endless. You've got to consider all of these posts, not just one statement in isolation because that's most likely what a tribunal would do.

The danger with relying on the relatively myopic view set

---

that they will carefully scrutinize every aspect of the code, including the commentary.

forth in the California opinion is that the California opinion was an academic exercise. The Committee was presented with a few hypothetical comments and it evaluated those communications in isolation. That would probably not happen in the real world. If someone finds him- or herself before a disciplinary board in real life, the board isn't going to review that lawyer's posts in isolation—it's far more likely that they'll look at the posts in the context of the lawyer's larger social media presence. Don't think so? Just go back to the Horace Hunter decision we discussed on the section about blogging. Look at how deeply the court reviewed Hunter's blog—the content, the platform—it was all inspected very closely.

Similar to the mindset of the court in *Hunter*, a tribunal who is asked to opine on whether a lawyer's social media post is a communication that triggers the ethics rules is going to have to view that situation the same way all tribunals review every matter put before them—on a case-by-case basis. Even if they are only presented with a single post for review, the investigators will most likely use their subpoena power to check into the profile and see what else is being said by the offending lawyer. They'll ask whether they are truly looking at a solitary post or even a few errant posts. They'll also check whether those posts gather together to represent a pattern of self-promotion.

The reality is that most lawyers commingle content and vary the quantity, quality, and frequency of their posts. When a tribunal reviews a lawyer's social media profile they're going to consider those posts in their totality. Based on that, and all of the foregoing, I believe that if you commingle content, there is a very high probability that tribunals will find that most self-promoting posts about your services that are made on your personal social media page will be considered "communications" that are subject to the advertising rules.

Admittedly, my interpretation is a broad one, but that's where the industry appears to be going. As you've seen elsewhere in this book, that notion is consistent with a movement throughout the rules. The attitude is all about "broader." The new language we're seeing in the rules is capturing more conduct. The standards are getting higher.

Incidentally, I realize that some people might think I've gone too far with my analysis above. There may be people who disagree about whether these posts are really covered

§ 5:8

by the rules. Maybe you don't think that a tribunal would take such a broad view. Regardless, that won't impact the rest of the analysis. We can all agree that there are some self-promotional posts that would certainly be considered "communications" which are covered by the rules. For instance, everyone would agree that a blatant statement like, "Come hire me, I'm a great lawyer and I can help you with your estate planning" would constitute an ad under almost any standard.

Don't get too excited about all of this. Let's keep things in perspective—all that I've concluded above is that the rules apply. I didn't opine on whether the statements were prohibited, or if they constituted a violation of the rules. All we're saying is that the rules apply, which means that our comments are subject to the standard set forth in the rules. But what does that mean? Let's examine the implications of concluding that our posts are subject to the rules on attorney advertising.

§ 5:9 The application of Rule 7.1 to advertising

You might recall that Rule 7.1[1] governs the content of our ads. Just to remind you of what it states, here's the rule again:

Rule 7.1. Communications concerning a lawyer's services

A lawyer shall not make a false or misleading communication about the lawyer or the lawyer's services. A communication is false or misleading if it contains a material misrepresentation of fact or law, or omits a fact necessary to make the statement considered as a whole not materially misleading.

There's an important section of the commentary to review in this context as well. Note what Comment [1] states:

[1] This Rule governs all communications about a lawyer's services, including advertising permitted by Rule 7.2. Whatever means are used to make known a lawyer's services, statements about them must be truthful.

[Section 5:9]
[1]Del. Prof. Conduct R. 7.1.
7.1 http://courts.delaware.gov/rules/DLRPCFebruary2010.pdf. Pages last checked by the author August 13, 2013.

The comment confirms that if our posts are considered to be advertising communications, the rule applies. Note something interesting, however. The comment gives us another reason to believe that this rule applies to our social media posts. Even if you don't agree that all of our social media posts about our professional life will be considered to be advertising communications, they might still otherwise be covered by Rule 7.1. Notice that the rule doesn't actually govern "ads"; rather, it is a prohibition against misleading communications about ourselves or our services. The commentary reiterates that the rule is supposed to be broadly applied and it states that Rule 7.1 governs "all communications about a lawyer's services." Of course, the analysis of whether a post constitutes a communication "about a lawyer's services" is likely to be quite similar to the discussion we had earlier. In the end, I'm going to argue that such a term will be broadly applied.

Before we get into the impact of Rule 7.1, let's consider one more important point about the breadth of the rule. Consider the following example. I was asked to deliver a CLE program in Cincinnati recently, and when I was finished I went to the airport to catch my flight home. As is usually the case, my flight was delayed. While I was drinking my coffee and eating what was probably a $45 sandwich I posted a Tweet like this one:

> Boo hoo poor me. Stuck in Cincy b/c of a late plane. #airportliving. I'll be back in Ohio in a few months. Want me to speak at your firm at that time? Then call me![2]

Well, that wasn't exactly what I said—I altered the post somewhat for the purposes of this example to make it blatantly promotional so there's no question about the advertising nature of the communication. I feel like I need to give you that disclaimer, lest you think that I'm too pushy in my own social media presence (I'm not one of *those* guys). But it's probably accepted by all that this is a statement inviting the attention of potential clients and would be subject to the advertising rules.

But is it really subject to the rules? After all, I'm not practicing law on behalf of a client, I'm teaching law at firms, bar associations, and other CLE providers. Does that change whether my statements are subject to the rule? I think not. Rule 7.1 doesn't have any limiting language in it. It doesn't

---

[2]Not sure why that # is in there? It's called a hashtag. Go look it up.

say that a lawyer shouldn't make false or misleading communications when acting on behalf of a client. It says that a lawyer can't make false or misleading communications about his or her services, without any further limitation. I'm a lawyer and these are my services. Making misrepresentations about my services is very likely going to trigger the rule.

I know what you're thinking—there he goes again, advocating the overly broad interpretation. I understand your skepticism, but I believe that the broad interpretation is warranted. Lawyers who aren't practicing law are disciplined by ethics tribunals all the time. The most famous case in recent history is former President Bill Clinton who lost his license to practice law in Arkansas.[3] At the time he was a full time politician and not actively practicing law at all. The point is, the disciplinary authorities have not been afraid to extend their enforcement arms in the direction of lawyers who aren't even engaged in the profession. Thus, the broad application of the rules is probably warranted.

Once again, my tendency to assert a wide reach of the rules won't affect our analysis. Let's return to those posts that we all agree are clearly covered by the rules and review the implications of applying Rule 7.1. Let's change my hypothetical post to something we can all agree upon:

> "Boo hoo poor me. Long divorce trial and I'm tired. Matrimonial work is my bag. Want me to represent you in your breakup? Then call me!

This is clearly an advertising communication, but is it a "false or misleading communication" that violates the rule? There doesn't seem to be anything so offensive or outlandish in the statement. It tells the reader that I was on trial and that I do matrimonial work, which seems harmless enough. But what if I fibbed? What if I wasn't actually on trial . . . what if I was actually sitting on my behind in my bathrobe all day watching The Simpsons (which I've been known to do). To take it a step further. What if I don't even do matrimonial work? Maybe I was a real estate lawyer for my whole career and am now looking to change my practice and this is a way to attract my first matrimonial client. Are these "misleading statements" as envisioned by the rule?

---

[3]See the New York Times article at http://www.nytimes.com/2001/10/01/national/01WIRE-CLIN.html, last checked by the author on February 4, 2014.

The first statement is clearly a problem. I claimed to be on trial in a divorce matter, but I wasn't. It's not even a half-truth, it's a whole untruth. Some might want to claim that the second statement isn't necessarily misleading—the statement about matrimonial law being my bag even though I've never actually had a matrimonial client. One might argue that saying that something "is my bag" could simply mean that it's an interest of mine. Once again, the commentary provides some guidance. Rule 7.2 Comment [2] states, in part, "A truthful statement is also misleading if there is a substantial likelihood that it will lead a reasonable person to formulate a specific conclusion about the lawyer or the lawyer's services for which there is no reasonable factual foundation."

The reason I included that matrimonial work "is my bag" was to get the reader to think that it's my area of specialization—I wasn't just quoting a line from an Austin Powers movie. There was a specific reason to include that text. In this case, like most instances, the post was carefully crafted so I could make an important promotional point in a cheeky, noticeable manner (because that's what people often do on social media). Here I wanted to get the reader to think that divorce cases are the kind of work that I do and that I have experience in the field.

It seems that there is a substantial likelihood that a member of the public who reads my post will get that message. They will formulate the conclusion that I have experience in matrimonial law, but there is no reasonable factual foundation for that conclusion. Thus, the statement appears to be a misleading statement under Rule 7.1.

Even though the statements are clear misrepresentations, the analysis doesn't stop there. There's another key word we need to evaluate to determine if these misrepresentations trigger the rule. We must determine whether that misrepresentation is material. Rule 7.1 states that, "A communication is false or misleading if it contains a *material* misrepresentation of fact or law, or omits a fact necessary to make the statement considered as a whole not materially misleading."[4]

Black's Law Dictionary[5] defines "material" as "Important; more or less necessary; having influence or effect; going to

---

[4]Del. Rule 7.1, emphasis added.
[5]Black's Law Dictionary 5th Edition, 1981.

the merits . . ." Thus, we need to determine whether your lie about being on trial is "important." Would your statement that matrimonial law is my bag qualify as being "more or less necessary"? The answer in both cases is probably yes. The purpose of this post was to attract potential clients. Not just any clients, matrimonial clients. That's clear because you specifically asked for people to call you if they were looking for divorce representation. Thus, the statement about having been on trial for a matrimonial matter and having experience in that area of the law was a critical part of your self-promotion as a matrimonial lawyer. Plus, if someone did respond, it's likely that your claims to be an experienced matrimonial lawyer would be a motivating factor in getting that client to call. Then the misleading statements would have had "influence or effect" on their decision which strengthens the idea that the content of the post was materially misleading.

Practice point: Step away from the rule book for a moment. I'm big on making sure that we take these analyses and apply them to real life and I want you to think about how this scenario might play out in real life. One day in your practice you might find yourself scrutinizing a self-promoting post that you're about to release to the Facebook world. You might realize that the statement is somewhat misleading. Here's what I want you to know: If, while evaluating whether you're about to make a post that is violative of Rule 7.1, you find yourself obsessing over whether the misleading statement is *materially* misleading . . . . that's when an alarm bell should be going off in your head. That's when your heightened state of awareness should start to play the soundtrack in your mind. Maybe you should avoid the statement all together? While I can't say that for sure, what I can say is that you should at least pause and realize that when you're analyzing the *extent* of your misrepresentation, you're already in a dangerous situation.

There's another reason why your evaluation of the extent of your misrepresentation should be of great concern. That's because it might not matter. Your misrepresentation doesn't necessarily have to be material to be actionable under the rules, and that's apparent when we evaluate another rule that might be determinative.

§ 5:9

There are five rules in the ethics code that deal with misrepresentation —Rules 7.1,[6] 8.1,[7] 4.1,[8] 3.3,[9] and 8.4.[10] If you review the text of each rule, you'll notice that the first four have a materiality requirement. For instance, we saw above that Rule 7.1 prohibits a "material misrepresentation of fact or law." Similarly, Rule 8.1 references a "false statement of material fact," Rule 3.3(a)(1)[11] addresses the failure to correct a "false statement of material fact or law," and Rule 4.1 deals with making "a false statement of material fact or law." The fifth rule, however, has no such limitation. Rule 8.4 doesn't have any materiality requirement. Rule 8.4 simply states that "It is professional misconduct for a lawyer to . . .(c) engage in conduct involving dishonesty, fraud, deceit or misrepresentation . . ."

One could read this rule to prohibit any type of misrepresentation by a lawyer. According to the rule, there's no reason to consider whether the post was *materially* misleading—the fact that it was a misrepresentation at all triggers the rule. And it goes even further. Not only do we need to be concerned about the quality of the content (whether the misrepresentation is material), but we also need to be concerned about the context of the content.

Notice that Rule 8.4(c)[12] doesn't say that it only applies when we're working on behalf of a client or when we're mak-

---

[6]Del. Prof. Conduct R. 7.1.

7.1 http://courts.delaware.gov/rules/DLRPCFebruary2010.pdf. Pages last checked by the author August 13, 2013.

[7]Del. Prof. Conduct R. 8.1.

8.1 http://courts.delaware.gov/rules/DLRPCFebruary2010.pdf. Pages last checked by the author August 13, 2013.

[8]Del. Prof. Conduct R. 4.1.

4.1 http://courts.delaware.gov/rules/DLRPCFebruary2010.pdf. Pages last checked by the author August 13, 2013.

[9]Del. Prof. Conduct R. 3.3.

3.3 http://courts.delaware.gov/rules/DLRPCFebruary2010.pdf. Pages last checked by the author August 13, 2013.

[10]Del. Prof. Conduct R. 8.4.

8.4 http://courts.delaware.gov/rules/DLRPCFebruary2010.pdf. Pages last checked by the author August 13, 2013.

[11]Del. Prof. Conduct R. 3.3(a)(1).

3.3(a)(1) http://courts.delaware.gov/rules/DLRPCFebruary2010.pdf. Pages last checked by the author August 13, 2013.

[12]Del. Prof. Conduct R. 8.4(c).

8.4(c) http://courts.delaware.gov/rules/DLRPCFebruary2010.pdf. Pages last checked by the author August 13, 2013.

§ 5:9   NAVIGATING LEGAL ETHICS

ing posts about our services. In fact, a strict reading of the text reveals that it goes way beyond anything that might be work related. The reality is that the prohibition against acting in a misleading and deceitful manner applies beyond our practice. Thus, heed Rule 8.4(c) and be careful at all times—misleading social media posts that aren't work related could still give you a disciplinary headache. Note that this is consistent with the concept I've asserted before which states that what we do outside the office matters. We see that distinction between our personal and professional lives is gone in many ways and it's particularly apparent when using social media.

To some extent Rule 8.4(c) trumps the other four rules regarding misrepresentation and it makes you wonder why the drafters let that happen. Why even have some of the other rules if you're going to have this catch-all rule? I'm not so sure why the drafters built the code this way and there might be something in the legislative history that explains it, but I don't really care that much. As my wife says, "it is what it is." Rule 8.4(c) happens to cast a very wide net and there's a lot of lawyer behavior that could be caught in this net. The reality is that Rule 8.4 hangs beneath the entire code and catches the bad conduct that slips through the rest of the rules.

Once again I'm advocating a broad interpretation of the rules. Once again, you might think I'm taking it too far. But (once again) remember what I said in the introduction. I'm a firm believer that if you do something repulsive, they're going to find a way to get you. Rule 8.4(c) is one of the rules that the disciplinary boards run to when they want to get you for bad conduct.

This entire analysis is a chore. Sifting through each one of our social media posts with such a fine-tooth comb can be a maddening effort. But this is the level of analysis that you need to go through if you're going to use social media in a promotional manner. Reviewing every social media post for possible misrepresentations can be an arduous task and seems out of step with the rest of society. I mean, people fib on social media all the time. Embellishment about one's abilities and qualifications is almost a national past time on Facebook. But what might be right for some, isn't necessarily right for members of the bar. We are held to a different standard than the rest of society and this is just another example.

Practice Point: How might this come up in real life? Let's

face it, it's not likely that a disciplinary board is going to go on a "post-hunt." But what's more likely to happen is that the board will be investigating some other claim and stumble upon some concerning posts. Perhaps a client complained that you didn't communicate with them adequately pursuant to Rule 1.4. One of your defenses might be that you communicated through texting and even some direct messages on Facebook or LinkedIn. Then, the board might review your account history to verify that you've actually been communicating, and that's when they might run across some problematic posts. Remember, the disciplinary authorities don't always have to restrict their investigation to the items complained about in the grievance. If some other violation is revealed during the course of their investigation, they are probably permitted to look into it further.

§ 5:10 Other technicalities

Let's step away from posts for a moment and talk about some of the other technicalities of the advertising rules. Don't forget everything we've talked about, however, because we're going to circle back and see how those technicalities apply to posts in a moment.

Claims of Specialization

I mentioned earlier that the official justification for lawyers to promote themselves is because the public can get better information about the legal services that are available to them. But when we allow lawyers to advertise, we also know that there is a high possibility that some of us might act in a misleading manner. Thus, the purpose of rules like Rule 7.1[1] is to regulate how lawyers speak about themselves so the public can be protected from the unscrupulous members of the bar.

But Rule 7.1 isn't the only rule that governs how lawyers are permitted to talk about themselves. That rule talks about the general category of prohibited statements (those that are false and misleading), but there are other rules that get

---

[Section 5:10]

[1]Del. Prof. Conduct R. 7.1.
7.1 http://courts.delaware.gov/rules/DLRPCFebruary2010.pdf. Pages last checked by the author August 13, 2013.

specific. Rule 7.4,[2] for instance, deals with our claims of specialization. It's widely accepted that lawyers can't run around calling themselves "experts" in a field of practice. That might be acceptable puffery in another profession, but it's misleading in the practice of law. Rule 7.4 gives specific instruction on how we're allowed to communicate that our practice is tailored toward a particular area of law. It states:

Rule 7.4. Communication of fields of practice and specialization

(a) A lawyer may communicate the fact that the lawyer does or does not practice in particular fields of law.

(b) A lawyer admitted to engage in patent practice before the United States Patent and Trademark Office may use the designation "Patent Attorney" or a substantially similar designation.

(c) A lawyer engaged in Admiralty practice may use the designation "Admiralty," "Proctor in Admiralty" or a substantially similar designation.

(d) A lawyer shall not state or imply that a lawyer is certified as a specialist in a particular field of law, unless:

(1) the lawyer has been certified as a specialist by an organization that has been approved by an appropriate state authority or that has been accredited by the American Bar Association; and

(2) the name of the certifying organization is clearly identified in the communication.

Even though the language in the black letter rule sounds a bit restrictive, the drafters gave us some relief from that harshness elsewhere. It appears that they saw the need to strike a balance between the necessity for regulation of the profession and the reality of life in the practice. In doing so, they showed how this rule overlaps somewhat with the more generic Rule 7.1. The drafters noted in the commentary that, ". . . A lawyer is generally permitted to state that the lawyer is a "specialist," practices a "specialty," or "specializes in" particular fields, but such communications are subject to the

---

[2]Del. Prof. Conduct R. 7.4.

7.4 http://courts.delaware.gov/rules/DLRPCFebruary2010.pdf. Pages last checked by the author August 13, 2013.

"false and misleading" standard applied in Rule 7.1 to communications concerning a lawyer's services."[3]

It's important to understand the rationale for the seemingly contradictory sentiments in the rule and commentary. The drafters must have understood that lawyers want to be clear about the areas of law that they practice. They must have realized that lawyers would want to tout their unique abilities in a particular field of law, especially if they'd been honing their skills in that practice area for many years. In this case, the lawyer's own self-interest happens to advance the core motivations for permitting lawyer promotion all together—the idea of getting valuable information into the hands of the public. Surely, clients want to know which lawyers focus on difficult areas of law so that they can factor it into their lawyer-selection decision making process.

Like always, however, it's important to check the language of your individual state ethics code because not all states are as permissive as the ABA drafters. Many states didn't adopt the commentary language which allows lawyers to use the term "specialist." Look at Ohio's Comment [1] to Rule 7.4, for instance, and you'll see that the phrase discussed above simply isn't there. Likewise, New York's code allows lawyers to list the area of law that they practice and even state that their practice is limited to certain types of law, but the rule specifically prohibits use of the term "specialist." New York Rule 7.4(a) states that, "the lawyer or law firm shall not state that the lawyer or law firm is a specialist or specializes in a particular field of law, except as provided in Rule 7.4(c)" (subsection (c) only permits the use of the term "specialist" if the lawyer received a formal designation by some organization or authority). North Carolina has similar language in its Comment [1] to Rule 7.4 which provides, "To avoid misrepresentation and deception, a lawyer may not communicate that the lawyer has been recognized or certified as a specialist in a particular field of law," unless they received an official designation. In fact, many states have eschewed the ABA approach and have adopted a more restricted standard.

The prohibition against identifying ourselves as experts or specialists has implications in the social media world. The obvious way it applies is when we talk about ourselves, generally. Thus, whether we're referring to ourselves in a

---

[3]Del. Rule 7.4, Comment [1].

§ 5:10   NAVIGATING LEGAL ETHICS

blog, a post, or any other format, we can't refer to ourselves as a "specialist" if our rules prohibit use of that term. But a few decisions have extended this restriction to other parts of social media.

The New York State Bar Association[4] discussed how this restriction would apply to our profiles on certain social media sites. The Bar was asked to opine on whether a firm that has, "created a page on LinkedIn . . . can, in the 'About' segment of the listing, include a section labeled 'specialties.' " LinkedIn had a separate section which allowed the user to enter several terms in a subsection of their profile called "Specialties" and the Bar was considering whether that section was something lawyers could use. The Bar said no. They stated,

> A lawyer or law firm listed on a social media site may, under Rule 7.4(a), identify one or more areas of law practice. But to list those areas under a heading of "Specialties" would constitute a claim that the lawyer or law firm "is a specialist or specializes in a particular field of law" and thus, absent certification as provide in Rule 7.4(a), would violate 7.4(a). *[citation omitted]* Op 972 at 2.

It seems likely that most states would agree with this reasoning, given that many states have similar restrictions to that which we find in the New York code. If your state adopts this line of thinking, it has a significant practical effect. If you are entering your information in a profile of some website and you see a section with a separate category called "Specialties," you probably want to avoid entering any text. That's easy enough to understand, but the application of this concept in the world of social media can get tricky.

We need to be diligent in scrutinizing the details of our profiles to ensure we comply with this technical rule requirement. For instance, while we want to be sure that we don't use a profile section with an inappropriate heading, it may not be obvious what label the profile section will actually contain. You might be entering your information into a generic text box, but when you save that information, the profile section of the page could default to a prohibited term. One "click," and the site pops up the term "Specialty." We need to be diligent to make sure that doesn't happen.

Also, social media platforms are constantly changing. A section that might not have an offending label today could be

---

[4]New York State Bar Association Ethics Opinion 972 (6/26/13).

changed overnight and we might not even know it. Website designers constantly make subtle changes without our knowledge. LinkedIn, for instance, no longer has "Specialties" as a separate category. For reasons unknown to me, the platform eliminated the separate category and combined the text that was previously in that section with the language that is in the "Summary" section of the user's profile. However, when the programmers made that change and moved the language into the Summary, they kept the phrase "Specialties" in the text. Thus, a lawyer in a state that shares the New York view needs to manually edit their profile and remove the term "Specialties" from their profile.

Notice another interesting comment in that New York opinion. The Bar noted that the rule permits certified specialists to list that designation, but it doesn't permit the law *firm* to make such a designation. The Bar reminded us that. ". . . Rule 7.4(c) does not provide that a law firm (as opposed to an individual lawyer) may claim recognition or certification as a specialist, and Rule 7.4(a) would therefore prohibit such a claim by a firm." NY Bar Op. 972 at 2. Thus, if your firm has its own page on a social media site, it wouldn't be appropriate to make a generic reference to a certification. Presumably, it would be okay if the language in the firm profile tied the certifications to the particular attorneys. The point is, watch out for the details. They matter in the world of social media and this type of thing can very easily slip through the cracks. Scrutinize!

One last key comment about NY Bar Opinion 972. As we've just read, the Opinion dealt with the specific issue of whether a lawyer could list some areas of practice in a category entitled "specialties." There are a lot of other profile categories that are found in different social media platforms, however, and the Bar made short mention of that. In fact, it was a little too short for my taste. The Bar wrote, "We do not in this opinion address whether the lawyer or law firm could, consistent with Rule 7.4(a) list practice areas under other headings such as 'Products & Services' or 'Skills and Expertise.' "[5] Quite frankly, I get frustrated from comments like this.

Whoever asked the question that was the impetus for Opinion 972 obviously limited their question to the issue of specialities. But while they conducted their review of that is-

---

[5] New York State Bar Association Opinion 972 at 2.

§ 5:10   NAVIGATING LEGAL ETHICS

sue, the Bar clearly realized that there were other categories that a lawyer might run into, some of which might be called "Products & Services" or "Skills and Expertise." So the Bar gave us their disclaimer: "Hey lawyers, we talked about *specialties*, but nothing else. We're not opining on those other categories." Why not?! If the Bar knows that those other categories exist and that lawyers will need to address them, why not take the extra step and give us your opinion on whether they are appropriate? The opinion's disclaimer provides cover for the Bar, but it doesn't provide guidance for the lawyers. Consider that issue in light of "Endorsements." I'm particularly frustrated because one of the categories they mentioned, "Skills and Expertise" is a big issue right now.

Endorsements

LinkedIn has a function that allows people to "endorse" other users for particular skills and expertise. Here's how that works: users will sometimes have a notification pop up on their screen that will ask them whether they want to endorse a fellow user. The image below is a screenshot from my profile which shows how the notification looks.

Once you press the "Endorse" link, the endorsement is sent to that other user. In other circumstances, you can choose from a pre-determined list of skills categories and once a category is selected the user being endorsed will receive a notification that the first user has made the endorsement. If the endorsements are accepted by the user you're endorsing, the skill will then be listed on the endorsed user's profile page. I guess it's a way of adding a little credibility to one's profile. When someone reviews your profile, it looks good if other people have acknowledged your particular skills and expertise. Below is a screenshot from my LinkedIn page that shows how it looks when an endorsement is made.

84

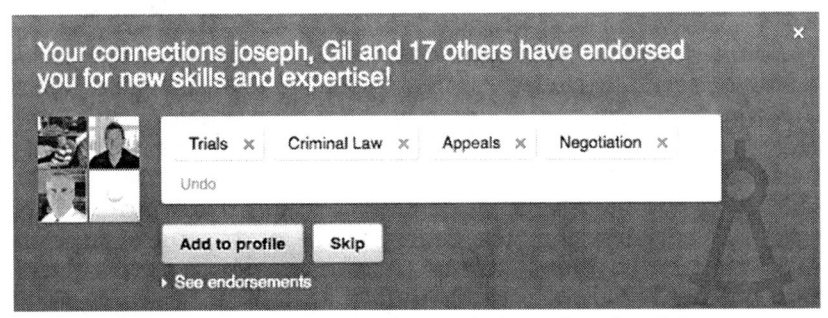

The problem that we need to ask in a legal ethics context is twofold. First, can we accept the endorsements? Second, even if we can accept the endorsements, what if we're being endorsed for an area of law in which we don't have very much experience? Regarding the former question, we got some direction from the State of Florida.

In a letter dated September 11, 2013, an Assistant Ethics Counsel at the Florida Bar opined in response to an inquiry about this very topic. Counsel noted that the Florida rules only permitted a lawyer to claim specialization if that lawyer had an accredited certification of some sort. Counsel further stated that "Based on these rules, it is staff's position that you may not list your areas of practice under the header 'Skills and Expertise' as you are not board certified."[6] I think there's a small flaw in one part of the opinion—they referred to New York's Opinion 972 in support of their opinion. But as I mentioned earlier, the New York Bar Association made a disclaimer about the "Skills and Expertise" heading and refused to render an opinion on that aspect of the issue. Regardless, the Florida Opinion is instructive. Clearly, some boards won't see a distinction between "Specialties" and "Skills and Expertise." In those jurisdictions, a lawyer should not accept an endorsement which conveys knowledge in a particular area of law.

Notice an additional nuance in the rule, however. Let's say that you're in a jurisdiction that adopted the New York/Florida position and the state only permits lawyers to list areas of specialization if they are certified. Let's further assume that you have the proper specialization credentials in a particular field and someone sends you an endorsement for that area of law. In that case, you'd feel justified in accepting it to your profile. However, simply accepting the listing of that specialty area of law might not be sufficient.

---

[6] Florida Letter 9/11/13 at 1.

§ 5:10   NAVIGATING LEGAL ETHICS

Rule 7.4(d)[7] permits lawyers to state that they are "certified as a specialist in a particular field of law," but the commentary gives further direction. It states that if you're going to make that assertion, then you must also include the name of the certifying organization. Specifically, Rule 7.4, Comment [2] states, "In order to insure that consumers can obtain access to useful information about an organization granting certification, the name of the certifying organization must be included in any communication regarding the certification." This allows the public to look into the certifying organization to confirm the legitimacy of the certification, among other things. Remember—it's all about protecting the public and arming them with the information they need to protect themselves. The point: Listing the area of specialty in the endorsement section, by itself, might not be enough. You probably also need to include the name of the certifying organization elsewhere in your profile.

The issue of endorsements is a little thorny when we talk about the recommendations that refer to specific areas of law. "Securities Law," "Bankruptcy"—these are areas which are clear indication of a specialization which trigger Rule 7.4. But the issue doesn't seem so confusing when we evaluate the more generic topic of "skills." If someone wants to endorse you for "Legal Writing" or "Public Speaking" you're probably not going to raise the ire of the disciplinary authorities. Those phrases don't constitute a "particular field of law" so Rule 7.4(a) would probably not apply. There doesn't seem to be any other restriction on such endorsements, provided that they're truthful . . . which leads us to the second major issue dealing with endorsements.

Let's set the stage: We've determined that listing a skill, by itself, probably isn't problematic. Let's also eliminate a prior problem we discussed and assume that we're in a jurisdiction that allows a lawyer to accept endorsements that state an area of law that you practice. So we're in a jurisdiction where the idea of the endorsement is permitted. The question remains, however: What if an endorsement that we receive is not accurate? Are we allowed to accept the endorsement? Take a peek at the screenshot from my profile above. Apparently, people in the social media world have endorsed me for Trials, Criminal Law, Appeals, and Negotiation.

---
[7]Del. Prof. Conduct R. 7.4(d).

7.4(d) http://courts.delaware.gov/rules/DLRPCFebruary2010.pdf. Pages last checked by the author August 13, 2013.

Unfortunately, however, I don't have a smidgen of experience in either Criminal Law or Appeals. Can I accept the endorsement? Another endorsement in the screenshot above is for "Trials." In my career I've done a couple of trials, but not a whole lot. I've conducted some bench trials and years ago I did some municipal court trials when I was a local prosecutor, but those were glorified hearings. I wouldn't consider myself experienced in trial work, per se. Plus, the people who have endorsed me for "Trials" don't have any personal knowledge of any of my (limited) trial experience. In this case I know who those people are and I know we've never worked on any trials together.

It seems nonsensical to endorse someone if you don't actually know if they have experience in the topic, but it happens all the time. We mentioned earlier that the endorsements are most likely there because the addition of these labels adds credibility to your profile, and the idea that an independent person sent you this endorsement presumably adds another layer of credibility. Thus, people might be motivated to endorse you for a category that the computer suggests even if they don't have any personal experience with you in that area. Stated simply, they may just think it's a nice thing to do for someone. They may even believe that, in doing so, you'll return the favor someday. This is part of the culture of social media.

Back to my lack of actual trial experience. If I don't consider myself to actually possess the skill for which I'm being endorsed, isn't it misleading to allow that endorsement to appear on my profile? For that we need to revisit our earlier analysis of Rule 7.1. Remember, Rule 7.4's commentary states that "communications are subject to the 'false and misleading' standard applied in Rule 7.1 to communications concerning a lawyer's services." As a result, we must inquire whether the endorsement constitutes a "communication" that is governed by the advertising rules.

We need to ask whether the endorsement "invite[s] the attention of those seeking legal assistance" per the ABA-style commentary in Rule 7.1. Here's what the endorsements on LinkedIn look like when they're displayed my profile.

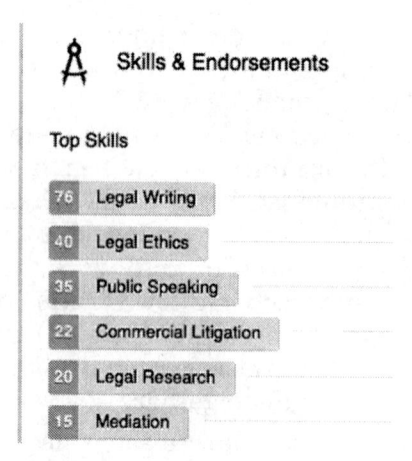

> **Skills & Endorsements**
>
> Top Skills
>
> - 76 Legal Writing
> - 40 Legal Ethics
> - 35 Public Speaking
> - 22 Commercial Litigation
> - 20 Legal Research
> - 15 Mediation

Remember, the layout could change over time and these types of endorsements could be different on various sites. We're not so concerned with the style of the layout, as much as the fact that these endorsements are being displayed all together.

If you take my earlier argument to its extreme, then you could argue that almost any communication about our services that we make on social media could be a "communication" that triggers the rules. Even though we didn't make the statement about our skills and expertise, one could argue that by allowing this endorsement to exist on our profile we are permitting this communication to be made. I know what you're thinking—this sounds like even more of a stretch than our earlier discussion. Maybe, but I happen to think that it's an accurate argument. If you ascribe to my view, then you've made "a false or misleading communication about the lawyer or the lawyer's services" that violates Rule 7.1. Of course, the analysis isn't complete because you need to determine whether it's a "material misrepresentation." As usual, that would depend on the circumstances—and this time even I think that's a tough argument to make.

I admit that getting Rule 7.1 to apply here would be an uphill battle. I respect the view that the mere listing of a skill, without any further elaboration might not qualify as inviting the attention of someone seeking legal assistance per Rule 7.1's commentary. Even more, I concur in the judgment that such a bare communication like the listing of a category/skill label might not be considered a "material" misstatement. But I still think you have a problem. I think that this is good example of how the misleading statements that don't fit perfectly into rules like Rule 7.1 will get caught in the net cast by Rule 8.4(c).

Remember that Rule 8.4(c) doesn't have the limiting "materiality" element. That rule states that it is professional misconduct to "engage in conduct involving dishonesty, fraud, deceit or misrepresentation." It's a broad restriction that captures far more activity. In addition, the action that triggers Rule 8.4 is broad. The rule simply says that a lawyer shall not "engage in conduct" that violates the rule. The act of accepting an endorsement seems like an overt action that would constitute "engaging in conduct." It's an affirmative step that is taken by the lawyer and, but for the conduct, there would have been no misleading language on the profile page. Beware of Rule 8.4 at all times—it sneaks up on you.

Testimonials

The "Endorsements" function on LinkedIn is only one place where other people can leave comments about you on your profile page. The other related (and dangerous) function is with testimonials. LinkedIn allows you to provide "Recommendations" for other users. This is simply an opportunity for you to give a testimonial to someone else. The (presumably) kind words you'll say about that individual is then displayed on their profile page to add credibility to that user, similar to the concept we discussed above regarding Skills & Expertise.

Here's how the LinkedIn feature works: when you view another person's profile, a prompt appears asking if you'd like to recommend the person whose profile you're viewing, like this:

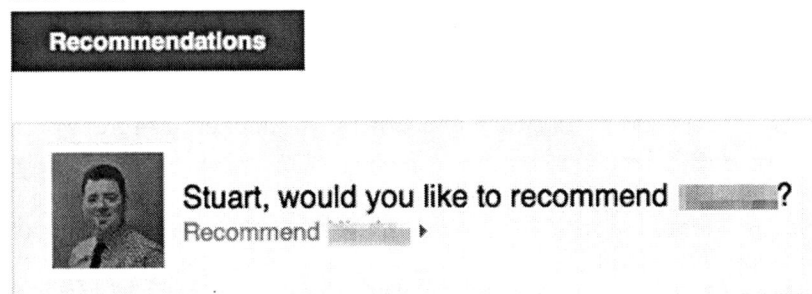

Recommendations

Stuart, would you like to recommend ▨▨▨?
Recommend ▨▨▨ ▸

If you choose to follow the links, eventually your recommendation will appear on that person's profile page as a testimonial:

§ 5:10

> 1 recommendation

Business Development and Operations

It was a real pleasure working with Stuart on his "How to be a Powerful and Ethical Legal Negotiator" seminar. He was able to blend ethical admonitions, negotiation strategy, and good humor into a program that was as entertaining as it was... View ↓

This functionality is by no means restricted to LinkedIn. One doesn't need this specific platform to leave a testimonial for others because there are a variety of opportunities for someone to make flattering comments about a lawyer on social media. For example, if a lawyer maintains a blog, a member of the public could write some testimonial and insert it into the comments section after a blog post. It's easy on other platforms as well—someone could write a complimentary statement about a lawyer on that lawyer's Timeline in Facebook. There are multiple variations. But much like everything that occurs on social media, there are ethical concerns for lawyers when other people give us testimonials.

Once again, I want to direct your attention to the core motivation behind the rules—to protect the client and protect the public. The drafters are concerned with misleading statements that can misrepresent the lawyer in the eyes of the public. Misleading testimonials are a way that lawyers might manipulate unwitting members of the public and the drafters in many jurisdictions have created closely tailored rules in response. The concern was best described by the Supreme Court of California several decades ago. The court in *Belli v. State Bar of California*,[8] addressed flashy statements made by a lawyer that were designed to attract attention to his services. The opinion states that, "Exposition of an attorney's accomplishments in an effort to interest persons . . . is one thing," but suggesting that clients will be, "dazzled by the services they have received from the attorney . . . is quite another." Thus, the court acknowledged that some statements are okay, but there are limits (a shocker, I'm sure).

Since the concern we have over testimonials is that they might constitute misleading statements about a lawyer or our services, we must go back to the rule that we referenced elsewhere, Rule 7.1. Recall that the ABA-recommended language that was adopted in states like Delaware reads:

---

[8]10 Cal.3d 824, L.A. No. 30120, Supreme Court of California (1974)], found on http://scocal.stanford.edu/opinion/belli-v-state-bar-27779, last checked by the author on December 1, 2013.

Advertising § 5:10

Rule 7.1. Communications concerning a lawyer's services

A lawyer shall not make a false or misleading communication about the lawyer or the lawyer's services. A communication is false or misleading if it contains a material misrepresentation of fact or law, or omits a fact necessary to make the statement considered as a whole not materially misleading.

Remember, however, that the ABA-suggested language represented a compromise among the various members of the drafting committee. There's usually a debate among the drafters when they're creating the rules—some members of the drafting committee argue for a more stringent rule while others advocate looser language. That argument replays itself when the rules are adopted at the state level and it means that there are sometimes very different versions of a particular rule among jurisdictions. This is particularly true of the rules that deal with advertising, including Rule 7.1. In order to evaluate the issue around testimonials we must consider the spectrum of rules from various states. And remember that despite the variations, each rule is concerned with the same thing—making sure that lawyers don't manipulate other people.

Some jurisdictions outright prohibit testimonials. Take Arkansas' Rule 7.1 for example—which states that testimonials are false and misleading by definition. Here's the text:

Rule 7.1. Communications Concerning a Lawyer's Services

A lawyer shall not make a false or misleading communication about the lawyer or the lawyer's services. A communication is false or misleading if it:

(a) contains a material misrepresentation of fact or law, or omits a fact necessary to make the statement considered as a whole not materially misleading;

(b) is likely to create an unjustified expectation about the results the lawyer can achieve, or states or implies that the lawyer can achieve results by means that violate the rules of professional conduct or other law;

(c) compares the lawyer's services with other lawyers' services, unless the comparison can be factually substantiated; or

(d) **contains a testimonial or endorsement.** *[emphasis added]*

91

§ 5:10 NAVIGATING LEGAL ETHICS

Others jurisdictions prohibit testimonials, but leave a window open for their use provided that a disclaimer is present. California's Rule 1-400 is an example:

> Pursuant to rule 1-400(E) the Board has adopted the following standards, effective May 27, 1989, unless noted otherwise, as forms of "communication" defined in rule 1-400(A) which are presumed to be in violation of rule 1-400:[9]
>
> * * *
>
> (2) A "communication" which contains testimonials about or endorsements of a member **unless such communication also contains an express disclaimer such as "this testimonial or endorsement does not constitute a guarantee, warranty, or prediction regarding the outcome of your legal matter."** *[emphasis added]*

Still other jurisdictions permit testimonials, but they put restrictions on their content. A good example is North Carolina's Rule 7.1, which reads in part:

> **Rule 7.1. Communications Concerning a Lawyer's Services**
>
> (a) A lawyer shall not make a false or misleading communication about the lawyer or the lawyer's services. A communication is false or misleading if it:
>
> (1) contains a material misrepresentation of fact or law, or omits a fact necessary to make the statement considered as a whole not materially misleading;
>
> **(2) is likely to create an unjustified expectation about results the lawyer can achieve, or states or implies that the lawyer can achieve results by means that violate the Rules of Professional Conduct or other law;** or
>
> **(3) compares the lawyer's services with other lawyers' services, unless the comparison can be factually substantiated.** *[emphases added]*

Your obligations, as always, are dictated by the terms of your local rule and there are vastly different requirements, depending on the style of Rule 7.1 to which you must adhere. If you're in a state where there is an outright prohibition on testimonials, like Arkansas, then you obviously can't include any on your website. It also means that you can't place them

---

[9]http://rules.calbar.ca.gov/Portals/10/documents/2013_CaliforniaRulesofProfessionalConduct.pdf, last checked by the author on December 3, 2013.

on your social media profile pages, provided that you agree with our earlier discussion that those profiles are the functional equivalent of a website. Consistent with this logic, you also probably can't accept "Recommendations" on LinkedIn from a client, colleague, business partner, or anyone else for that matter. That "Recommendation" is clearly a testimonial, so it would be prohibited in a state that has a rule prohibiting testimonials.

What if you're in North Carolina or a jurisdiction with a similar rule? It depends upon what the recommendation/testimonial actually says. What if someone offers you a recommendation that states,

> Stuart Teicher got me out of a drunk driving ticket because he's awesome. He can do the exact same thing for you, too. CALL HIM!!

It's hard to imagine a more blatant way to "create an unjustified expectation about the results the lawyer can achieve."[10] Clearly, such a testimonial would violate the rule.

Likewise, you'd be in a bad ethical place if someone offered you a recommendation that stated, "I've used Joe Shmoe and I've used Stuart Teicher and I'll tell you what . . ..Stuart Teicher is waaaay better than Joe Shmoe." That would violate the prohibition on comparing a lawyer's services without a factual basis.[11]

What about the jurisdictions like Delaware that adopted the model rule-style text? There appears to be a broader standard—the lawyer must simply refrain from making statements that are "misleading." That includes testimonials, of course. And as we pointed out above, the ABA's version of Rule 7.1 doesn't have any language regarding unjustified expectations or comparative statements in the black letter portion of the rule. Be careful, however, because this is an example of how the commentary can sneak up and bite you from behind. You're not necessarily immune from the limiting language because the ABA-style rule refers to those other restrictions in Comment [3] to Rule 7.1:

> An advertisement that truthfully reports a lawyer's achievements on behalf of clients or former clients may be misleading if presented so as to lead a reasonable person to form an unjustified expectation that the same results could be obtained

---

[10] North Carolina Rule 7.1(a)(2) to (3).
[11] North Carolina Rule 7.1(a)(3).

§ 5:10   NAVIGATING LEGAL ETHICS

for other clients in similar matters without reference to the specific factual and legal circumstances of each client's case. Similarly, an unsubstantiated comparison of the lawyer's services or fees with the services or fees of other lawyers may be misleading if presented with such specificity as would lead a reasonable person to conclude that the comparison can be substantiated. The inclusion of an appropriate disclaimer or qualifying language may preclude a finding that a statement is likely to create unjustified expectations or otherwise mislead a prospective client.

So what's the bottom line? If you display a testimonial on your website (which includes accepting a recommendation on LinkedIn) in a jurisdiction that bans testimonials, you've broken the rules. However, if you're in a jurisdiction that permits testimonials but puts restrictions on their content, displaying a testimonial is okay, provided that the testimonial doesn't violate the unjustified expectation standard, doesn't make a prohibited comparative statement and isn't otherwise misleading. That's probably the case in an ABA-style state as well, given the language in the commentary of Rule 7.1.

There's a little wrinkle here that must be addressed. At first, this won't even appear to be an issue worth discussing, but the realities of social media platforms throw a teeny monkey wrench into the machine. The issue comes back to whether you, personally, are making a communication.

§ 5:11 Controlling statements about you that are made by others, and "making" a communication

When you receive a recommendation on LinkedIn, you, personally, didn't place the testimonial on your profile. It's added to your profile by someone else. Another LinkedIn user writes the recommendation and sends it to your page. Of course, the recommendation/testimonial doesn't actually appear on your site unless you accept it. You need to take some action to allow the testimonial to appear on your profile.

Have you, personally, made the communication such that the rule is violated? Rule 7.1[1] states that, "A *lawyer* shall not make a false or misleading communication about the lawyer

---

[Section 5:11]

[1]Del. Prof. Conduct R. 7.1.

or the lawyer's services." [emphasis added]. You didn't initiate the testimonial; someone else started that process. It seems almost certain, however, that that you will be considered to have "made" the communication. You took an affirmative step to accept the testimonial and allowed it to remain on your profile. Thus, common sense dictates that you made the potentially offending communication.

The issue gets a bit muddled, however, when you look at something like blog post comments. If you maintain a blog, any member of the public could place a testimonial on that blog by making the testimonial in a comment to one of your posts. Depending on how a blog is programmed, that testimonial might be added to the blog without any action by the blog owner.

Of course, a lawyer could avoid this situation by "moderating" comments on their blog. That means that a lawyer could choose to require that all comments be reviewed and approved by the lawyer before they are permitted to appear on the blog. What's key, however, is that the ability to moderate comments is something that must be selected in a blog's settings. The blogger must actually go to the settings module of a blog and tell the blog whether the owner is requiring posts to be moderated before they can be exhibited on the website. In real life bloggers often choose not to moderate comments. Sometimes it's done out of ignorance—the blogger isn't very advanced and they don't know that they even have the ability to select a "moderate first" option. It's common, however, for bloggers to specifically forego moderating comments because it's consistent with the idea of encouraging the free flow of ideas on the Internet. While that might sound overly philosophical, there is a practical aspect to this approach. Many savvy social media users consider the credibility of a blog to be greatly enhanced if it allows comments to be posted without a filter. That extra element of credibility might be important to a lawyer who is using the blog in a self-promotional effort.

Thus, a lawyer-blogger could choose not to moderate comments. In that case, any comment made to a blog will be automatically posted to the site. Once that's done, a testimonial might be made by a member of the public and it would appear on the lawyer's site without any further affir-

---

7.1 http://courts.delaware.gov/rules/DLRPCFebruary2010.pdf. Pages last checked by the author August 13, 2013.

§ 5:11

mative act by the lawyer, and that might be a problem.[2] To determine whether we have an ethical violation we're forced to revisit Rule 7.1.

Review the text of the rule again (for the up-teenth time): "A lawyer shall not make a false or misleading communication about the lawyer or the lawyer's services." But the initial question in this analysis isn't about the misleading nature of the text—it's whether a lawyer is deemed to have "made" the communication all together. There is nothing in the Rule or commentary to Rule 7.1 that addresses whether the lawyer is deemed to have made a communication when someone else makes a statement about that lawyer and inserts the statement directly onto a lawyer's social media page. Common sense may dictate that you "make" a communication when you specifically approve someone's statement and permit it to be placed on your site. It's not so clear, however, whether you've "made" a communication if all you did was sit passively by and another person placed their comments on the site without moderation.

One could argue that the lawyer isn't sitting passively by. The lawyer took an affirmative action by selecting the "no moderation" setting on the blog. In a situation where a lawyer purposely set their blog in that manner, the lawyer made a choice to permit comments to be posted without the requirement of prior review. Then, while there is no affirmative act to allow each individual comment, there was an overall decision to allow every comment. Seen in that light, it seems as if the lawyer "made" the communication and that it would be covered by Rule 7.1. Once making that determination, you'd need to evaluate if the comment was a misleading testimonial or otherwise violated Rule 7.1, consistent with our discussion above.

I submit that it is conceivable, even likely, that a disciplinary authority would feel the same way. It's a mildly far-reaching concept—that a lawyer can be deemed to have "made" a comment that is covered by Rule 7.1 by virtue of choosing certain blog settings. But it's not so far out there. The truth is, it's no different from a lawyer 20 years ago handing a person a piece of paper and saying, "I'm sending this newsletter to the public. Write whatever you want on it and I'll send it to everyone, regardless of what it says." In both cases, the lawyer permitted the offending statement to be released to the public.

---

[2] We're assuming that we're in a jurisdiction where testimonials aren't outright forbidden, of course.

It seems like the key factor is "control." In all of the foregoing situations, the lawyer was able to control what was released to the public. The lawyer either specifically approved each testimonial for publication on his or her blog with knowledge of its conduct, or the lawyer knowingly allowed every testimonial to be published on his or her blog, regardless of its content.

§ 5:12 Being aware of statements about you that are made by others and "making" a communication

In all of the foregoing situations, however, the lawyer was aware that something was being said. Either they accepted a recommendation or moderated a blog comment. Even in the case where a blog comment was unmoderated and posted on a lawyer's blog, it's very likely going to be something the lawyer "should have" been aware of. After all, it's your site. However, there are situations where a lawyer might not be aware that they're being talked about on the Internet all together. Maybe someone mentioned you on another person's website or in a comment to some blog post somewhere in the social media universe. Once again, common sense peeks in. If a lawyer doesn't know that there are statements being made about them that constitute violations of the rules, they can't be held responsible.[1] However, the key factor in these situations appears to be awareness. Once the lawyer finds out that these statements are out there, a duty to do something about it kicks in. This was addressed by the South Carolina Bar in Ethics Advisory Opinion 99-09.

In the facts before the South Carolina Bar, a lawyer's clients created a web page that discussed ongoing litigation without the lawyer's knowledge or direction. The Bar found that the effect of the webpage was to advertise the lawyer's services and attract potential clients for similar matters. The Bar determined that the advertising rules applied to that type of communication. Even though the site was created without the lawyer's knowledge, the Bar imposed various duties upon the lawyers once they became aware of the existence of the site. Regarding advertising, in particular, the Bar stated:

[Section 5:12]

[1]Remember, I'm not the disciplinary authority. These are just my educated opinions.

§ 5:12   NAVIGATING LEGAL ETHICS

If the web page does not comply with the rules on advertising, the attorneys should counsel the client about any omissions and advise the client about how the web page could be changed to comply with those rules. If the client refuses to bring the page into compliance, the lawyer should give serious consideration to withdrawal from representation to avoid any impression that the lawyer has authorized or adopted the client's continued use of the web page.[2]

There were a host of other ethical concerns that the Bar discussed in their opinion, beyond just advertising. The point, however, is that once you learn that someone is talking about you on the Internet and that those communications violate the ethics rules, there is a duty to do something about it. How we define the extent of our responsibilities depends on the circumstances. If we control the website, then we must remove offending material or otherwise bring the contents into compliance. If we don't control the website, opinions like South Carolina 99-09 require us to approach the site owner and get them to change the content of their site to bring it into compliance.

§ 5:13 A specific problem with control and awareness: Lawyer rating sites

The South Carolina opinion above probably made you wrinkle your nose because it reveals a significant issue. When it comes to people speaking about lawyers in ways that might cause ethical violations, we must understand that there is a perfect storm of sorts that is brewing on the Internet. There are situations where a lawyer may be both unaware that people are talking about them and also be unable to control what is being said about them. This happens on "lawyer rating" websites. These websites use information obtained through requests to state courts and bar associations under the Freedom of Information Act and create web site entries for lawyers whose information is retrieved from these FOIA requests.[1] The website creates a listing for each lawyer and that listing is published for the entire world to see without the prior knowledge of any individual lawyer.

What's concerning about these sites is that they allow people to post comments about the lawyer. Another opinion

---

[2]South Carolina Advisory Opinion 99-09.

[Section 5:13]

[1]South Carolina Bar Ethics Advisory Opinion 09-10.

ADVERTISING § 5:13

out of South Carolina explained the sites best.[2] Note that the impetus for the opinion appears to have been the site http://www.AVVO.com, commonly called "Avvo," but that actual site wasn't actually named in the opinion. Instead, they call it "Company X":

> The website also feathures (sic) "client ratings." Anyone can submit a client rating about any lawyer, and the lawyer may invite current and former clients to submit ratings. Client ratings do not impact an attorney's internal rating by Company X, but the client comments are prominently posted on the attorney's listing. While Company X monitors and inspects client ratings and peer reviews, attorneys are unable to control who endorses or rates them.

That last comment was the kicker, right? Not only might the lawyer be unaware that the listing and comments exist, but even if they become aware, the lawyer does not have the ability to control who writes the comments that are attached to the lawyer's individual listing. Many lawyers don't like this for obvious, practical reasons. It's not very appealing to know that there are sites that potentially allow people to post unflattering comments about our services. However, the ethical considerations are real as well. While people might be out there bad-mouthing you, there are also potentially well-meaning people singing your praises. In that case you might have clients or other individuals posting what amounts to testimonials that violate Rule 7.1, but an attorney would not have any ability to alter it.

Incidentally, in case you're not familiar with the concept, the inability to alter comments is not so unusual on the web. Many sites believe that the free-flow of information is enhanced by allowing people to post their unfiltered opinions. The theory is that the credibility of ratings websites is dependent upon allowing all comments to be posted, regardless of their merit. Of course that means that some outlandish opinions will be cast. But the belief is that the crazies out there will be exposed by the masses and their nutty opinions will be ignored.

If a lawyer is unaware that the listing exists, then they're most likely in the clear, consistent with our prior discussion. But what about when they become aware? The question becomes (1) whether and (2) when lawyers are responsible for the comments posted by others which may be attached to

---

[2]South Carolina Bar Ethics Advisory Opinion 09-10.

§ 5:13

the lawyer's listing. The South Carolina opinion addressed that concern in its ruling. Note that the following text is consistent with our earlier discussion about testimonials. The Bar stated in South Carolina Op. 09-10:

> Lawyers are responsible for all communications they place or disseminate, or ask to be placed or disseminated for them, regarding their law practice, and all such communications are governed by Rule 7.1 of the Rules of Professional Conduct. See Cmt. 1 ("This Rule governs all communications about a lawyer's services . . . Whatever means are used to make known a lawyer's services, statements about them must be truthful.") (emphasis added). However, a lawyer is not responsible for statements about the lawyer or the lawyer's practice that are not placed or disseminated by the lawyer. Statements made by Company X on its website about a lawyer are not governed by the Rules of Professional Conduct unless placed or disseminated by the lawyer or someone on the lawyer's behalf.

So according to South Carolina, if you didn't place or disseminate the information on a lawyer rating website, you're not responsible for its content. This is certainly supported by common sense. If we didn't post the offending text and we didn't ask someone to post it, then we can't be liable for its content. But the second question remains. When. At what point are we deemed to be responsible? When is our duty to act triggered? It appears that our responsibilities kick in when we take some control of the listing.

The lawyer ratings sites allow lawyers to "claim" their listing. Once the lawyer claims the listing, they have the ability to update their profile information. In case you're curious about the website's business model, they encourage you to claim the profile for free and then they try to make money by getting lawyers to upgrade their listing to a premium version. These lawyer rating sites present themselves as a marketing tool for lawyers, allowing them to connect with potential clients.

It is the "claiming" of the website that triggers a lawyer's duty, according to the South Carolina Bar. In Opinion 09-10 the Bar stated, ". . . to 'claim' one's website listing is to 'place or disseminate' all communications made at or through that listing after the time the listing is claimed . . ." Thus, the ethical duties attach when you claim the website.

Remember not to pigeonhole this issue—the concepts aren't restricted to ratings websites. In fact, the South Carolina opinion acknowledged that there may be other platforms on which similar concerns may arise and ethical duties are imposed. Some name brands mentioned in the opinion are Martindale-Hubbell, SuperLawyers, LinkedIn, and Avvo. As a result, Opinion 09-10 states, "Likewise, a lawyer who adopts or endorses information on any similar web site becomes responsible for confirming all information in the lawyer's listing to the Rules of Professional Conduct."

Thus, according to South Carolina, the duty to be responsible for what people say about you on these websites is triggered when a lawyer "claims" the website or "adopts or endorses information" on these sites. And don't get caught up in the technicalities of the terminology—Opinion 90-10 states that, "The language employed by the website for claiming a listing is irrelevant (Martindale.com, for example, uses an "update this listing" link for lawyers to claim their listings)." Essentially, these appear to be acts that indicate that we are accepting some modicum of control over the site, however limited that might be. The South Carolina opinion confirms that "Regardless of the terminology, by requesting access to and updating any website listing (beyond merely making corrections to directory information), a lawyer assumes responsibility for the content of the listing." And once that happens, the duty is clear. According to Opinion 90-10, "By claiming a website listing, a lawyer takes responsibility for its content and is then ethically required to conform the listing to all applicable rules." So according to South Carolina, the lawyer's duty is to conform the website listing.[3]

§ 5:14 Total lack of control: The inability to force conformance

The responsibility to control what other people say about us on the Internet is bigger than just lawyer rating websites. What if we notice someone making a problematic post about our services elsewhere on the Internet? Our review of these various opinions might make us believe that we are required to approach the offending poster and ask that they bring their site/comment into compliance. And unfortunately, that might be all we're able to do—our efforts to get the poster to

---

[3]On a separate note, recall the discussion we had about our profile pages on social media and the duty that their content conform to Rule 7.2. That issue applies to lawyer rating websites too. In fact, the issues regarding profiles and how they are the functional equivalent of a personal website apply to all similar profiles and listings. Don't get lulled into thinking that those concerns were only about Facebook or LinkedIn.

§ 5:14 NAVIGATING LEGAL ETHICS

"conform" will probably be nothing more powerful than politely asking the writer to remove or amend their comment. But that might prove ineffective. You could ask someone to amend their comments, but that doesn't mean they're going to do it—commenters on the Internet aren't required to listen to you. They don't have to change their comments if they don't want to and sometimes there's nothing you can do to get them to alter what they've said about you.

Even on other ratings websites like Yelp, the comments made by others are usually not within our control—very often you can't change a comment by a public user. And if our control over the site is limited, then how do we comply with our duty to conform? The answer appears to be that you need to do your best to disassociate, or distance yourself from the offending post.

Recall the earlier South Carolina opinion where a client had posted problematic information about a lawyer that ended up constituting advertising. In that opinion the distancing/disassociation consisted of withdrawing from the representation. There the Bar stated, "If the client refuses to bring the page into compliance, the lawyer should give serious consideration to withdrawal from representation to avoid any impression that the lawyer has authorized or adopted the client's continued use of the web page."[1]

The other South Carolina opinion (regarding lawyer ranking websites) gives guidance as well. In a bit of tough love, it states that, "If any part of the listing cannot be conformed to the Rules (e.g., if an improper comment cannot be removed), the lawyer should remove his or her entire listing and discontinue participation in the service."[2] That appears to be the Bar's version of distance/disassociation in that context.

This isn't quite perfect guidance. In the former scenario (the client who posted information about you), one can envision situations where a lawyer no longer represents a person who makes an ethically troublesome post (or maybe even never represented that person). In the lawyer ratings website instance, you might not have the power to remove the entire listing. Sometimes the best you can do is cancel a subscription to a website and make a hollow demand of the website owner/poster that the offending material be deleted. Unfortu-

[Section 5:14]
[1]South Carolina Advisory Opinion 99-09.
[2]South Carolina Advisory Opinion 09-10.

nately, chances are high that they won't comply. In that situation, your options are limited.

It appears that the most you can do amounts to nothing more than "disavow" the posting/listing and its contents. Quite frankly, I don't even know how you'd do that, practically. Do you post a comment on your listing saying that you've abandoned it? Of course, even if you find a good way to disavow the contents, it's tough to say whether a disciplinary board would accept that. Would disavowing the website be enough to absolve you of liability? If so, was the manner in which you disavowed adequate?

South Carolina Opinion 09-10 mentioned a sort of hybrid option—an act one can take which lies somewhere between successfully conforming the listing and deleting the listing all together. A disclaimer. When reminding lawyers that they can't allow publication of comments that violate the rules (such as setting unjustified expectations), Opinion 99-10 states that a disclaimer might let the attorney avoid ethical liability for such a comment. Specifically, the Bar wrote, "The inclusion of an appropriate disclaimer or qualifying language may preclude a finding that a statement is likely to create unjustified expectations or otherwise mislead a prospective client." The problem is that this direction raises more questions than it answers.

There are a ton of issues, each of which gets more confusing when you change even the slightest variable. For instance, when is it appropriate to make a disclaimer? When will a disclaimer suffice, instead of actually changing or deleting the comment? Is a disclaimer okay if you try to get a comment amended but you're unsuccessful? How much of an effort must you make in order for a disclaimer to be a responsible next step? Does using a disclaimer allow you to avoid all liability? Does it depend on what the disclaimer says? Where does the disclaimer get posted? It's almost as if the Bar is saying, "*Well, we guess you could try a disclaimer . . . that would probably work sometimes . . . but we're not quite sure.*" Personally, I think that if they were going to mention the possibility of using a disclaimer, they should have given some clear guidance in that regard.

Writing a disclaimer seems like a form of self-help. A lawyer is likely to engage in that type of self-help when they don't feel they have any other recourse. An example would be a time when a lawyer asks someone to amend a comment they've made about the lawyer, but the commenter refuses

§ 5:14   NAVIGATING LEGAL ETHICS

to do so. In many cases a lawyer feels that they have no choice but to post a response, which tries to negate the offending comment.

However, going down that road gets dangerous for a lawyer. Remember the disciplinary matter in Illinois that we discussed elsewhere in this book.[3] In that case there was a deterioration of the relationship between the lawyer and client. Eventually, the client posted a review on Avvo that stated, "She only wants your money, claims "always on your side" is a huge lie. Paid her to help me secure unemployment, she took my money knowing full well a certain law in Illinois would not let me collect unemployment. [N]ow is billing me for an additional $1500 for her time." The Avvo posting was removed, but a second, similar posting was made by the client. When that second posting appeared, the lawyer responded by saying,

> This is simply false. The person did not reveal all the facts of his situation up front in our first and second meeting [sic] When I received his personnel file, I discussed the contents of it with him and informed him that he would likely lose unless the employer chose not to contest the unemployment . . . Despite knowing that he would likely lose, he chose to go forward with a hearing . . . I dislike it very much when my clients lose but I cannot invent positive facts for clients when they are not here . . . I feel badly for him but his own actions in beating up a female coworker are what caused the consequences he is now so upset about.[4]

The problem with this posting was best explained by the hearing board which held,

> "By stating in her . . . posting that Rinehart beat up a female coworker, Respondent revealed information that she had obtained from Reinhart about the termination of his employment. Respondent's statements in the posting were designed to intimidate and embarrass Rinehart and to keep him from posting additional information about her on the Avvo website." The board found the lawyer in violation of the rule on confidentiality (1.6), no substantial purpose other than to embarrass, delay or burden (4.4) and for conduct prejudicial to the administration of justice (8.4).

There's an obvious difference here. The statements made by the client don't appear to be testimonials that violate the ethics rules. Instead, they're simply comments that are not

---

[3]In the Matter of Betty Tsamis, Illinois Commission No. 2013PR00095.

[4]In the Matter of Betty Tsamis at 3.

pleasing to the lawyer. Regardless, this is the kind of tit-for-tat that can occur once you start to engage in asking people to change their comments on these types of websites. The lawyer makes a request of a commenter, it's not honored, and the lawyer then feels that they must take matters into their own hands.

You're probably reading this right now and thinking to yourself, "Yeah, but I wouldn't be stupid . . . I wouldn't go that far." Be careful. Remember what I said earlier about the lack of a soundtrack in real life. There isn't any warning sign that appears when you're about to make a mistake. There isn't any string section that will start to play to give you a heads up. You can sit back in a comfortable chair today and judge whether you would have taken a similar path to that lawyer, but you might do the very same thing if you were in her situation.

The reason I brought up this example is because I want you to see how easy it is to get into a dangerous place when trying to request that someone change their comments on the web. Self-help can be a slippery slope and we must understand the pitfall—it's all part of developing the heightened state of awareness we need to properly protect ourselves from dangerous ethical violation.

I've posed a series of questions in this section but I've left many of them unanswered. I wish I could give you the answers to those questions, but I can't. They simply haven't been resolved and they most likely won't be resolved until some ethics authority is presented with the fact of a real-life disciplinary matter. So what's a lawyer to do if you're faced with these concerns? You need to take the same steps you'd take whenever you find yourself facing an ethics questions that is not addressed by the rule. I believe that the prudent lawyer should engage in CYA-squared (CYA^2). *Craft Your Argument and Cover Your....umm... Behind.*

First, *Craft Your Argument*. Attempt to comply with the black letter rule as much as possible. Then, for those issues that fall in the grey area, evaluate your proposed conduct in light of several key factores: Consider the direction given in the commentary to the rule, the underlying purpose of the particular rule in question, and the primary goal of the rules in general. When you decide on a particulare course of conduct, *Cover Your... Behind*. Write a detailed memo to the file that explains how you arrived at your decision. Explain your rationale and cite your support. Basically, lay out the defense that you'd provide to the ethics authorities if they required you to do so.

Granted, this might not be a golden ticket to ethics salvation. There is no guarantee that an ethics authority will agree with your decision, but that holds true in every ethics dilemma that deals with an issue in the grey area. The way I see it, the best you can do is make an educated decision that is supported by the rules and memorializes your thought process to prove your intent to comply with the rules.

§ 5:15 Copies of advertisements

We've seen in other contexts that the advertising rules are laced with technicalities. Each of those requirements is all geared toward the same thing—protecting the public and protecting the client. For example, in the section on virtual offices we discuss some states' requirement that an actual office address be included in all ads. In the section on testimonials we noted that some states require disclaimers. The purpose of those requirements is to protect the public, whether it's by providing them with important information about the lawyer's location or including key information that will avoid misunderstandings/deception. Toward that end, many states have an additional requirement—copies.

Some states have a requirement that copies of all advertisements be kept by the firm for a certain amount of time after it's disseminated. Idaho's Rule 7.2(b) requires that, "A copy or recording of an advertisement or communication shall be kept for two years after its last dissemination along with a record of when and where it was used."[1] That's a popular provision you see in many jurisdictions. Still other jurisdictions go even farther and require that the copy of the ad be filed with a governmental agency or the state bar. Nevada, for instance, contains the following language in its version of Rule 7.2:

Rule 7.2A. Advertising Filing Requirements.[2]

(a) Filing requirements. A copy or recording of an advertisement or written or recorded communication

---

[Section 5:15]

[1]http://isb.idaho.gov/pdf/rules/irpc.pdf, last checked by the author December 22, 2013.

[2]http://www.leg.state.nv.us/CourtRules/RPC.html, last checked by the author, December 22, 2013.

ADVERTISING § 5:15

published after September 1, 2007, shall be submitted to the state bar in either physical or digital format within 15 days of first dissemination along with a form supplied by the state bar. If a published item that was first disseminated prior to September 1, 2007, will continue to be published after this date, then it must be submitted to the state bar on or before September 17, 2007, along with a form supplied by the state bar.

(b) Failure to file. A lawyer or law firm's failure to file an advertisement in accordance with paragraph (a) is grounds for disciplinary action. In addition, for purposes of disciplinary review pursuant to Supreme Court Rule 106 (privilege and limitation), when a lawyer or law firm fails to file, the 4-year limitation period begins on the date the advertisement was actually known to bar counsel.

The Rule in Texas is pretty specific and it's been updated in light of some modern media options. Rule 7.07(b) requires that a lawyer,

". . . file with the Advertising Review Committee of the State Bar of Texas . . . a copy of each of the lawyer's advertisements in the public media. The filing shall include:

(1) a copy of the advertisement in the form in which it appears or will appear upon dissemination, such as a videotape, audiotape, DVD, CD, a print copy, or a photograph of outdoor advertising;

(2) a production script of the advertisement setting forth all words used and describing in detail the actions, events, scenes, and background sounds used in such advertisement together with a listing of the names and addresses of persons portrayed or heard to speak, if the advertisement is in or will be in a form in which the advertised message is not fully revealed by a print copy or photograph;

(3) a statement of when and where the advertisement has been, is, or will be used . . ."

If you were to review the different state rules that require submission of lawyer ads to an official agency, you'd see that the Nevada and Texas rules appear to be a bit harsh. Should we say "stringent" instead? While the language may be somewhat tough, the requirement is for good reason. The State of Kansas provided justification for the copy-retention requirement in its comment [5] where is said, "Paragraph (b) requires that a record of the content and use of advertising

§ 5:15 NAVIGATING LEGAL ETHICS

be kept in order to facilitate enforcement of this Rule."[3] Thus, whether the copy of the ad is kept in the lawyer's office or forwarded to some governmental agency, the purpose for the requirement is the same—to keep a copy of the advertising communication so that it can be reviewed in case there is an enforcement issue.

The idea of retaining, and even filing copies wasn't such an onerous requirement in the days where advertisements consisted of display ads in a newspaper or isolated radio spots. But it's quite difficult to apply in the world of social media. We've seen throughout this chapter that the number of different types of self-promoting communications that are subject to the rule has increased. Directories, blogs, profiles, tweets, posts . . . the list is almost endless. But while the way we communicate has changed, the way the states apply the rules has not. There continues to be remarkable consistency.

Some of the new advertising communications fall into existing exemptions. Take South Carolina, for example. We discussed South Carolina's Opinion 09-10 in which the Bar was presented with lawyer rating sites like Avvo. To a certain extent, these sites are similar to attorney directories. Under the South Carolina rules, directories (even though they are technically advertisements) are exempt from the filing requirement. The Bar stated that that exemption also applies to online directories:

> "In order to be exempt from the filing requirement of Rule 7.2(b), an advertisement must be limited to directory information only and must not be disseminated through a public medium. Comment 5 to Rule 7.2 specifically excludes from the filing requirement "basic telephone directory listings, law directories such as 'Martindale Hubbell' or a desk book created by a bar association." The Comment does not address online versions of such directories; however, to require lawyers to file copies of online directory listings would be to require them to file copies of not only Martindale.com listings, but the South Carolina Bar's online directory listing as well. The Committee does not believe the Court intended the rules to require such filing and therefore does not believe that an online listing containing only directory information must be filed pursuant to Rule 7.2(b).

However, very often the online directories add more infor-

---

[3]http://www.kscourts.org/rules/Rule-Info.asp?r1=Rules+Relating+to+Discipline+of+Attorneys&r2=9, last checked by the author on December 22, 2013.

mation than just an attorney's listing. In fact, that's exactly what happens on the Avvo site and other brand name lawyer rating/listing sites that were the subject of the opinion. The Bar stated that when the site changes from a traditional directory and becomes something more, the copy-retention requirements kick in.

> However, if an online listing is updated to include anything beyond directory information (which includes "the name of the lawyer or law firm, a lawyer's job title, jurisdictions in which the lawyer is admitted to practice, the lawyer's mailing and electronic addresses, and the lawyer's telephone and facsimile numbers," according to Comment 5), then 7.2(b) requires that a copy be filed with the Commission."

Thus, while the exemption applies to some online directories, that exemption is narrowly construed. If it's simply an online version of a good-old fashioned directory, then it gets the benefit of the exemption. Otherwise, it doesn't.

That's a consistent application of an existing rule and, from a policy point of view it makes sense. A directory is harmless enough. Once we start to editorialize, however, there's a greater need to keep an eye on what lawyers say. That's most likely the reason that other states have continued to apply the copy-retention and filing requirements to other social media communications.

Texas directly addressed the copy/filing requirement for certain social media communications in its Interpretive Comments. They stated that "Landing Pages such as those of Facebook, Twitter, LinkedIn, etc. where the landing page is generally available to the public are advertisements. Where access is limited to existing clients and personal friends, filing . . . is not required."[4] The Bar also discussed other social media communications when it said, "Blogs and status updates considered to be educational or informational in nature are not required to be filed . . . However, attorneys should be careful to ensure that such postings do not meet the definition of an advertisement subject to the filing requirements."[5] Thus, the Texas position is clear and consistent: if the communication is an ad and the public sees it, it must be filed. California came to the same position, and then some.

You might recall the State Bar of California Standing

---

[4]Texas Interpretive Comment 17(C).
[5]Texas Interpretive Comment 17(D).

§ 5:15 NAVIGATING LEGAL ETHICS

Committee on Professional Responsibility and Conduct Formal Opinion No. 2012-186. We discussed it earlier when we considered social media posts and whether they constitute advertising communications. In that opinion, the Bar noted that there are some instances where self-promotional posts would be subject to the rules. The opinion also stated that such posts constitute advertising communications and, "a true and correct copy of any communication must be retained by Attorney for two years." The fact that these were web-based communications didn't matter. The Bar stated that, "[The Rule] expressly extends this requirement to communications made by 'electronic media.' "[6] While that position makes theoretical sense, it creates an enormous amount of practical problems. Worse yet, many of these problems can't be answered without further guidance from the authorities. For instance, how exactly do you keep copies of communications?

In the days when paper ruled the earth it was easy to keep copies. If you printed an ad in the newspaper, or you ran off 200 brochures, you could keep an extra copy (or photocopy) in a file somewhere. But with websites and social media accounts, it's not so easy. How do you make a copy of something on the Internet? And what do you have to copy? If you're a social media user who promotes your practice online significantly, then you're talking about making a "copy" of your entire social media existence. How does one accomplish that, practically?

Some sites might archive your social media account— both the profile and everything you communicate. Presumably that would be acceptable, provided that you could access the archived copy upon demand.[7] But even if the site archives everything and keeps that archive for the period required by the rule, it's still unclear whether that archiving qualifies as "keeping a copy" under the rule. California seems to think so because they stated in Opinion 186, "If Attorney discovers that a social media website does not archive postings automatically, then Attorney will need to employ a manual method of preservation, such as printing or saving a copy of the screen." Did you get that? Print screen (or screen capture, for you younger folk), may be required. That seems to create a practical nightmare.

---

[6] California Opinion No. 2012-186 at 5.

[7] As usual, that's only MY presumption, not the official word of any disciplinary authority.

It probably wasn't that big a deal when websites first became popular because they were programmed, thrown up into cyberspace, and static for quite a while. But in the world of social media things change constantly. There are tweaks and new posts happening constantly and that means a whole lot of screen snaps. Tinker with your profile? Print the screen. Write a new blog post? Print the screen. Comment on a blog somewhere in a manner that constitutes a statement about your services covered by Rule 7.1? Print the screen. Make a post on your Facebook page that's a "communication" per the rule? Print the screen.

That's not all. Most states require that you keep a copy of the ad for several years from the date of its dissemination. How do you measure the time? If you create a profile, that's Day One, right? But what if you amend it or add some data? Does that set you back to Day One? The same problem exists with other types of communications. We know that status updates or "posts" could be communications that are subject to the rules. Does that mean that you need to start running the two-year copy-retention period from the date that each post is disseminated? Oy vey.

But that's not all. You might be in a state that requires filing copies of the ads with some governmental agency. Again, depending on your use, that may mean that you need to send a printout of a screen snap every day. It's dangerous even if you're not a power user—you may be the type that makes some self-promoting move on social media infrequently. Then it's easy to forget/fail to appreciate that the particular communications you made have triggered the rules and need to be filed.

It's unclear how this will play out. Several jurisdictions have given special attention to social media matters. You can see above the Interpretive Comments in Texas, Opinion 186 in California and The Florida Revised Guidelines from April of 2013. The Philadelphia Bar Association Professional Guidance Committee also chimed in regarding solicitations. They stated that comments made in chat rooms that constitute solicitations according to the rules are subject to the copy-retention rules.[8] But even though those opinions addressed many details, they haven't talked about some of the practical obstacles. Note, however, that the basic principle has been consistent: If the communication is an ad, it's subject to the rules—all of the rules.

---

[8]Philadelphia Professional Guidance Committee Opinion 2010-6 at 5.

§ 5:15   NAVIGATING LEGAL ETHICS

I can understand the argument that one would make to the disciplinary authorities—that they should carve out exceptions for certain requirements if they are overly burdensome. But I'll tell you the truth—I'm not so sure they'll do it. The danger of deception and the potential to mislead the public with things like social media posts and blog comments is so great that I think the authorities will simply leave the rules as they are and deal with the cases on an individual basis. Specifically, they'll deal with it when some violation needs to be adjudicated.

My position in that regard is further bolstered by California's approach to disclaimers. The following example also shows how so many of these advertising issues are intertwined.

In California's Opinion 186, the Bar explained that a post which exhorted, "Who wants to be next?" is a communication that is subject to the advertising rules. However, they also found that it constituted a solicitation. Specifically, the Bar stated, " 'Who wants to be next?' when viewed in context, seeks professional employment for pecuniary gain."[9] As a result, the rules regarding solicitation applied. In California's case, that meant affixing a disclaimer to the solicitation as required by rule. The Bar held that the post violated the rule because it did not, "bear the word 'Advertisement,' or 'Newsletter,' or words to that effect."[10] Of course, it's impractical to require such a disclaimer on something as short as a social media post. The Bar acknowledged that fact, but their response was, basically, "tough." Specifically the opinion states:

> Attorneys may argue that including this wording for each 'communication' posting would be overly burdensome, and destroy the conversational and impromptu nature of a social media status posting. The Committee is of the view, however, that an attorney has an obligation to advertise in a manner that complies with applicable ethical rules. If compliance makes the advertisement seem awkward, the solution is to change the form of advertisement so that compliance is possible.

That's a tough stance. It's telling us that if a lawyer in California makes a social media posting that constitutes a communication subject to the rules, that lawyer needs to include a disclaimer on that post. The Bar doesn't care if

---
[9]California Opinion 186 at 4.
[10]California Opinion 186 at 4.

that mandate is impractical. The rule says what it says and if you can't comply, then there's a simple way to get around it—just make sure that you change your post so it doesn't trigger the rule.

Despite their tough stance, the California Bar acknowledged that it might not be possible for lawyers to comply with every technical requirement. For instance, they noted that the rules require disclaimers to appear in "12-point print on the first page."[11] The Committee clearly understood that complying with the font size requirement might be a problem when it stated, "The Committee recognizes that certain social media postings may not allow for the user to choose the font size of postings, and this technical compliance . . . may be impossible."[12] Unfortunately, rather than make a determination whether non-compliance in that regard would be acceptable, the Committee punted. They threw it back to the drafters and stated, "It may be that the State Bar needs to review such standards to bring them current in the face of the prevalence of electronic communications."[13]

Of course, the Bar then muddies the water even more significantly in a footnote. In the tucked-away clause it notes that you might be able to cure this by creating a "Fan Page" on Facebook and you could place the disclaimers there. However, in that case you're placing the disclaimer on the page, not each individual post. Thus, the directive in the body of the opinion seems to contradict the statement in the footnote. I don't know if the drafters understood that conflict. Did they understand that you could make individual postings on a "Fan Page?" That footnote actually creates more misunderstandings, and they would have been better off leaving it out all together.

What does this tell us? First, there is a real conflict between the technicalities of the advertising rules and the realities of social media use for self-promotional purposes. What's clear, however, is that the Bar association position is that the fundamental principles of the rules will not be compromised. They're going to continue to apply the rules as carefully as before, even if it causes some burden on the lawyer. If the things you say on social media are considered

---

[11]California Opinion 186.
[12]California Opinion 186.
[13]California Opinion 186.

§ 5:15   NAVIGATING LEGAL ETHICS

a communication that's covered by the rules, chances are high that the copy-retention rule will apply. It doesn't matter if it's going to be difficult to comply with that rule—the objective is to protect the public, not make advertising easier for the lawyer. Of course, the California opinion also illustrates that at some point there will be technicalities that even the harshest of disciplinary authorities might believe are unreasonable. The problem is that no one knows which technicality will be overlooked, by whom, and under what circumstances.

I'm sorry. I wish I could say, "Here's the rule." But the truth is, the footnote fiasco alone proves that the states themselves don't quite know how to deal with this.

Unfortunately, the thorniest issues will continue to go unresolved until an ethics authority addresses them in an actual disciplinary case. Until then, your best option is something I mentioned at the end of § 5:14, CYA^2. Simply restated, CYA^2:

First, *Craft Your Argument*. Attempt to comply with the black letter rule as much as possible. Then, for those issues that fall in the grey area, evaluate your proposed conduct in light of several key factores: Consider the direction given in the commentary to the rule, the underlying purpose of the particular rule in question, and the primary goal of the rules in general. When you decide on a particulare course of conduct, *Cover Your... Behind*. Write a detailed memo to the file that explains how you arrived at your decision. Explain your rationale and cite your support. Basically, lay out the defense that you'd provide to the ethics authorities if they required you to do so.

There is no guarantee that an ethics authority will agree with your decision, but that holds true in every ethics dilemma that deals with an issue in the grey area. The way I see it, the best you can do is make an educated decision that is supported by the rules and memorialize your thought process to prove your intent to comply with the rules.

§ 5:16 Advertising in the future

As the Internet advances, new opportunities for self-promotion appear. There are an ever-increasing number of platforms that allow lawyers to advertise their wares and things like Facebook pages or Avvo listings are just the tip of the iceberg. The problem is that not all of these new ad vehicles are permitted by the ethics rules.

Example: viral videos are all the rage these days. These are funny, provocative, scary, or otherwise interesting video clips that are so unique that social media users feel the need to share them with all of their social media contacts. The videos are shared on Facebook, retweeted on Twitter, or posted to whatever social media account you prefer and they spread quickly through the Internet world. Once it's attained a large following it's considered to have "gone viral." Companies that sell everything from razorblades to razorbacks are aware of the power of the viral video, so it's been co-opted in the advertising world. A great example is the recent clip featuring professional baseball player, Evan Longoria.

In that video, Longoria is being interviewed by a news reporter, while a teammate takes batting practice in the background. During their conversation, the teammate hits a foul ball that takes off straight toward the unsuspecting interviewer. The viewer sees the errant shot screaming toward the pair, a disaster about to occur as the ball closes in on the reporter's head. At the last moment, however, Longoria makes a barehanded grab, snaring the ball just before it strikes the interviewer. It was an unbelievable save. So unbelievable that people questioned whether it actually happened.

Many believed that the video was manufactured and that it was actually a Gillette ad.[1] CBS news reported on the ad and gave several reasons for why it seemed to be a promotion (there were Gillette logos all over the place, the reporter didn't flinch, etc.). They even noted that, "The real/fake guessing game is part of the video's charm . . ."[2] Both of those factors— the incredible content and the mystery— contributed to the ad going viral. Conventional wisdom supports that (1) it was a Gillette ad, (2) it was fake, and (3) it was effective because a ton of people saw it. Sure, it may have been a lie, but that hasn't stopped it from being effective. Nor has it stopped other businesses from pursuing that advertising strategy. There's something that would stop lawyers from pursuing that strategy, however. You guessed it, the ethics rules.

[Section 5:16]

[1] http://mashable.com/2011/05/16/evan-longoria-gillette-2/.

[2] http://www.cbsnews.com/news/longorias-bare-hand-catch-is-probably-a-stunt-for-gillette-heres-why-it-worked/.

Lawyers would probably be prohibited from disseminating deceptive viral ads. A law firm that might create a video which contained a false factual scenario like the Longoria ad (allegedly?), would likely run afoul of Rule 8.4(c). That section of the rule on misconduct states that, "it is professional misconduct for a lawyer to . . . engage in conduct involving dishonesty, fraud, deceit or misrepresentation." While an intriguing ad is not per se deceptive, the Longoria ad appears to be a complete fabrication. In fact, as we saw from the CBS comment above, the debate over whether the action in the ad is bona fide is part of the allure of the ad. One could even argue that the element of potential deception might be a critical part of the ad all together. What's clear, however, is that ads which amount to blatant lies would most likely be considered a violation of Rule 8.4(c).

Such ads would also likely violate Rule 7.1. That rule, which prohibits false or misleading communications, states that "a communication is false or misleading if it contains, 'a material misrepresentation of fact.' " Given that the entire ad is a misrepresentation, it's pretty much a no-brainer that Rule 7.1 would prohibit lawyers from creating such ads to promote their services.[3]

---

[3]Incidentally, if you're in California, fake viral ads face a particular hurdle because of the contents of Rule 6158, which states, "In advertising by electronic media, to comply with Sections 61571.1 and 6157.2, the message as a whole may not be false, misleading, or deceptive, and the message as a whole must be factually substantiated. The message means the effect in combination of the spoken word, sound, background, action, symbols, visual image, or any other technique employed to create the message. Factually substantiated means capable of verification by a credible source."

Chapter 6

Solicitations

§ 6:1 The theory behind the rule
§ 6:2 How the rule is built
§ 6:3 Direct messages as solicitation
§ 6:4 Texting as solicitation
§ 6:5 Daily-deal websites may also be off limits
§ 6:6 If technology changes, the application of the rule could change
§ 6:7 Beware of shortcuts: Hyperlink disclaimers are not always permitted
§ 6:8 Beware of shortcuts: The specific words in disclaimers matter
§ 6:9 When real-time electronic contact is not a prohibited solicitation

> KeyCite®: Cases and other legal materials listed in KeyCite Scope can be researched through the KeyCite service on Westlaw®. Use KeyCite to check citations for form, parallel references, prior and later history, and comprehensive citator information, including citations to other decisions and secondary materials.

§ 6:1 The theory behind the rule

An entire rule is reserved for a method of business development that is particularly concerning to the drafters. That's solicitation and it's dealt with in Rule 7.3.[1] Take a moment to read the rule, then we'll talk about how it's built and the implications for social media.

Rule 7.3. Direct contact with prospective clients

(a) A lawyer shall not by in-person, live telephone or real-time electronic contact solicit professional employment from a prospective client when a significant motive

---

[Section 6:1]

[1]Del. Prof. Conduct R. 7.3.
7.3 http://courts.delaware.gov/rules/DLRPCFebruary2010.pdf. Pages last checked by the author August 13, 2013.

for the lawyer's doing so is the lawyer's pecuniary gain, unless the person contacted:

(1) is a lawyer; or

(2) has a family, close personal, or prior professional relationship with the lawyer.

(b) A lawyer shall not solicit professional employment from a prospective client by written, recorded or electronic communication or by in-person, telephone or real-time electronic contact even when not otherwise prohibited by para-graph (a), if:

(1) the prospective client has made known to the lawyer a desire not to be solicited by the lawyer; or

(2) the solicitation involves coercion, duress or harassment.

(c) Every written, recorded or electronic communication from a lawyer soliciting professional employment from a prospective client known to be in need of legal services in a particular matter shall include the words "Advertising Material" on the outside envelope, if any, and at the beginning and ending of any recorded or electronic communication, unless the recipient of the communication is a person specified in paragraphs (a)(1) or (a)(2).

(d) Notwithstanding the prohibitions in paragraph (a), a lawyer may participate with a prepaid or group legal service plan operated by an organization not owned or directed by the lawyer that uses in-person or telephone contact to solicit memberships or subscriptions for the plan from persons who are not known to need legal services in a particular matter covered by the plan.

This is, in my opinion, the most counterintuitive rule in the code. Here's why: A prospective client is a business opportunity for a lawyer. So what is a lawyer's reaction when they learn about a prospective client? We want to run to them. We want to approach them and tell them how we could help them so that they could get their matter resolved and we could put some money into our pocket. It's a win-win, right? However, this rule doesn't tell us to approach the prospective client. Instead, the rule tells lawyers that when we see a business opportunity, we must run the other way.

Okay, it's not quite that literal, but when you review the actual text of the rule you can see that it's not that far off. Rule 7.3 uses a variety of tactics ranging from outright prohibition from contact to carefully tailored disclaimers and each is designed to ensure that lawyers don't approach prospective clients the wrong way. The reason for employing such restrictions is clear: because lawyers have superpowers.

Lawyers have the ability to make the common layperson do whatever we want. We have "the force". . . we have extra-sensory-manipulative abilities . . . call it whatever you want, but clearly we have some super-human ability to get the common person to succumb to our every desire.

Attorneys might not be quite that powerful, but let's face it, we have a particular ability to manipulate. When you combine our schooling with the advocacy skills that we've honed over the years and throw in the fact that most laypeople don't have as intimate an understanding of the legal system as we do, one can see why lawyers really do have a particular ability to take advantage of others. The drafters understand that reality.

The drafters know that the prospective client is in a vulnerable position. A layperson in that situation might be confused, scared, apprehensive, eager for help, or all of the above. The combination of these factors might cause even the most sophisticated, educated layperson to let their guard down. Thus, the prospective client is in an inherently vulnerable position. The drafters are concerned that unscrupulous lawyers will see that vulnerability as an opportunity to manipulate that person. The lawyer might get the prospective client to make a decision that is in the best interest of the lawyer, rather than the client.

The rule regarding solicitation is part of a group of rules that set forth a code-wide obligation to avoid taking advantage of vulnerable people. Consider the above rule, along with Rule 1.14[2] (Clients With Diminished Capacity) and Rule 4.3[3] (Dealing with Unrepresented Person). Each of the groups addressed in those rules is in a vulnerable situation. A person with diminished capacity is unable to made decisions for themselves, thus they might not be able to look after their own best interest. A layperson who is unrepresented (our concern in Rule 4.3) is operating in a procedurally

---

[2]Del. Prof. Conduct R. 1.14.
1.14 http://courts.delaware.gov/rules/DLRPCFebruary2010.pdf. Pages last checked by the author August 13, 2013.

[3]Del. Prof. Conduct R. 4.3.
4.3 http://courts.delaware.gov/rules/DLRPCFebruary2010.pdf. Pages last checked by the author August 13, 2013.

§ 6:1   NAVIGATING LEGAL ETHICS

complicated system where small missteps could have large substantive implications. They do so without any professional guidance. Similarly, the prospective client (our concern in Rule 7.3) is vulnerable to the manipulation of a lawyer.

The rules that govern each instance put some sort of affirmative duty on us to ensure that we don't take advantage of those people. Whether it's seeking the appointment of a guardian (Rule 1.14),[4] making it clear that we are not disinterested (Rule 4.3), or the combination of restrictions set forth in Rule 7.3. Let's look into those prohibitions a bit further.

§ 6:2 How the rule is built

The rule on solicitation is divided up by method of contact. It starts with Rule 7.3(a)[1] where it addresses the type contact that's most dangerous to prospective clients (sometimes I'll call them "targets," which seems appropriate). That includes "in-person, live telephone or real-time electronic contact." You can see that the rule imposes almost draconian restrictions on a lawyer's use of these methods. You can't solicit prospective clients in that manner unless the target is also a lawyer or you know them really well. Basically, the rule is telling us that you can't solicit prospects using one-on-one methods unless they can protect themselves— either because they are equipped by training or by familiarity.

Skip down to subsection (c). That section addresses written contact.[2] That's certainly a form of solicitation that needs to be monitored, but it's less intensive than the real-time contact addressed in (a), so it gets different treatment by the rules. Since it's less problematic than the intense efforts set

---

[4]Del. Prof. Conduct R. 1.14.
   1.14 http://courts.delaware.gov/rules/DLRPCFebruary2010.pdf.
Pages last checked by the author August 13, 2013.

[Section 6:2]

[1]Del. Prof. Conduct R. 7.3(a).
   7.3(a) http://courts.delaware.gov/rules/DLRPCFebruary2010.pdf.
Pages last checked by the author August 13, 2013.

[2]Note that I jumped over (b). That subsection tells us when any type of solicitation is off limits like when you're coercing someone or they've explicitly asked you not to engage them. It's important, it's just not relevant to our discussion. Personally, I think it interrupts the flow of the rule and the drafters should have put it either before or after the other subsections, for clarity's sake.

SOLICITATIONS § 6:4

forth in (a), there isn't any restriction on the type of person that a lawyer could contact via written solicitation. However, there are requirements like disclaimers that need to be affixed to such contacts. It's important to review the rules on solicitations for your own jurisdiction because this is one of the rules that local drafters like to tinker with. There are a host of particular restrictions that drafters place on solicitations and the rules sometimes vary greatly from state to state.

§ 6:3 Direct messages as solicitation

It's pretty easy to detect many solicitations in social media. The most obvious are direct messages that are sent between SM users. These communications are almost exactly like e-mail because they're sent from one particular user, directly to a specified recipient. It's not like posts where a user's overall network can see the message; rather, these messages are similar to a private message between two individuals.

Common sense (as well as some decisions from around the country) dictates that direct messages would constitute, "written, recorded or electronic communication" described in Rule 7.3(c). As a result, direct messages which satisfy the other elements of a solicitation would be covered by the rules.

§ 6:4 Texting as solicitation

Earlier we discussed text messaging and how the Ohio Board of Commissioners on Grievances & Discipline held that texting is an advertising communication that's both covered and permitted by the ethics rules. However, texting touches on a bunch of ethical issues including solicitation.

Ohio gave us a specific definition of this mode of communication when it explained, ". . . text messaging systems allow users to write and send messages using the keypads on their cell phone. Users can also send . . . text messages to and from email addresses or instant messaging applications directly to and from the recipient's mobile phone."[1] We discussed earlier that as a typed message it falls under the definition of both an "electronic communication" and a "writ-

---

[Section 6:4]
[1]Ohio Opinion 2013-2 at 1, citation omitted.

§ 6:4

ten communication," thus subjecting it to Rules 7.2[2] and 7.1.[3] But as an electronic communication, texting is also subject to the rules on solicitation, so there are Rule 7.3[4] implications to consider.

The Ohio decision notes that texting is not a live telephone conversation, nor does it occur in real time, so it's not a real-time electronic contact and Rule 7.3(a) would not be implicated.[5] Rather, "the Board's view is that a standard text message is more akin to an email." That doesn't mean that texting is free of regulation as a solicitation, it simply means that we need to proceed to the next section of the rule to understand its limitations. Remember, that's how the rule is built—the rule categorizes solicitations by the degree of pressure that a tactic puts on the target of the solicitation. Thus, we proceed to Rule 7.3(c),[6] which addresses written solicitations. As you would imagine, this raises some other practical issues that are tough to manage.

Rule 7.3(c) requires that a label be placed on every written solicitation which warns the target that they are receiving a solicitation. The Ohio-specific version has some additional requirements, thus, Opinion 2013-2 states that. ". . . the text message must notify the recipient of the means by which the lawyer learned of the need for legal services . . . and include 'ADVERTISING MATERIAL,' or 'ADVERTISEMENT ONLY' at both the beginning and ending of the message. These descriptors must be conspicuous and in capital letters as designated in the rule."[7] Including the requisite disclaimers might seem awkward, but the opinion makes it clear that the technicalities must be complied with nonetheless.

---

[2] Del. Prof. Conduct R. 7.2.

7.2 http://courts.delaware.gov/rules/DLRPCFebruary2010.pdf. Pages last checked by the author August 13, 2013.

[3] Del. Prof. Conduct R. 7.1.

7.1 http://courts.delaware.gov/rules/DLRPCFebruary2010.pdf. Pages last checked by the author August 13, 2013.

[4] Del. Prof. Conduct R. 7.3.

7.3 http://courts.delaware.gov/rules/DLRPCFebruary2010.pdf. Pages last checked by the author August 13, 2013.

[5] Ohio Opinion 2013-2 at 5.

[6] Del. Prof. Conduct R. 7.3(c).

7.3(c) http://courts.delaware.gov/rules/DLRPCFebruary2010.pdf. Pages last checked by the author August 13, 2013.

[7] Ohio Opinion 2013-2 at 6.

SOLICITATIONS § 6:5

It's important to remember that all state-specific additional requirements for solicitations must be met when one uses text messages in this manner. That can get quite burdensome, and in some cases, difficult to apply. For instance, Ohio has a provision that you see in many states—the lawyer is forbidden from sending a solicitation within 30 days of certain accidents. Even after that time elapses, the rule requires that the lawyer's solicitation include the text of a document called, "Understanding Your Rights."[8] One might argue that including these few sentences in a text message makes the communication a bit bulky, but that doesn't matter. The Opinion even acknowledged some difficulties when it noted that the practical constraints of the texting platform might make it difficult to comply with that requirement. For example, the length of the statement, "may cause the message to be split into multiple messages or fail to transmit in its entirety."[9] Despite that practical obstacle, the Board stuck to its ethical guns. It noted that the commentary to the rule specifically stated that the language be "included with the communication," thus the full text of the statement must appear in the body of the communication.[10]

§ 6:5 Daily-deal websites may also be off limits

Entrepreneurs are finding new ways to harness the power of the Internet for marketing purposes all the time. Lately, "daily-deal" websites such as Groupon or Living Social have become popular. The Alabama State Bar explained how those sites work as follows:

> These "daily deal" websites typically contact the consumer via email and give the consumer the opportunity to purchase a certificate for services or products from a retailer at a discounted rate of 50% or greater. The proceeds from each sale are typically divided on a 50-50 split between the website and the retailer. For example, a law firm would agree to sell a coupon entitling the purchaser to $500 worth of legal services for a discounted rate of $250. The purchaser or prospective client would pay the website $250 and would receive a certificate for $500 to redeem for legal services with the law firm. The certificate may or may not have an expiration date. From the

---

[8]Ohio Opinion 2013-2 at 7, citing Ohio Rule 7.3(e).
[9]Ohio Opinion 2013-2 at 7.
[10]Ohio Opinion 2013-2 ar 7.

§ 6:5   NAVIGATING LEGAL ETHICS

sale, the website would keep 50% of the revenue, $125 in this case, and remit the remaining $125 to the law firm.[1]

Several states have opined on the permissibility of the websites, so too has the American Bar Association Standing Committee on Ethics and Professional Responsibility.[2] The most comprehensive analysis of the rules that are implicated is probably set forth in the Arizona opinion. The ABA's Formal Opinion 465 is pretty good too—it addresses all of the issues raised by the states and also give a little more depth to some of the principles behind the issues.

Some of the opinions approve of the use of daily-deal sites, some forbid it, and others say it's not forbidden but it's really difficult to use them and stay within ethical bounds. Interestingly, almost all of the opinions evaluate the same rules and debate the same ethical issues. They simply come down on different sides of the debate. While there are about 10 separate ethical issues that are in play, the seminal issue is about sharing fees.

Some states see the payment of money from the customer to the web site as a legal fee. According to that view, when the website retains a portion of the proceeds they are sharing the legal fee in violation of Rule 5.4.[3] That's why Arizona opined that "the business model contemplated would violate the fee sharing prohibition . . ."[4] The question of whether the payment constitutes a "fee" is a threshold issue, because if you can't get past that, you simply don't have to evaluate all the other ethical questions. For instance, it doesn't matter if there is a potentially misleading statement in the website's offering that violates Rule 7.2.[5] You never have to evaluate that issue if you're forbidden from using the site because it constitutes impermissible fee sharing.

[Section 6:5]

[1]Alabama State Bar Opinion R0-2012-01.

[2]Arizona (Ethics Opinion 13-01), North Carolina (2011 Formal Ethics Opinion 10), South Carolina (Ethics Advisory Opinion 11-05), Indiana (Opinion No.1, 2012-JDH-1), Alabama (Ethics Opinion R0-2012-01).

[3]Del. Prof. Conduct R. 5.4.

5.4 http://courts.delaware.gov/rules/DLRPCFebruary2010.pdf. Pages last checked by the author August 13, 2013.

[4]Arizona Ethics Opinion 13-01.

[5]Del. Prof. Conduct R. 7.2.

7.2 http://courts.delaware.gov/rules/DLRPCFebruary2010.pdf. Pages last checked by the author August 13, 2013.

Other states get past the fee sharing issue. South Carolina, for instance, believed that the money paid is not a lawyer's fee, rather:

> The fee charged by a company for use of its services (i.e., a percentage of the money paid by the customer for the discounted coupon) constitutes the payment of 'the reasonable cost of advertisements or communications' permitted under Rule 7.2(c)(1) and not the sharing of a legal fee with a nonlawyer prohibited by Rule 5.4.[6]

Thus, if the state sees the payment as an advertising cost, rather than a legal fee, then you might be permitted to use the site.[7] However, even if you get over that initial hurdle, you must go further and review the myriad of other ethics issues that surround the use of these sites. Those are pretty tough to wade through, which is why even the states that don't outright prohibit these sites strongly caution against their use. Thus, Arizona stated, "Practitioners are discouraged from using an Internet marketing voucher or coupon system and, if they opt to do so, they must proceed with caution and only after careful consideration and analysis of the ethical rules and implications."[8]

What you'll find after reading the opinions is quite frustrating. Different jurisdictions look at the exact same issues, evaluate nearly identical rules, and sometimes come out completely differently on the topic. There are 10 or so other issues that every state seems to review and some states come to completely different conclusions. That doesn't bode well for someone who wants to use these sites and happens to be in a state that has not made a decision on the matter.

If you're in a state that has not yet opined on the topic, you're in a really tough position. That's because every single ethics rule that is implicated is imminently resolvable. In my opinion, it's completely possible for a rational reviewer to interpret each issue and state, "as long as you are careful, as long as you understand these issues and navigate them properly, then the use of those sites passes ethical muster." But it's equally possible for the authorities in your state to say that they don't agree with that position. They could go

---

[6] South Carolina Ethics Advisory Opinion 11-05.

[7] Interestingly, South Carolina went further and said that even if the payment is seen as a fee, the sharing is still justified under the rule because it does not interfere with the professional independence of a lawyer. South Carolina Ethics Advisory Opinion 11-05.

[8] Arizona Ethics Opinion 13-01.

§ 6:5   NAVIGATING LEGAL ETHICS

the way of North Carolina and South Carolina and say that the sites are not permitted. They might also take Indiana's approach and say, they're not forbidden, but you probably shouldn't use them. Or, they might go Alabama's way and say *no, you can't do it.* You just don't know.

One thing that's for sure is that if you're in a state that permits the use, you need to be super careful. There are a significant number of ethical minefields to navigate and doing so is very difficult. The use of these sites is indeed "fraught with danger" as the Indiana Bar stated.[9]

§ 6:6 If technology changes, the application of the rule could change

It's been my experience that a lot of the opinions addressing social media use, and advertising in particular, have little nuggets of danger sprinkled throughout. It's up for debate whether the opining authorities place these gems in the opinions purposefully, but when I see them I want to point them out. The Ohio opinion on texting/solicitation dropped two such morsels.

The foregoing analysis all presumed that texting is a form of written communication, and we applied Rule 7.3(c)[1] as a result. It was a safe presumption, since the Ohio Board actually said that the communication tool was written. However, the drafters of the opinion left open a small window and acknowledged that there might be a cause for a change in their analysis. On page 5 of Opinion 2013-2, the Ohio Board stated, "Lawyers may likewise solicit clients using test[2] messages so long as the technology used to implement the text message does not generate a real-time or live conversation."[3] The drafters acknowledged that as technology advances, the texting feature could morph so that it ultimately becomes something similar to real-time communication. If that were to happen, then the restrictions in Rule 7.3(a) would kick in and the near-prohibition on contact would apply.

The Ohio Board noted that some problematic situations al-

---

[9]Indiana Opinion No. 1, 2012-JDH-1, Conclusion.

[Section 6:6]

[1]Del. Prof. Conduct R. 7.3(c).

7.3(c) http://courts.delaware.gov/rules/DLRPCFebruary2010.pdf. Pages last checked by the author August 13, 2013.

[2]This must have been a typo- they meant "text," I'm sure.

[3]Ohio Opinion 2013-2 at 5.

ready exist in this regard. In the footnote the Board added that "'voice-texting' apps, for example, can be used to decrease real-time conversations that combine voice and text."[4] While these apps aren't prevalent as of the date of this writing, it's possible that they might become more commonplace as time goes on. In that case, we'll need to re-evaluate the rule on solicitation and how it applies to texting.

Here's the other issue in the opinion that concerns me. As we've discussed, the opinion makes clear that texting is a written form of communication and it's governed by Rule 7.3(c). The Board spent most of the opinion addressing the implications of that section of the rule. However, there's one line in the opinion that raised my eyebrows. The Board stated, "Because most text messages are received on cellular phones, which are often carried on one's person, lawyers should be sensitive to the fact that a text message may be perceived as more invasive than email."[5] They mentioned it in the context of coercion—they were reminding the reader that Rule 7.3(b)[6] prohibits such conduct. However, I think there is a deeper meaning.

I think that the drafters are giving us a warning. There could be a time that texting would demand a more strict application of the rules. Remember that in real life the specific facts of a case are critical in determining whether a lawyer will be liable for an ethical violation. That's an obvious statement in every legal dilemma, but it seems like we end up saying, "it depends on the facts" a bit more often when we evaluate our ethical obligations as opposed to other areas of the law. It seems like the Board could envision a situation where the particular contents of a text message, when combined with the circumstances of the solicitation and the fact that texting is more invasive than email, ends up putting an inordinate amount of pressure on the target. That pressure and the resulting potential manipulation by the lawyer could be worse than it would have been in the case of an email message. Remember that we're talking hypotheticals here—it's tough to say exactly how the various forces would align to create a more pressure-filled scenario, but it seems like the Board is acknowledging that it might occur.

---

[4] Ohio Opinion 2013-2 at 5, citation omitted.
[5] Ohio Opinion 2013-2 at 6.
[6] Del. Prof. Conduct R. 7.3(b).
   7.3(b) http://courts.delaware.gov/rules/DLRPCFebruary2010.pdf. Pages last checked by the author August 13, 2013.

§ 6:6   Navigating Legal Ethics

In that case, the more "invasive" nature of the communication might lead to harsher penalties. The larger lesson is to beware . . . even though these communications are similar to methods that we've used for many years, they are all still somewhat unique. The application of the rules could be tweaked, depending on the attendant circumstances.

§ 6:7   Beware of shortcuts: Hyperlink disclaimers are not always permitted

The practical difficulty in complying with these rules has caused some lawyers to seek shortcuts that allow the lawyer to satisfy the rule in a less burdensome manner. Thus, in the context of texting, the Ohio Opinion acknowledged that due to the practical constraints of including the lengthy contents of the required disclaimer in the text, "some Ohio lawyers have included an Internet link in their text message solicitations that allow . . . the prospective client to view the . . . statement on the lawyer's website."[1] This seems like a perfect solution, doesn't it? If the requisite disclaimer text is too bulky, just provide an Internet link that leads the reader to the text. That way the necessary information is only one click away. The prospective client can go read that language if they choose to do so. Then, the message sent via text is cleaner and not so unwieldy. (Don't get excited yet . . . read on.)

We see this approach all the time outside the law. A banner ad on your cell phone might have very little text, but after one click of the screen, you're directed to a page with lots more information. However, this is a great example of how a common practice in the rest of the world is not always a permitted practice in the practice of law. In fact, the Ohio Board said that that approach is not permitted in the world of legal ethics.

In Ohio's opinion about texting, the Board addressed whether a lawyer could comply with its obligation to provide disclaimer information by providing a hyperlink to the requisite text. The Board rejected that approach when it stated that, "simply providing an Internet link to the . . . statement does not comply with Prof.Cond.R. 7.3(e)."[2] Basically, the Board took a very literal view of the way the rule

---

[Section 6:7]

    [1]Ohio Opinion 2013-2 at 7.
    [2]Ohio Opinion 2013-2 at 7.

was written. They confirmed that, "The rule requires that the statement be 'included with the communication' and the Supreme Court's announcement at the end of the statement similarly indicates that the solicitation 'must include' the statement."[3] The Board also acknowledged that there might be alternative shortcuts that lawyers find applicable and they headed those off at the proverbial pass as well. "Similarly, the Board believes that attachments of photographs containing the statement fail to satisfy Prof.Cond.R. 7.3(e)."[4]

This decision wasn't made simply for formality's sake. With every such opinion it's important to hearken back to the motivation behind the rules. That is what ultimately guides us when we evaluate other technologies that might not be specifically addressed by the black letter code. In this case remember that the justification for the rule that restricts solicitation is to protect the vulnerable. It's to ensure that a lawyer does not take advantage of someone in a difficult situation. The purpose of providing the specific cautionary language required by the rule on solicitation is to allow the target of a solicitation to realize that they have choices at the moment they are being solicited. If you force the target to hunt down the language, there is less of a likelihood that they will see the disclaimer in a timely manner (if at all) and that increases the chance that the target will be manipulated. The Ohio board confirmed that when they stated that their position, "ensures that all recipients, regardless of the features on their cellular phones or service plans, have immediate access to the information"[5]

One can see how this potential shortcut would apply to other delicate instances. For example, in the section on virtual offices we will discuss the requirement that an advertisement set forth the name and office address of a lawyer. Specifically, the Delaware rules state in Rule 7.2(c), "Any communication made pursuant to this rule shall include the name and office address of at least one lawyer or law firm responsible for its content." Now imagine that your firm wants to advertise with banner ads on cell phones. These are small ads that appear on the bottom or top of the screen when you launch certain apps. The ads are usually

---

[3]Ohio Opinion 2013-2 at 7.
[4]Ohio Opinion 2013-2 at 7.
[5]Ohio Opinion 2013-2 at 7.

very limited in space, so there's very little text. It may be physically impossible, or simply impractical, to fit the name and address of the lawyer responsible for the ad's content, no less any disclaimers that might be required by a particular state's rule. But the requisite information could be one click away. One small touch on the screen, and the reader could be transported to a page that has everything listed in detail. Decisions like Ohio 2010-2, however, appear to put the kibosh on such a practice.

The foregoing analysis demonstrates why you need to look at the rules from the client's perspective, not the lawyer's. The drafters take a literal approach to the rules because it is consistent with the purpose behind the code. They're not trying to ensure that the lawyer has an easy time complying with a technicality; they're trying to ensure that the protection afforded to the prospective client is actually received. A further expression of this principle can be found in a recent decision in Illinois.

§ 6:8 Beware of shortcuts: The specific words in disclaimers matter

In January 2012, the Illinois Bar Association issued Advisory (ISBA) Opinion No 12-04 in which they opined on the requirement that certain solicitations be labeled as "Advertising Material." Specifically, the ISBA learned that some firms who were sending out brochures about their services were not affixing the "Advertising Material" to the brochure; rather, they substituted the language, "Promotional Materials." The ISBA said that such a practice violated Rule 7.3(c) and stated:

> . . . labeling of the communications to solicit professional employment in question as "promotional materials" does not comply with the requirements of this Rule. While the terms "advertising" and "promotional" may be similar, we believe RPC 7.3's specific use of the term "Advertising Material," highlighted by quotation marks, is a clear indication of the mandatory nature of the use of that specific term *[citation omitted]*.[1]

Thus, firm brochures that were sent to prospective clients as solicitations needed to have the specific term, "Advertising Material" affixed to the communication. While one could

---

[Section 6:8]
[1]ISBA Opinion 12-04 at 2.

argue that this is nothing more than a strict reading of the rules, I believe that they stuck to a literal interpretation of the rule because the words mean something. The specific word "advertising" puts the target on guard in a way that "promotional material" would not. "Advertising" gives a clear warning to the target of manipulation, one that is readily understood the first time it's read. "Promotional Material," on the other hand, is more of a vague, watered down disclaimer. The drafters of both the Illinois Rule and the ISBA Opinion most likely felt the same way. As you can see (and similar to other decisions), the rationale for being a stickler was all about protecting the prospective client.

Yet in the same opinion, the ISBA appears to be inconsistent. Later on they state that, "the labeling requirements of Rule 7.3(c), only apply to communications employed in the direct written, recorded or electronic solicitation of prospective clients known to be in need of legal services. Communications sent in response to requests from potential clients and general announcements do not require the special labeling. RPC 7.3, Comment [7]"[2]

Are they saying what I think they're saying? That not all communications to prospective clients need to have the required disclaimers? How do you make sense of that? It's simple, really—just note that the key phrase is, "in response." In this part of the opinion they're not talking about communications that are initiated by the lawyer, they're talking about communications that are initiated by the potential client, to which a lawyer responds. The required disclaimer is not necessary if the communication is a response. Thus, the ISBA isn't carving out any exception; rather, they're just saying that if you're sending a communication in response to someone's request for information, you're not soliciting someone as envisioned by the rules.

Once again, it's consistent with the deeper meaning of the code. If a potential client asks a lawyer for information, the potential client initiated the contact. They made the choice to seek you out, which means that you are the target, not the prospective client. In that instance, the need to put the potential client on guard about your desire to woo them as a client is not necessary. Presumably, they contacted you for that very reason. That's why the ISBA says that the disclaimer isn't necessary. This would be helpful in evaluating other, similar contacts with prospective clients.

---

[2]ISBA Opinion 12-04 at 2.

§ 6:8   NAVIGATING LEGAL ETHICS

Consider as an example a lawyer who has an established social media presence—a Facebook page, a blog, and a twitter page perhaps. She hears about an interesting change in a regulation, then writes a blog post about it which attracts the attention of a potential client. If that potential client sends her a tweet, then the lawyer's response is not considered a solicitation. It won't need to have all the disclaimers that would have been required had they initiated the contact.

All of this applies to the larger issue of ethical use of social media pretty clearly. What we see is that states are not likely to look favorably upon shortcuts and substitutions to the requirements of the rules. Whether it's providing a link to access requisite disclaimers instead of setting forth the lengthy text, or messing around with the specific language that's mandated in such a disclaimer, the authorities are consistent. The public must be protected and the underlying principles of the rules will not be compromised. The platform is not determinative . . . it's the goals of the system that prevail.

§ 6:9 When real-time electronic contact is not a prohibited solicitation

None of the rules operate in a vacuum. Sometimes the underlying principles for some code sections cause a tribunal to relax the rules, rather than interpret them more strictly. Nowhere was that more evident than when the Philadelphia Bar Association Professional Guidance Committee addressed solicitation in its Opinion 2010-6.[1] In that opinion, the Committee grappled with chat-room communication and whether such communication is real-time electronic communication, and thus prohibited by the rule on solicitation. It began by acknowledging the reason for the rule:

> The purpose behind this Rule is to prohibit what is referred to as 'direct solicitation' because of the concern about an inherent potential for abuse where a non-lawyer is engaged by a trained advocate in a direct, interpersonal encounter and, potentially feeling overwhelmed and not able to fully evaluate all the

---

[Section 6:9]
[1]June 2010.

available alternatives before immediately retaining the offending lawyer, feels pressured to engage the lawyer.[2]

That rationale is the reason that intense communications like in-person discussions and live telephone calls are prohibited forms of solicitations, except under very tailored circumstances. The Committee stated that the concept was intended to be extended to the world of technology when it stated, "The notion behind the adoption of the words 'real-time electronic communication' plainly was to ensure the rule would apply to what were then referred to as 'chat rooms,' website communication forums where one might interact on a real-time basis with other persons . . . ."[3]

However, the Philadelphia Committee drew a distinction. Chat rooms, they said, are "different from in-person direct communication and telephone calls. In the latter kinds of in-person communications with an overbearing lawyer, the prospective client can walk away or hang up the phone, but it is socially awkward to do so in the face of a determined advocate. In the former, however . . . a recipient can readily and summarily decline to participate in the communication."[4] The Committee believed that in the case of chat rooms, the prospective client has the ability to " 'turn off' the soliciting lawyer and respond or not as he or she sees fit . . . ."[5]

In a departure from established doctrine, the Committee stated that even though the rule referred to "real-time electronic communication" and the ABA reporter to the Model Rules specifically stated that such language refers to chat rooms, they still didn't feel bound to apply the rules as the ABA drafters intended. A key justification for the Committee's divergence in that regard was that they believed, "that the social attitudes and developing rules of Internet etiquette are changing."[6] Basically, the opinion acknowledged that norms have changed and that means that the application of the rules should change. Specifically, they said, "with

---

[2]Philadelphia Bar Association Professional Guidance Committee 2010-6 at 2.

[3]Philadelphia Bar Association Professional Guidance Committee 2010-6 at 3.

[4]Philadelphia Bar Association Professional Guidance Committee 2010-6 at 5.

[5]Philadelphia Bar Association Professional Guidance Committee 2010-6 at 6.

[6]Philadelphia Bar Association Professional Guidance Committee 2010-6 at 6.

the increasing sophistication and ubiquity of social media, it has become readily apparent to everyone that they need not respond instantaneously to electronic overtures, and that everyone realizes that, like targeted mail, emails, blogs and chat room comments can be readily ignored, or not, as the recipient wished.[7] Thus, the pressure that is inherent in real-time communication is simply not present in chat room conversations, given the realities of social media use today.

Some realities of social media use have even changed from the time the opinion was written. In particular, chat rooms aren't as prevalent today as they once were. The place that most people are using a similar style of communication is through the "chat" function on platforms like Facebook. In that situation, two users who are logged onto the social media platform at the same time can converse in real time. A review of both types of chats shows that they are, functionally speaking, the same thing. Thus, it appears that the Philadelphia opinion would most likely apply to Facebook-style chat just as it applies to chat rooms.

But what does it all mean? Is the Philadelphia decision turning the rule on its head? While on its face this decision might seem contradictory to the rules, a deeper review of the rationale reviews that it is wholly consistent with the underlying principles for the rule on solicitation.

The rule on solicitation was created to prevent lawyers from manipulating people in a vulnerable position. The more dangerous the communication, the more restrictive the treatment. Here, the drafters are saying that behavior once considered dangerous, no longer presents such a danger. As a result, the level of restriction can be altered. The rule didn't change for the dangerous stuff—live communications, for instance, are still treated restrictively. Thus, the underlying rationale of the rule is intact.

This decision acknowledges that the rules have a tough time keeping up. It is a prime example of how the tweaks to the existing standards will most likely come from interpretive opinions, rather than wholesale rule amendment. Sure, the ABA amended their model rules and the states will be considering those changes over the upcoming years, but the immediate change comes from the advisory opinions and disciplinary cases.

---

[7]Philadelphia Bar Association Professional Guidance Committee 2010-6 at 6.

§ 6:9

Danger Zone Alert #1: One must note that even though the Philadelphia Committee issued this opinion, the State of Pennsylvania has not changed their ethics rule to conform. Thus, you're probably going to be able to claim the decision's protection if you're in Philadelphia, but not so much in other states. Heck, they may not even agree in other parts of Pennsylvania. So what does this opinion do for us? It helps us defend ourselves. You might find yourself before a tribunal where you need to justify your own chat communications that appear to run afoul of the rule. In that case, you might want to make an argument similar to that set forth in the Philadelphia opinion and now you know that you have that rationale in your pocket. But there's a broader lesson of defense, as well.

The Philadelphia decision gives each lawyer theoretical direction that you could follow when making your own evaluations of new technologies. Remember that when the Committee conducted their evaluation, their motivation was singular—to ensure that the fundamental goals of the code are advanced. Thus, they spent a significant amount of time exploring the underlying purpose of the code before they evaluated the new technology. That's what each lawyer must do whenever we face a technethics question. Because even when we advocate that the rules need to be modified, the best argument is one that argues for a new application of the rules that is consistent with the underlying goals of the code.

Danger Zone Alert #2: The Philadelphia opinion left us one of those little nuggets of danger that I mention every once in a while. In classic style, the drafters of the opinion left us with a warning when they stated:

> . . . there might be some types of social media, not directly involved in this inquiry that are so similar to an in-person communication or telephone call that use of them for solicitation is barred. For example, it is possible to conduct chat rooms over the Internet in which the participants communicate in tea-time by voice over IP. That could be and likely is, real-time electronic communication.[8]

There are two lessons we get from this passage. First, the drafters are saying that certain modes of communication might look like the kind of chat they're addressing in the opinion but they aren't really the same thing. Opinion 2010-6

---

[8]Philadelphia Bar Association Professional Guidance Committee 2010-6 at 7.

§ 6:9   NAVIGATING LEGAL ETHICS

dealt with real-time written communication. Voice over IP is not the same thing—voice over IP is more like a phone call. In that case, the technology would fall into the Rule 7.3(a) method of solicitation and the harsher restrictions would apply. Thus, when you're conducting your own analysis about the permissibility of a particular type of technological communication, be careful that you critically evaluate each such technology. Different types of communication may have similarities, but there could be fundamental differences that warrant very different treatment under the rules. Incidentally, now you can see what I meant in the beginning of the book when I talked about competence and Rule 1.1.[9] Staying competent, staying cutting-edge, and understanding the nuances of the latest technology is a must.

The second lesson is a bit more conceptual. The drafters are also telling us to watch how technology evolves. You don't see many chat rooms using voice over IP, but it's certainly a possibility. Things might evolve so that voice over IP becomes more popular. The drafters don't know if that technological change will occur, but they are acknowledging that it's a possibility. And that's what this passage is really about—change. The drafters are telling us that if the communication methods change in a way that makes the underlying concerns about pressure and manipulation more of a concern, then that will trigger the more restrictive approach to solicitations. In other words, if the technology changes and the concerns return, then the old way of looking at this communication will apply once again.

---

[9]Del. Prof. Conduct R. 1.1.
   1.1 http://courts.delaware.gov/rules/DLRPCFebruary2010.pdf. Pages last checked by the author August 13, 2013.

Chapter 7

The Hazards of Being Helpful

- § 7:1 An introduction to being helpful
- § 7:2 Beware of assisting *that guy*
- § 7:3 Inadvertently establishing a lawyer-client relationship
- § 7:4 Practicing outside our jurisdiction
- § 7:5 Unauthorized practice of law—Assisting laypeople
- § 7:6 Is there a duty to defriend?
- § 7:7 Ignoring the not-so-hidden, hazardous realities of the Internet

> **KeyCite®:** Cases and other legal materials listed in KeyCite Scope can be researched through the KeyCite service on Westlaw®. Use KeyCite to check citations for form, parallel references, prior and later history, and comprehensive citator information, including citations to other decisions and secondary materials.

§ 7:1 An introduction to being helpful

Sometimes we do obviously stupid things on social media which get us into ethical trouble. Other times we wander upon a hidden hazard that causes problems. Keep your eyes open for these dangers that sometimes go unappreciated.

§ 7:2 Beware of assisting *that guy*

One of the benefits of social media is that help is just click away. We can find case law, statutes, treatises, you name it. We also have a large amount of human resources at our disposal—our social media contacts. If we find ourselves tackling a legal question with which we're not familiar, we need go no further than our LinkedIn network to find an attorney who can give us the assistance we need.

This goes beyond just looking for help on an isolated question. The rules grant us even more permission to seek assistance from our colleagues. A review of the rules reveals that we're actually permitted to take cases that deal with areas of the law where we may not have prior experience so

§ 7:2 NAVIGATING LEGAL ETHICS

long as we acquire the requisite competence by conferring with other members of the bar. Rule 1.1, Comment [2] (Competence), gives direction in that regard:

> [2] A lawyer need not necessarily have special training or prior experience to handle legal problems of a type with which the lawyer is unfamiliar . . . A lawyer can provide adequate representation in a wholly novel field through necessary study. Competent representation can also be provided through the association of a lawyer of established competence in the field in question.

There are two sides to this issue, however. While the code grants us the ability to seek assistance from our colleagues, it also grants our colleagues the ability to seek assistance from us. Those of us who are established in a particular area of law know that it's not uncommon to attract other lawyers who need assistance. In fact, if you're a thought leader in your practice area—maybe you're a proficient blogger or a prominent member of a bar committee—you might very well be a target for lawyers who need assistance. There's nothing wrong with that on its face. After all, if a lawyer has a question, why not go to the guru for help?

Many of us willingly help other lawyers who seek our assistance and there is plenty of justification for doing so. Helping out another person seems like the right thing to do, plus our concepts of professionalism espouse that we should be assisting our colleagues when they need our assistance. As a result, many lawyers give our struggling brethren the guidance they seek and it most cases there isn't any problem. But watch out for *that guy*.

You know who *that guy* is. We have all met some version of *that guy*. He's the one who shows up late for a closing, forgets his motion papers at the office, walk around with a shirttail out of his pants, or all of the above. Of course, this isn't gender specific—*that guy* could be *that gal*. Regardless of gender, be careful. Helping *that guy* could spell trouble. It's interesting, because this isn't a problem when we run into *that guy* in real life. In the face-to-face world, we can see *that guy* coming a mile away and we know to avoid getting too involved with him. Our internal warning system sounds loudly. The problem is that on social media, we have the buffers.

Social media desensitizes us to some dangers and masks others. One such danger is that you don't know who people really are in the virtual world. People often hide their true personalities behind the Internet. The person with whom you are corresponding could be wearing a shirt and tie in their tightly cropped profile pic, but for all you know they could be wearing Spiderman pajama bottoms. But the real danger in the helping this colleague is that you don't know what *that guy* will do with the information you provide. *That guy* could end up committing malpractice or violating the ethics rules. And you and I both know that if he gets into trouble, he's throwing you under the wheels of the cyber-bus.

It's a real dilemma, because as we mentioned before, our professionalism concepts encourage us to help others. But this concern doesn't mean that we should avoid helping our colleagues in need. We need to simply be aware that there are hazards to being helpful and each of us must do whatever we can to remove the buffers. Protect yourself. Conduct your own due diligence into people who approach you on the Internet before you offer assistance.

§ 7:3 Inadvertently establishing a lawyer-client relationship

I present to you the following example. What's the problem with these facts?

> *An acquaintance writes a post on your Facebook page congratulating you on being named "Real Estate Lawyer of the Millennium." A few days later she asks you if it's possible for a person to appeal their residential property taxes. You respond with some basic information. A day later, she asks you where she could find the forms to file the appeal. You give her the web address. A day after that, she sends you an e-mail with some comparable sales and asks you whether you think they're any good.*

Hopefully there's a red light flashing before your mind's eye right now, or maybe a red flag waving back and forth . . . or some other type of warning sign. The issue that I hope you've noticed is that the lawyer in this example might be on their way to forming a lawyer-client relationship with the person seeking information.

As we can see from this fact pattern, the formation of the lawyer-client relationship doesn't always jump out at you. Heck, it would be nice if a doctor came barreling down a hallway, pulled down his or her mask and shouted, "CONGRATULATIONS, MR. TEICHER, IT'S A BRAND NEW BABY CLIENT!" Unfortunately, we don't always get that

§ 7:3   NAVIGATING LEGAL ETHICS

kind of notice. In fact, attorney-client relationships could be (and often are) created by course of conduct. In those instances there might not be any formal statement of the commencement of the relationship.

I've always believed that the best generic definition of when a lawyer-client relationship is created comes from the landmark case, *Togstad v. Vesely, Otto, Miller & Keefe*, decided by the Minnesota Supreme Court in 1980.[1] Specifically, the Court stated in Footnote [4], ". . .'[a]n attorney-client relationship is created whenever an individual seeks and receives legal advice from an attorney in circumstances in which a reasonable person would rely on such advice.' " *[citation omitted]*.[2] That's exactly what appears to be happening in the example above. The person with whom you communicated asked for some information, and as the exchange of messages continued, you got closer and closer to providing information upon which the person expected to rely.

One can see how this problem is of particular concern in the world of social media. Social media is all about exchanging information. It's dominated by the concept of engaging in conversation with the larger Internet community. The probability of inadvertently forming a lawyer-client relationship increases exponentially when you're involved in a medium where that level of communication is prevalent. Throw in the norms—where asking questions and seeking free advice is commonplace—and you've got a potent mix.

The key is for lawyers to maintain a heightened level of awareness. Be on guard for the ethical implications of your seemingly innocuous online conversations. They're never really harmless. In reality, they could be birthing you a brand new baby client.

§ 7:4 Practicing outside our jurisdiction

In a medium where there is consistent interaction with people who could easily become our clients, there arises one other related concern. Not only should we worry about inadvertently forming attorney-client relationships, but we

---

[Section 7:3]

[1]http://scholar.google.com/scholar_case?case=8498879200867285465&q=togstad+v.+miller&hl=en&as_sdt=6,33, last checked by the author January 11, 2014.

[2]291 N.W.2d 686 (1980).

need to be equally on guard about forming those relationships with people outside of the jurisdiction where we are licensed to practice. If we do that, we would end up practicing law outside of our jurisdiction, violating Rule 5.5.[1]

Rule 5.5. Unauthorized practice of law; multijurisdictional practice of law *(in part)*

(a) A lawyer shall not practice law in a jurisdiction in violation of the regulation of the legal profession in that jurisdiction, or assist another in doing so.

(b) A lawyer who is not admitted to practice in this jurisdiction shall not:

(1) except as authorized by these Rules or other law, establish an office or other systematic and continuous presence in this jurisdiction for the practice of law; or

(2) hold out to the public or otherwise represent that the lawyer is admitted to practice law in this jurisdiction.

* * *

At its most basic level, Rule 5.5 prohibits us from practicing in states where we're not licensed. The concept is simple enough, but it's one of those things that can sneak up and bite you on the behind when you're not expecting it. It's a double whammy of sorts. You might not be expecting to inadvertently form a lawyer-client relationship with a person you're speaking to on line (thus the use of the word *inadvertent*). If that's the case, then you're certainly not going to realize that the brand new baby client is actually located in a state where you're not licensed.

Whether your actions rise to the level of the actual practice of law depends upon your local standards. That is confirmed in Rule 5.5, Comment [2] which states, "The definition of the practice of law is established by law and varies from one jurisdiction to another." What's clear, however, is that you need to get that soundtrack playing in your head. You need to train yourself to hear the danger coming on the ethical horizon. And that means all the danger—not just the formation of the relationship but the issues that might follow as well.

[Section 7:4]

[1]Del. Prof. Conduct R. 5.5.

5.5 http://courts.delaware.gov/rules/DLRPCFebruary2010.pdf. Pages last checked by the author August 13, 2013.

§ 7:5 Unauthorized practice of law—Assisting laypeople

Rule 5.5[1] is probably best known for the aforementioned ban on practicing outside your jurisdiction, but it also prohibits assisting someone else in the practice of law when they are not permitted to do so. Comment [1] to Rule 5.5 states, ". . . Paragraph (a) applies to unauthorized practice of law by a lawyer, whether through the lawyer's direct action or by the lawyer assisting another person."

That means that you can't help another lawyer practice in a jurisdiction where they're not permitted by the bar. There's another angle about which to be aware because the comment also prohibits you from assisting another "person." That word encompasses plain-old regular people too. Thus, the rule prohibits you from helping a layperson engage in the practice of law when that layperson is not licensed to do so.

Stay on guard against the latter situation, in particular. It's possible that a layperson could contact you via social media to ask for assistance in a particular legal matter. They might say it's their own case, or they might create some other seemingly harmless justification for needing the information. Remember, however, that we don't really know many of the people with whom we interact on social media, nor do we know what they will be doing with the information we provide. Continue to exercise that heightened state of awareness—be aware about the potential danger of assisting another in the unauthorized practice of law.

No Establishment of a Systematic and Continuous Presence

There is a more social media-centric topic that grows out of Rule 5.5. Recall that subsection (b) states that, "A lawyer who is not admitted to practice in this jurisdiction shall not: (1) except as authorized by these Rules or other law, establish an office or other systematic and continuous presence in this jurisdiction for the practice of law . . ." At its most basic level, the rule is trying to avoid people from, say, Cincinnati, swimming across the river into Kentucky to set up shop for the practice of law when they aren't licensed in that state. But it's no longer restricted to a question of physical location.

[Section 7:5]

[1]Del. Prof. Conduct R. 5.5.

5.5 http://courts.delaware.gov/rules/DLRPCFebruary2010.pdf. Pages last checked by the author August 13, 2013.

Indeed, the commentary to Rule 5.5 acknowledges that when it states, "[4] Presence may be systematic and continuous even if the lawyer is not physically present here. Such a lawyer must not hold out to the public or otherwise represent that the lawyer is admitted to practice law in this jurisdiction."

The concern in the social media context is whether a lawyer is in danger of establishing a systematic and continuous *virtual* presence for the practice of law. Once again, when using a medium that has the exchange of information and the engagement in conversation as its primary tool, this becomes a realistic issue.

Let's say, for instance, that there is a lawyer licensed only in Kansas who practices health care law. He or she is so enamored with the Massachusetts health care system that they engage in social media communications galore. Maybe they post blog comments on articles written about the topic on the online version of various Massachusetts newspapers. They might engage Massachusetts law firms in conversation on their social media pages. They might also engage members of the public in Massachusetts in conversations about the state's health care law on the lawyer's own social media accounts. For the purposes of this hypothetical, assume that this activity is consistent and done often. The creation of these contact points could lead to a systematic presence in Massachusetts. Sure, it's debatable whether the presence has actually been created and whether the rule has been violated based on these facts. After all, how many such contact points need to be established, before you establish a continuous virtual presence? I don't know, but you can certainly see the danger looming.

One doesn't need to consider such an elaborate scheme to see how this issue could be a problem. Virtual law offices (VLOs) are becoming far more prevalent these days.[2] If one's entire professional existence is online and virtual, then there is a significant possibility that one might establish themselves in a jurisdiction where they're not licensed. Incidentally, don't read that statement as a knock on VLOs— I'm not saying they should be outlawed because of that concern, I'm just noting that it's a real possibility.

In fact, the ABA thinks it's a real possibility as well. In June of 2012 the ABA released an issues paper where they

---

[2]Virtual Law Offices are discussed at length elsewhere in this book.

§ 7:5   NAVIGATING LEGAL ETHICS

acknowledged the systematic and continuous virtual presence problem and sought feedback about whether the issue warranted amending the Model Rules.[3] Personally, I haven't seen any movement by the ABA on this topic as of the date of this writing. But that doesn't matter for our purposes. What I want you to know is that, if they are thinking about it, you should be thinking about it. The point we're making here is that you should be aware of this issue and avoid falling into its trap.

§ 7:6 Is there a duty to defriend?

Here's a scenario for you to chew on: You're "friends" with your layperson-neighbor on Facebook. For whatever reason, that layperson-neighbor becomes an opposing party in a lawsuit —say that you represent a client and the layperson-neighbor is represented by separate counsel. The question is, can you remain Facebook friends? Or stated more formally, can we stay connected with a layperson on social media when that layperson's status changes from a social acquaintance to an opposing party who is represented by counsel?

The answer isn't so clear (thus its inclusion in the "hidden hazards" section). The rule that is implicated is Rule 4.2[1] because the individual is represented by counsel.[2] It reads:

Rule 4.2. Communication with person represented by counsel

In representing a client, a lawyer shall not communicate about the subject of the representation with a person the lawyer knows to be represented by another lawyer in the matter, unless the lawyer has the consent of the other lawyer or is authorized to do so by law or a court order.

Let's dispense with a few easy issues at the outset: First, the fact that this person was a social acquaintance before

---

[3]http://www.americanbar.org/content/dam/aba/administrative/ethics_2020/20120619_draft_release_for_comment_rule_5_5_comment_4_virtual_practice.authcheckdam.pdf, last checked by the author on January 14, 2014.

[Section 7:6]

[1]Del. Prof. Conduct R. 4.2.

4.2 http://courts.delaware.gov/rules/DLRPCFebruary2010.pdf. Pages last checked by the author August 13, 2013.

[2]If the individual was not represented by counsel you'd go to Rule 4.3.

they became a party in the suit doesn't matter. Comment [2] to the rule states that, "This Rule applies to communications with any person who is represented by counsel concerning the matter to which the communication relates." Second, it doesn't matter if you start the conversation or your neighbor starts it. Comment [3] says that it's off limits either way. Specifically, it states, "[3] The Rule applies even though the represented person initiates or consents to the communication. A lawyer must immediately terminate communication with a person if, after commencing communication, the lawyer learns that the person is one with whom communication is not permitted by this Rule." Third, all of this only applies if you're talking about the case. So if you ask your neighbor about who got kicked off Project Runway last night, that's okay, right? That communication is not "about the subject of the representation," as stated in Rule 4.2, so you're probably in the clear.

But what if the neighbor isn't talking to *you* at all? Also, what if you're not doing any talking; rather, you're just listening. That's where this gets murky.

A more realistic scenario is that you spend some time eavesdropping on your neighbor's social media page watching to see if he or she makes any comments about the ongoing litigation. Maybe the neighbor will have an open conversation with their lawyer about matters—sure, the neighbor's lawyer is probably committing an ethics violation in doing so, but things like that happen. Or maybe the neighbor is posting incriminating pictures. Who knows—there could be tons of helpful information for you to glean. Can you lurk? Note that this is different from the scenarios we presented in the investigation section of this book because here you didn't ask to be friended in advance of litigation. Instead, you were a pre-existing connection, one that was made before any adversarial situation was created.

It may be distasteful, but the question is whether it's an ethics violation. The way I see it, this ultimately boils down to whether your eavesdropping is considered a "communication" per Rule 4.2. As you've likely read elsewhere in this book, the question of what exactly is a "communication" has been hotly debated in other contexts (see the section on advertising and solicitation, for instance). The somewhat elusive definition of that word is a key question in the world of social media because it often determines whether an ethical rule will be triggered. In this scenario, it's not so clear. (What else is new, right?)

§ 7:6 NAVIGATING LEGAL ETHICS

The advent of social media has transformed the way the word "communication" is defined. In the past, one would have expected that there would be some sort of statement, writing, or other verbalization by a lawyer in order for a "communication" to be deemed to have taken place. But as we saw in the investigations section of this book, that isn't always the case. You might recall that we discussed the New York City Bar Association Formal Opinion No. 2012-2, which evaluated whether an attorney may research a juror through social media websites. There, the City opined that such research was proper, provided that no communication with the juror occurs.[3] However, the Opinion defined what constitutes a "communication" very broadly. It stated that,

> . . . if an attorney views a juror's social media page and the juror received an automated message from the social media service that a potential contact has viewed her profile . . . the attorney has arguably "communicated" with the juror. The transmission of the information that the attorney viewed the juror's page is a communication that may be attributable to the lawyer . . .[4]

Thus, according to this Opinion's reasoning, a lawyer might not have to say anything at all and they still might be deemed to have been "communicating" with the target. According to the New York City Bar, simply making the lawyer's presence known is enough to constitute a communication.

Certainly, this opinion is limited. It's a New York City decision (it isn't even a statewide opinion), and it's limited to the question of juror research. But like many of the other opinions we've reviewed, it's indicative of the way disciplinary authorities are evaluating these questions. It needs to inform our actions in social media. It impacts how we view the example above.

We can see that it's not out of the realm of possibilities for a disciplinary authority to consider the lurking/eavesdropping/listening to the layperson's website to be a "communication" that runs afoul of Rule 4.2. I'd expect that there would need to be some other attendant circumstances, but one thing that the New York City Opinion makes clear, is that verbalization isn't necessarily one of them. The old common-sense definition of what constitutes a "communication" isn't dispositive any more.

---

[3]New York City Formal Opinion 2012-2 at 4.
[4]New York City Formal Opinion 2012-2 at 4–5.

And don't forget the old fall-back rule for the disciplinary authorities: the rule I call "the Stupid Rule," Rule 8.4[5] (Misconduct). If your actions go beyond merely eavesdropping to the point that the authorities believe that you acted in a deceptive manner, then they might claim that the action violated Rule 8.4(c)[6] as well.

This is a toughie because the issue could be argued convincingly both ways. There's a good argument for claiming that the continued connection is permissible, but there's an equally compelling case for de-friending. Personally, I would err on the side of caution and de-friend (not that you're surprised about that position—I'm sure I've made my overly cautious nature quite clear). Among the reasons I believe that is because of the adage I've stated elsewhere in this book—if you do something repulsive, they're gonna find a way to get you. Depending on the particular facts of the case, your stalking-like behavior in this example might very well be seen as repulsive.

§ 7:7 Ignoring the not-so-hidden, hazardous realities of the Internet

There are hidden hazards that are missed, then there are not-so-hidden hazards that are ignored. There's a case out of Rhode Island that aptly illustrates the latter category. *In the Matter of Donal F. DeCicco*,[1] tells a tale of a lawyer trying to make some easy money on the Internet. In that case there was a sole practitioner who learned that lawyers could offer their services and be paid a fee to act as an "attorney pay master."[2] A lawyer who acts as a pay master is basically acting as an escrow agent who receives and holds monies that are due to a commodities broker and then disburses the funds to the broker after they receive confirmation that the

---

[5]Del. Prof. Conduct R. 8.4.

8.4 http://courts.delaware.gov/rules/DLRPCFebruary2010.pdf. Pages last checked by the author August 13, 2013.

[6]Del. Prof. Conduct R. 8.4(c).

8.4(c) http://courts.delaware.gov/rules/DLRPCFebruary2010.pdf. Pages last checked by the author August 13, 2013.

[Section 7:7]

[1]Case No. 2013-275-M.P., Rhode Island Supreme Court (October 17, 2013).

[2]DeCicco, Case No. 2013-275-M.P., at 1.

§ 7:7   NAVIGATING LEGAL ETHICS

funds were earned.[3] This particular lawyer created a website and offered his services in that regard.[4] You think you know the rest of the story, right? Lawyer gets involved with a scam client and loses a truckload of money. Sort of, but there's a wrinkle that makes the case even more concerning. In this case the lawyer actually asked the ethics authorities if the paymaster services were permissible.

The lawyer asked the ethics authorities whether he could engage in these services and counsel warned him against getting involved in it.[5] The lawyer was told by Rhode Island Disciplinary Counsel, "that attorneys are being specifically targeted by scam artists using the Internet, and that he was most likely becoming involved in a scam. The respondent chose not to heed that advice."[6]

The rest of the story is somewhat predictable (unfortunately). The lawyer was contacted by a potential client.[7] Over the course of a little over a month there were numerous wire and cash deposits to the lawyer's trust account totaling millions of dollars. The lawyer forwarded that money to institutions around the world, per the client's instructions.[8] The problem is that the lawyer never inquired about the source of the money, nor did he determine if the client was entitled to the money and, "did not question the legitimacy of these transactions."[9] When the lawyer learned that the client was defrauding people (and using the lawyer's trust account to do so), the lawyer stopped acting as an attorney pay master, contacted the authorities and cooperated with law enforcement officials.[10] No criminal charges were filed against the respondent.[11] The court held that the respondent violated both Rule 1.1[12] by not acting competently

---

[3]DeCicco, Case No. 2013-275-M.P., at 1.
[4]DeCicco, Case No. 2013-275-M.P., at 2.
[5]DeCicco, Case No. 2013-275-M.P., at 2.
[6]DeCicco, Case No. 2013-275-M.P., at 2.
[7]DeCicco, Case No. 2013-275-M.P., at 2.
[8]DeCicco, Case No. 2013-275-M.P., at 2, 3.
[9]DeCicco, Case No. 2013-275-M.P., at 3.
[10]DeCicco, Case No. 2013-275-M.P., at 3.
[11]DeCicco, Case No. 2013-275-M.P., at 3.
[12]Del. Prof. Conduct R. 1.1.
   1.1 http://courts.delaware.gov/rules/DLRPCFebruary2010.pdf. Pages last checked by the author August 13, 2013.

and Rule 1.15[13] for failing to hold the property of others "with the care required of a professional fiduciary."[14]

In previous sections we've seen how the buffers of the Internet cause us to let down our guard. In this section we go one step further. The *DeCicco* case combines the lure of easy money with the desensitizing buffers of the Internet. As a result, the offending lawyer went from simply missing a hidden hazard to disregarding an obvious danger. The lesson for lawyers using social media is that if you hear the soundtrack starting to play in the back of your mind, listen to the music—it's trying to tell you something.

---

[13]Del. Prof. Conduct R. 1.15.
    1.15 http://courts.delaware.gov/rules/DLRPCFebruary2010.pdf. Pages last checked by the author August 13, 2013.

[14]DeCicco, Case No. 2013-275-M.P., at 4.

Chapter 8

Other Ethical Issues Created by Technology

§ 8:1   Introduction to other technology
§ 8:2   Emails, yesterday and today
§ 8:3   Confidentiality and the cloud: The reasonable care standard
§ 8:4   Our fiduciary duty under Rule 1.15
§ 8:5   The extension of our duty to supervise
§ 8:6   The two facets of confidentiality
§ 8:7   The emerging affirmative duty to understand, anticipate, and act
§ 8:8   Is client consent required?
§ 8:9   Generally, no consent is probably required
§ 8:10 Exceptions exist, like sensitive information or express instruction
§ 8:11 Questions to ask
§ 8:12 Texting
§ 8:13 Mega issues with metadata
§ 8:14 What everyone's missing in the virtual law office debate
§ 8:15 The issues with wireless networks
§ 8:16 Implications for smart phones, iPads and other devices

> **KeyCite®:** Cases and other legal materials listed in KeyCite Scope can be researched through the KeyCite service on Westlaw®. Use KeyCite to check citations for form, parallel references, prior and later history, and comprehensive citator information, including citations to other decisions and secondary materials.

§ 8:1   Introduction to other technology

There are a myriad of other technologies being used in the practice of law today, beyond social media. The concerns for lawyers are wide-ranging.

With email, texting and other communication we're talking about the transmission of data from one person to

§ 8:1   NAVIGATING LEGAL ETHICS

another. We are concerned about the channels upon which that data travels—the highways our information rides along to get from place to place. When we take that information and put it on the Internet to move it we use the proverbial information superhighway. One question we need to ask ourselves is whether that highway is secure. Can anyone jump onto it and intercept the data we're moving?

What about getting onto that highway to begin with? Just like a car uses an onramp to access a highway, you plug a cable into your computer and that carries your information onto the Internet. Of course, we all know that you can access that information superhighway wirelessly these days, by using a wireless router to move the information from your computer to the Internet. But if we use that type of a wireless onramp, we have security issues. The data becomes vulnerable once we transmit it through the air. By connecting to a wireless router we essentially open up a door to our computer and invite other people to come in and see whatever we have loaded onto our computers. The whole question of wireless access is also raised when we talk about cell phones and tablets. Those devices access the Internet and transmit information using unsecured networks as well.

How about once it's on the highway being carried from place to place. Those carriers—the people who drive the information on the highways—they are moving that information by using potentially unsecured channels.

Mobile storage devices also present an issue because we are moving our client's data to a portable device like a flash drive or cell phone. We're still dealing with moving information and the data could get inadvertently released or lost.

Not only do we have issues of moving data (transmission), but we also have issues about situations where you move information to another place and leave it there to store it. Those storage companies, or "cloud storage" companies/websites end up storing the data on their own servers (in the cloud). Similarly, programs known as Software as a Service (SaaS) invoke all of the problems discussed above because you are sending data to another company that is used in their programs, thus creating transmission issues, wireless problems and storage concerns. Not sure what "the cloud" is all about? The Pennsylvania Bar Association Committee on Legal Ethics and Professional Responsibility explained these technologies clearly when it stated:

If an attorney uses a Smartphone or an iPhone, or uses web-based electronic mail (e-mail) such as Gmail, Yahoo!, Hotmail or AOL Mail, or uses products such as Google Docs, Microsoft Office 365 or Dropbox, the attorney is using "cloud computing." While there are many technical ways to describe cloud computing, perhaps the best description is that cloud computing is merely "a fancy way of saying stuff's not on your computer."[1] From a more technical perspective, "cloud computing" encompasses several similar types of services under different names and brands, including: web-based e-mail, online data storage, software-as-a-service ("SaaS"), platform-as-a-service ("PaaS"), infrastructure-as-a-service("IaaS"), Amazon Elastic Cloud Compute ("Amazon EC2"), and Google Docs."[2]

There are some common concerns among all of these technologies. For the most part, we're concerned about vulnerable technology—using the potentially unsecured Internet to move data and using potentially unsecured wireless routers and cellular networks to get the information onto the Internet in the first place. It's also about the place you're moving that data to. That's a concern whether you're moving it to a storage facility that's not on your computer or moving it into a program that utilizes that data and happens to be located in the cloud. The vulnerabilities of those technologies lead us to the primary ethical issues, which are the potential release or disclosure of confidential information (Rule 1.6),[3] and the potential loss of client information/property (a failure to safeguard client property per Rule 1.15),[4] and the duty to supervise the vendors (Rule 5.3).[5]

§ 8:2 Emails, yesterday and today

It has long been established that lawyers could send

[Section 8:1]

[1]Pennsylvania Bar Association Committee on Legal Ethics and Professional Responsibility Formal Opinion 2011-200, at 1, citing, Quinn Norton, "Byte Rights," Maximum PC, September 2010, at 12.

[2]Pennsylvania Bar Association Committee on Legal Ethics and Professional Responsibility Formal Opinion 2011-200 2011-200 at 1.

[3]Del. Prof. Conduct R. 1.6.

1.6 http://courts.delaware.gov/rules/DLRPCFebruary2010.pdf. Pages last checked by the author August 13, 2013.

[4]Del. Prof. Conduct R. 1.15.

1.15 http://courts.delaware.gov/rules/DLRPCFebruary2010.pdf. Pages last checked by the author August 13, 2013.

[5]Del. Prof. Conduct R. 5.3.

5.3 http://courts.delaware.gov/rules/DLRPCFebruary2010.pdf. Pages last checked by the author August 13, 2013.

§ 8:2   NAVIGATING LEGAL ETHICS

unencrypted email regarding client matters, but that wasn't always the case. When the technology was first developed, the powers that be were opposed to permitting such email communication. However, things changed in the late 1990s.

The American Bar Association (ABA) issued a formal opinion in 1999 which stated that there is a reasonable expectation of privacy despite the risk of interception and disclosure. The key development was that legislation was enacted making the interception of email a crime. In its Opinion, the ABA stated:

> The Committee believes that e-mail communications, including those sent unencrypted over the Internet, pose no greater risk of interception or disclosure than other modes of communication commonly relied upon as having a reasonable expectation of privacy. The level of legal protection accorded e-mail transmissions, like that accorded other modes of electronic communication, also supports the reasonableness of an expectation of privacy for unencrypted e-mail transmissions. The risk of unauthorized interception and disclosure exists in every medium of communication, including e-mail. It is not, however, reasonable to require that a mode of communicating information must be avoided simply because interception is technologically possible, especially when unauthorized interception or dissemination of the information is a violation of law. The Committee concludes, based upon current technology and law as we are informed of it, that a lawyer sending confidential client information by unencrypted e-mail does not violate Model Rule 1.6(a)[1] in choosing that mode to communicate. This is principally because there is a reasonable expectation of privacy in its use.[2]

States have since followed suit and permitted the use of unencrypted email in the practice of law. What's key here is that we see the standard clearly—the reasonable expectation of privacy. It's important to understand the standard/rationale for permitting such email communications, because it continues to be relevant today. As new technologies are developed, the authorities apply the same reasoning. Consider the recent furor over Gmail and other free email services.

[Section 8:2]

[1] Del. Prof. Conduct R. 1.6(a).

1.6(a) http://courts.delaware.gov/rules/DLRPCFebruary2010.pdf. Pages last checked by the author August 13, 2013.

[2] ABA Commission on Ethics and Professional Responsibility Formal Opinion 99-413.

In its Opinion 820, the New York State Bar Association opined about those free email systems.[3] The systems were a concern because of the business model that the systems use to keep the service free. Here's how they work: in return for providing the email service, "the provider's computers scan e-mails and send or display targeted advertising to the user of the service. The e-mail provider identifies the presumed interests of the service's user by scanning for keywords in e-mails opened by the user. The provider's computers then send advertising that reflects the keywords in the e-mail."[4] The obvious problem is that if we're using the email system for client work, then we're allowing the provider to scan confidential information.

When considering whether these new email systems would be permitted, the New York authorities first considered the rationale for permitting email back in the 1990s. Email was allowed because, "there is a reasonable expectation that e-mails will be as private as other forms of telecommunication and . . . therefore . . . a lawyer ordinarily may utilize unencrypted e-mail to transmit confidential information.[5] They applied that same reasoning to the question of free emails.

Even though the email messages in the current systems are scanned, the opinion noted that humans don't actually do the scanning. Rather, it's computers that take care of that task. Thus, they stated that "Merely scanning the content of e-mails by computer to generate computer advertising . . . does not pose a threat to client confidentiality, because the practice does not increase the risk of others obtaining knowledge of the e-mails or access to the e-mails' content."[6]

What the opinion is basically saying is that there continues to be a reasonable expectation of privacy in these email systems. Maybe the better way to phrase it is a reasonable expectation of "confidentiality," but the idea is the same. What's important to note is that the technology developed, but the standard that was applied remained the same.

---

[3]New York State Bar Association Committee on Professional Ethics Opinion 820 - 2/8/08.
[4]NYSBA Op. 820 at 2.
[5]New York State Bar Association Opinion 820 at 1.
[6]New York State Bar Association Opinion 820 at 2.

§ 8:3 Confidentiality and the cloud: The reasonable care standard

The early decisions that addressed technology didn't always talk about "cloud computing" in particular, but they set the standard that would be followed when that technology arrived. Thus, the State of Nevada addressed the ability of lawyers to store confidential client information and/or communications in an electronic format on a server or other device that is not exclusively in the lawyer's control.[1] The Committee found that it was ethically permissible and stated that, "If the lawyer acts competently and reasonably to ensure the confidentiality of the information, then he or she does not violate [the rules] by simply contracting with a third parity to store the information . . . ."[2]

The Committee said that the duty to save files on third party servers is the same as the duty to safeguard files that are put into third party warehouses, so contracting for such storage is not a per se confidentiality violation.[3] The lawyer wasn't strictly liable for an ethics violation "even if an unauthorized or inadvertent disclosure should occur."[4] Instead, the question was whether they exercised proper care. They articulated a standard that would be repeated in many following opinions when they said, "The lawyer must act competently and reasonably to safeguard confidential client information and communications from inadvertent and unauthorized disclosure."[5]

Similarly, New Jersey evaluated a technologically related issue—whether a lawyer can scan client files to a PDF, then archive them electronically and store those documents on the web.[6] Just like in Nevada, the concern was that Rule 1.6 requires "that the attorney 'exercise reasonable care' against

---

[Section 8:3]

[1]State Bar of Nevada, Standing Committee on Ethics and Professional Responsibility, Formal Opinion No. 33, February 9, 2006, at 1.

[2]Nevada Opinion No. 33, at 1.

[3]Nevada Opinion No. 33, at 1.

[4]Nevada Opinion No. 33, at 1.

[5]Nevada Opinion No. 33, at 1.

[6]State Bar of New Jersey, Supreme Court Advisory Committee on Professional Ethics, Opinion 701, April 10, 2006, 15 N.J.L. 897 April 24, 2006, at 2.

the possibility of unauthorized access to client information."[7] The New Jersey Committee echoed the Nevada findings and stated that,

> "Reasonable Care . . . does not mean that "the lawyer absolutely and strictly guarantees that the information will be utterly invulnerable against all unauthorized access . . . What the term 'reasonable care' means in a particular context is not capable of sweeping characterizations or broad pronouncements."[8]

Given the changing nature of technology, the New Jersey Committee was reluctant to make a particularly bold decision but they did provide some elaboration of what constituted "reasonable care." They stated that,

> "The Touchstone in using 'reasonable care' against unauthorized disclosure is that: (1) the lawyer has entrusted such documents to an outside provider in circumstances in which there is an enforceable obligation to preserve confidentiality and security, and (2) use is made of available technology to guard against reasonably foreseeable attempts to infiltrate the data. If the lawyer has come to the prudent professional judgment he has satisfied both these criteria, then 'reasonable care' will have been exercised."[9]

That phrase, "reasonably foreseeable" was an indication of things to come. In fact, the standard evolved in a decision out of Maine. Maine agreed that the lawyer needs to take reasonable steps to protect confidentiality but they went further and they stated that,

> "The lawyer would be well-advised to include a contract provision requiring the contractor to inform the lawyer in the event the contractor becomes aware of any inappropriate use or disclosure of the confidential information. *The lawyer can then take steps to mitigate the consequences and can determine whether the underlying arrangement can be continued safely.* (emphasis added).[10]

This is the first time we see an extended affirmative duty on the lawyer's part. Maine set forth the idea that the lawyer's duty is ongoing and that there may be a time where a lawyer needs to actually take some action to protect the client information.

---

[7]New Jersey Opinion 701, at 3.

[8]New Jersey Opinion 701, at 3.

[9]New Jersey Opinion 701, at 5.

[10]Maine Board of Overseers of the Bar, Opinion 194, issued June 30, 2008, at 2.

§ 8:3 NAVIGATING LEGAL ETHICS

Arizona reviewed a question that was analogous to cloud storage and added a further elaboration of what it meant to be exercising reasonable care. Arizona said that if you're going to use online storage sites, Competence (Rule 1.1)[11] demands that you understand them. Specifically, they stated that "the competence requirements . . . apply not only to a lawyer's legal skills, but also generally to 'those matters reasonably necessary for the representation.' " Therefore, as a prerequisite to making a determination regarding the reasonableness of online file security precautions, the lawyer must have, or consult someone with, competence in the field of online computer security."[12] In other words, in order to show that you're exercising reasonable care, you need to understand the systems or associate yourself with someone who has that understanding.

And there's something more—here we see a further expansion of the affirmative duty. Not only must we take reasonable precautions to protect confidentiality and security of client information, but, the committee acknowledged that as technology changes, certain protective measures might become obsolete.[13] Thus, the Committee warned that "As technology advances occur, lawyers should periodically review security measures in place to ensure that they still reasonably protect the security and confidentiality of the clients' documents and information."[14] Thus, there is a continuing obligation to revisit the reasonability of the security that our vendors are utilizing. In other words, we can't take the "stick our heads in the sand approach."

A year later, the State of Alabama agreed and stated that,

> Additionally, because technology is constantly evolving, the lawyer will have a continuing duty to stay abreast of appropriate security safeguards that should be employed by the lawyer and the third-party provider. If there is a breach of confidentiality, the focus of any inquiry will be whether the lawyer acted reasonably in selecting the method of storage and/or the third party provider.[15]

In the same year, the New York Bar Association elaborated

---

[11]Del. Prof. Conduct R. 1.1.

1.1 http://courts.delaware.gov/rules/DLRPCFebruary2010.pdf. Pages last checked by the author August 13, 2013.

[12]State Bar of Arizona, Opinion 09-04, 12/2009, at 1.

[13]Arizona Opinion 09-04 at 2.

[14]Arizona Opinion 09-04 at 1–2.

[15]Alabama Ethics Opinion 2010-02 at 16.

on that idea. In Opinion 842 they evaluated whether a lawyer could use an online data storage system to store and back up confidential client information. Like the other states that opined on the topic, they answered in the affirmative, subject to the same confidentiality concerns. They also confirmed the ongoing nature of the lawyer's duty if one were to make use of these systems. They stated:

> 10. Technology and the security of stored data are changing rapidly. Even after taking some or all of these steps (or similar steps), therefore, the lawyer should periodically reconfirm that the provider's security measures remain effective in light of advances in technology. If the lawyer learns information suggesting that the security measures used by the online data storage provider are insufficient to adequately protect the confidentiality of client information, or if the lawyer learns of any breach of confidentiality by the online storage provider, then the lawyer must investigate whether there has been any breach of his or her own clients' confidential information, notify any affected clients, and discontinue use of the service unless the lawyer receives assurances that any security issues have been sufficiently remediated. See Rule 1.4[16] (mandating communication with clients); see also N.Y. State 820 (2008) (addressing Web-based email services).[17]

In the following far less earth-shattering paragraph, the New York authorities also noted the need for lawyers to stay abreast of the law regarding technology. "Not only technology itself but also the law relating to technology and the protection of confidential communications is changing rapidly. Lawyers using online storage systems (and electronic means of communication generally) should monitor these legal developments, especially regarding instances when using technology may waive an otherwise applicable privilege. *[citation omitted]*."[18]

§ 8:4 Our fiduciary duty under Rule 1.15

In North Carolina we see an opinion that reveals the second of the three major ethical concerns with using cloud-based systems/software. That's the need to protect our

---

[16]Del. Prof. Conduct R. 1.4.

1.4 http://courts.delaware.gov/rules/DLRPCFebruary2010.pdf. Pages last checked by the author August 13, 2013.

[17]New York State Bar Association Opinion 842 (9/10.10) at 4.

[18]New York State Bar Association Opinion 842 (9/10.10) at 4.

§ 8:4 NAVIGATING LEGAL ETHICS

client's information with the care required of a fiduciary as set forth in Rule 1.15.[1]

Most people hear the Rule number "1.15" and think about trust accounts. It's true that the rule is most often invoked in our discussion about our client's money, but the rule actually has broader implications. Rule 1.15 governs our responsibilities with our client's property, and money is just one type of client property that we might hold. Another type of property is the client's file.

The hard copy of your client's file is the client's property and we also know that Rule 1.15 mandates that we take steps to safeguard that property. When you think about it, however, the digital version of your client's file is also their property—you're simply holding it in computerized form. Thus, if we release that to another individual (like a cloud storage vendor) we need to make sure that we're taking steps to safeguard that client property appropriately. That invokes Rule 1.15, which is why the North Carolina opinion states, "Rule 1.15 requires a lawyer to preserve client property, including information in a client's file such as client documents and lawyer work product, from risk of loss due to destruction, degradation, or loss. See also Rules of Professional Conduct 209 (noting the "general fiduciary duty to safeguard the property of a client")."[2]

In the end, the North Carolina authorities didn't provide any new ethical ideas; rather, they simply confirmed that using SaaS (cloud computing), in particular, was not a violation. Specifically, they stated, "Lawyers can use SaaS, 'provided steps are taken effectively to minimize the risk of inadvertent or unauthorized disclosure of confidential client information and to protect client property, including the information in a client's file, form risk of loss.' "

§ 8:5 The extension of our duty to supervise

The day-to-day realities of the practice reveal that lawyers are not the only individuals in the office about whom we must be concerned when we decide to use cloud technology.

[Section 8:4]

[1]Del. Prof. Conduct R. 1.15.
1.15 http://courts.delaware.gov/rules/DLRPCFebruary2010.pdf. Pages last checked by the author August 13, 2013.

[2]The North Carolina State Bar, 2011 Formal Ethics Opinion 6, Issued in January 27, 2012.

The commentary to Rule 1.6[1] confirms that: "[16]. . . A lawyer must act competently to safeguard information relating to the representation of a client against inadvertent or unauthorized disclosure by the lawyer or other persons who are participating in the representation of the client or who are subject to the lawyer's supervision." Various states have expanded upon that concept and discussed our larger responsibility to train our non-lawyer staff.

In an opinion we discussed earlier, the Maine Committee confirmed that the primary responsibility for confidentiality remains with the lawyer, but they also noted that the Maine rule "implies that lawyers have the responsibility to train, monitor, and discipline their non-lawyer staff in such a manner as to guard effectively against breaches of confidentiality. Failure to take steps to provide adequate training, to monitor performance, and to apply discipline for the purposes of enforcing adherence to ethical standards is grounds for concluding that the lawyer has violated [the rule]."[2]

In addition, our duties extend beyond keeping an eye on our in-house nonlawyer staff. The foundation for that was laid before the technology era when the Oregon State Bar addressed whether a lawyer could use a recycling service to dispose of client documents. The issue was whether doing so violated the rule on confidentiality because you would be exposing confidential client information to the recycling vendor. The opinion held that, "as long as Law Firm makes reasonable efforts to ensure that the recycling company's conduct is compatible with Law Firm's obligation to protect client information," using the service is permissible.[3] They further stated that "reasonable efforts include, at least, instructing the recycling company about Law Firms duties pursuant to Oregon RPC 1.6 and obtaining its agreement to treat all materials appropriately."[4] This is exactly the sentiment set forth by other bars regarding cloud computing vendors.

The Maine Committee noted that the technology vendor

[Section 8:5]

[1]Del. Prof. Conduct R. 1.6.

1.6 http://courts.delaware.gov/rules/DLRPCFebruary2010.pdf. Pages last checked by the author August 13, 2013.

[2]Maine Board of Overseers of the Bar, Opinion #194, Issued June 30, 2008, at 1–2.

[3]Oregon State Bar, Formal Opinion No. 2005-141, August 2005, at 386.

[4]Oregon Opinion 2005-141 at 386.

§ 8:5   NAVIGATING LEGAL ETHICS

needs to be supervised as well. While the lawyer doesn't directly train or monitor the service provider employees, "the lawyer retains the obligation to ensure that appropriate standards concerning client confidentiality are maintained by the contractor."[5]

The Oregon and Maine opinions marked the beginning of a trend, about which all lawyers must be aware. Over the past several years we've seen states expand upon the duty for lawyers to be responsible for non-lawyers who are working for the firm, but not necessarily inside the firm's office. This was further exhibited in North Carolina's Formal Ethics Opinion 6, in which they stated,

> Although a lawyer may use nonlawyers outside of the firm to assist in rendering legal services to clients, Rule 5.3(a)[6] requires the lawyer to make reasonable efforts to ensure that the services are provided in a manner that is compatible with the professional obligations of the lawyer. The extent of this obligation when using a SaaS vendor to store and manipulate confidential client information will depend upon the experience, stability, and reputation of the vendor. Given the rapidity with which computer technology changes, law firms are encouraged to consult periodically with professionals competent in the area of online security.[7]

New Hampshire went a little further and let us know that we can't pass the buck when it comes to the technology vendors. They made it clear that the duties of confidentiality and competence are ongoing and not delegable:[8]

> "When engaging a cloud computing provider or an intermediary who engages such a provider, the responsibility rests with the lawyer to ensure that the work is performed in a manner consistent with the lawyer's professional duties. Rule 5.3 (a). Additionally, under Rule 2.1, a lawyer must exercise independent professional judgment in representing a client and cannot hide behind a hired intermediary and ignore how client information is stored in or transmitted through the cloud.[9]

Recently, the ABA chimed in on the topic. In its most

---

[5]Maine Board of Overseers of the Bar, Opinion #194, Issued June 30, 2008, at 2.

[6]Del. Prof. Conduct R. 5.3(a).
   5.3(a) http://courts.delaware.gov/rules/DLRPCFebruary2010.pdf. Pages last checked by the author August 13, 2013.

[7]North Carolina's 2011 Formal Ethics Opinion 6.

[8]New Hampshire Opinion 2012-13/4, at 4.

[9]New Hampshire Opinion 2012-13/4, at 3.

recent batch of amendments, the ABA made a change to two letters in the title of Rule 5.3—that's right, I said two letters in the *title*—and that change has profound implications. Rule 5.3 used to be called, "Responsibilities Regarding Nonlawyer Assistants." However, how it's called, "Responsibilities Regarding Nonlawyer Assistance." Did you catch that? The last two letters of the final word—"Assistants" is now "Assistance." This is a big deal because it reflects a growing trend in the world of ethics. Yes, we are responsible for supervising our own staff, but today that duty extends to other parties like those that we would have once called "independent contractors." Anyone that we use in assistance, like vendors, is a party that we now have a duty to supervise. We get further guidance in this regard from new Comments [3] and [4] in Rule 5.3.[10]

What we notice from those comments is that this change was brought about mostly because (a) lawyers now outsource many of the tasks that used to be completed in house, and (b) there is an increased reliance on cloud storage and other technology-related vendors. Thus, the comments tell us that we must supervise nonlawyers outside the firm that we use for investigations, document management, cloud storage, etc., and the Comment also provides factors that should be considered when determining the extent of our obligations in these circumstances.

§ 8:6 The two facets of confidentiality

The commentary to Rule 1.6[1] mentions two important facets of the confidentiality issue about which all lawyers should be aware. As mentioned earlier, Comment [16] states, "A lawyer must act competently to safeguard information relating to the representation of a client against inadvertent or unauthorized disclosure by the lawyer . . ." Those two words, "inadvertent" and "unauthorized" have different, equally serious implications.

---

[10]Copyright restrictions prevent me from listing the comments here. Please review them on your own at your convenience. They can be found here: http://www.americanbar.org/content/dam/aba/administrative/ethics_2020/2012_hod_annual_meeting_105a_filed_may_2012.authcheckdam.pdf, last checked by the author on February 2, 2014.

[Section 8:6]
[1]Del. Prof. Conduct R. 1.6.
1.6 http://courts.delaware.gov/rules/DLRPCFebruary2010.pdf. Pages last checked by the author August 13, 2013.

§ 8:6   Navigating Legal Ethics

When most people think about the confidentiality issue, they worry about people breaking into websites to steal information. That's obviously a concern and such conduct would certainly constitute the "unauthorized" disclosure that's prohibited by the rule. Thus, we are properly concerned about security of the web-storage facilities that we use. But there's also that "inadvertent" term.

How could one "inadvertently" disclose confidential information in a cloud context? Sure, we could accidentally provide someone with our password, or be otherwise careless in our use of the system. But something that most lawyers don't realize is that we may be inadvertently granting people access to our client's confidential information by ignoring the "wrapping paper." Do you remember getting a gift on a special occasion as a kid? We tear off the wrapping paper almost mechanically and pursue our singular task of getting at the present that lies beneath the paper obstacle. The same thing happens when adults sign up for a new website—lawyers too. When we sign up for a cloud storage site, for instance, many of us put in our credit card information, quickly click the box that acknowledges that we've read the "Terms of Service," and we move on to playing with our new website-toy. The Terms of Service is our wrapping paper—more often than not, we mechanically check the box saying that we've read the terms, even though we haven't.

The reality, however, is that the Terms of Service is actually a contract that defines the relationship between the user and the cloud storage provider. Sometimes referred to as "Service Level Agreements," these contracts can grant the cloud website owner the right to access, own, and even disseminate the information you store on their site. Remember—the creators of these websites didn't write the SLAs with the rules of attorney ethics in mind. Pennsylvania acknowledged this problem when they stated, "The terms and conditions under which the 'cloud computing' services are offered, i.e., Service Level Agreements (SLAs), may also present obstacles to reasonable care efforts. Most SLAs are essentially 'take it or leave it,' *[citation omitted]* and often users, including lawyers, do not read the terms closely or at all. As a result, compliance with ethical mandates can be difficult."[2]

It's a bit easier to understand why states are so emphatic

---

[2]Pennsylvania Opinion 2011-200 at 11.

about stressing the lawyer's fiduciary duties when you consider the dangers presented by poorly crafted SLAs. There are a host of open issues regarding the data that lawyers turn over to cloud storage vendors and each involves potential disclosure or loss of client information. For instance, where are the vendor's servers located? Is it a secure area? Who has access to those servers? What are the vendor's backup policies? What are the procedures for catastrophic failure of the servers (*are* there backups)? What type of data encryption is being used?[3] What happens if there is a data breach?[4]

Thus, it's incumbent upon lawyers to review the terms of these SLAs to ensure that we don't "inadvertently" jeopardize our client's confidential information. There's hope, however, because the Pennsylvania opinion acknowledged that, "new competition in the 'cloud computing' field is now causing vendors to consider altering terms. This can help attorneys

---

[3] A more detailed description of the issues can be found online in the ABA's Issues Paper Concerning Client Confidentiality and Lawyer's Use of Technology, dated September 20, 2010.

[4] Pennsylvania Opinion 2011-200 at 11 noted the dangers of data breaches and pointed out an advancement in that regard. As of 2011, at least forty-five states had data breach notification. They provided a few clauses from Pennsylvania's notification law, 73 Penn.Stat. § 2303 (2011) ("Notification of Breach"), which states:

(a) GENERAL RULE. — An entity that maintains, stores or manages computerized data that includes personal information shall provide notice of any breach of the security of the system following discovery of the breach of the security of the system to any resident of this Commonwealth whose unencrypted and unredacted personal information was or is reasonably believed to have been accessed and acquired by an unauthorized person. Except as provided in section 4 or in order to take any measures necessary to determine the scope of the breach and to restore the reasonable integrity of the data system, the notice shall be made without unreasonable delay. For the purpose of this section, a resident of this Commonwealth may be determined to be an individual whose principal mailing address, as reflected in the computerized data which is maintained, stored or managed by the entity, is in this Commonwealth.

(b) ENCRYPTED INFORMATION. — An entity must provide notice of the breach if encrypted information is accessed and acquired in an unencrypted form, if the security breach is linked to a breach of the security of the encryption or if the security breach involves a person with access to the encryption key.

(c) VENDOR NOTIFICATION. — A vendor that maintains, stores or manages computerized data on behalf of another entity shall provide notice of any breach of the security system following discovery by the vendor to the entity on whose behalf the vendor maintains, stores or manages the data. The entity shall be responsible for making the determinations and discharging any remaining duties under this act.

§ 8:6

meet their ethical obligations by facilitating an agreement with a vendor that adequately safeguards security and reliability *[citation omitted]*.[5]

§ 8:7 The emerging affirmative duty to understand, anticipate, and act

I've tried to take the information that's been provided by the various state opinions and distill it down to some workable direction to attorneys. Here's how it looks to me:

All of these opinions make clear that we need to be competent and protect client confidentiality. In order to do that we need to understand the technological systems, understand the security precautions that the vendors use, supervise the vendors appropriately, ensure that the terms of service are adequate, and remember that the review of all of the foregoing is a continuing duty (plus some other stuff, but those are the biggies).

What's clear is that the opinions have created a significant affirmative duty for lawyers who choose to use cloud systems. *We have an ongoing obligation to understand, anticipate, and act.* We must understand the technology, the security, and the law. We must be able to anticipate security issues, problems presented by our nonlawyer staff, confidentiality concerns, and everything else. And if the situation requires it, we must act. We may be forced to change vendors, for instance, if we think our client's information is vulnerable. We may need to negotiate the terms of a Service Level Agreement. We may need to demand that the vendor change some protocol. It could be anything.

The point is that we can't sit idly by. Ignorance is not bliss, it's an ethical violation. If we are going to utilize these systems we need to continually stay up to date on all relevant variables. It's an active, ongoing process.

§ 8:8 Is client consent required?

If using the cloud to store client data is so fraught with peril, one must ask whether we need to get client consent before using those systems. The answer, like most ethics questions is, "it depends."

There isn't a particular ethics rule that addresses the

---

[5]Pennsylvania Opinion 2011-200 at 11.

question. The closest we come is Rule 1.2[1] which sets forth the allocation of decision making responsibility between the client and lawyer. Unfortunately, the rule provides scant guidance under normal circumstances and absolutely no direction regarding the use of technology.

One might wonder whether our duty to communicate with our client per Rule 1.4[2] might require client consent, but states like Ohio have refused to make that a requirement. They stated. "Rule 1.4(a)(2)[3] requires a lawyer to 'reasonably consult with the client' about how the client's objectives are to be accomplished. We do not conclude that storing client data 'in the cloud' always requires prior consultation, because we interpret the language 'reasonably consult' as indicating that the lawyer must use judgment in order to determine if the circumstances call for consultation."[4]

There are a few states, however, that give us direct guidance about when consent is or is not required.

§ 8:9 Generally, no consent is probably required

According to states like Nevada and New Hampshire, it appears that so long as the lawyer has fulfilled his or her ethical duties, the use of cloud storage would be within the lawyer's decision making authority.

The State of Nevada opined about whether a lawyer could store confidential information on a third party server without the client's consent. The Committee stated that it wasn't necessary to ask the client's consent before sending the information to electronic storage. The Opinion stated that the Supreme Court would prefer that the lawyer obtain the client's informed consent (not bad practical advice), but they nonetheless stated that, ". . . if the third party can be reasonably relied upon to maintain the confidentiality and

---

[Section 8:8]

[1]Del. Prof. Conduct R. 1.2.

1.2 http://courts.delaware.gov/rules/DLRPCFebruary2010.pdf. Pages last checked by the author August 13, 2013.

[2]Del. Prof. Conduct R. 1.4.

1.4 http://courts.delaware.gov/rules/DLRPCFebruary2010.pdf. Pages last checked by the author August 13, 2013.

[3]Del. Prof. Conduct R. 1.4(a)(2).

1.4(a)(2) http://courts.delaware.gov/rules/DLRPCFebruary2010.pdf. Pages last checked by the author August 13, 2013.

[4]Ohio State Bar Association, Informal Advisory Opinion 2013-02.

agrees to do so, then the transmission is permitted by the rules even without client consent."[1] New Hampshire confirmed that sentiment and stated:[2]

> As cloud computing comes into wider use, storing and transmitting information in the cloud may be deemed an impliedly authorized disclosure to the provider, so long as the lawyer takes reasonable steps to ensure that the provider of cloud computing services has adequate safeguards. Recent revisions to Comment [16] to the ABA Model Rule 1.6 note that "if the lawyer has made reasonable efforts to prevent the access or disclosure" of confidential information, then the unauthorized access to, or the inadvertent or unauthorized disclosure of, client information does not constitute a violation of a lawyer's duty of confidentially.[3]

§ 8:10 Exceptions exist, like sensitive information or express instruction

There are situations where client consent would be required. If, for instance, you were going to store particularly sensitive client data, you might need to get the client's consent before putting it on the Internet. This is what New Hampshire was getting at when they stated:

> Not all information is alike. For example, where highly sensitive data is involved, it may become necessary to inform the client of the lawyer's use of cloud computing and to obtain the client's informed consent. " 'Informed consent' denotes the agreement by a person to a proposed course of conduct after the lawyer has communicated adequate information and explanation about the material risks of and reasonably available alternatives to the proposed course of conduct." Rule 1.0(e).[1] The material risks and reasonably available alternatives will of course vary by client, scope of representation, the sensitivity of the stored or transmitted information, provider,

---

[Section 8:9]

[1]Nevada Opinion No. 33, at 4.

[2]New Hampshire Bar Association Ethics Advisory Opinion #2012-13/4 at 2.

[3]See, "American Bar Association Commission on Ethics 20/20, Report to the House of Delegates, Resolution, 105A Revised, p. 5. On behalf of the New Hampshire Supreme Court's Rules Committee, the Bar's Ethics Committee is currently reviewing the revision to Comment [16]. The proposed revision has not yet been recommended to the Rules Committee or adopted by the Supreme Court. New Hampshire Rules of Professional Conduct (last accessed December 27, 2012)."

[Section 8:10]

[1]Del. Prof. Conduct R. 1.0(e).

and other considerations *[footnote omitted]*. But if the information is highly sensitive, consent of the client to use cloud computing may be necessary.[2]

Additionally, you would need client consent to store client information on the Internet if you had previous express instructions not to do so. I realize that such a statement is patently obvious, but it was important enough for Massachusetts to mention in an opinion:

> Consistent with its prior opinions, the Committee further believes that Lawyer remains bound to follow an express instruction from his client that the client's confidential information not be stored or transmitted by means of the Internet, and that he should refrain from storing or transmitting particularly sensitive client information by means of the Internet without first seeking and obtaining the client's express consent to do so. *[footnote omitted]*.[3]

§ 8:11 Questions to ask

What we've seen from all these opinions is that lawyers have a responsibility to ask questions of their tech providers. The disciplinary code, "places on the lawyer the obligation to perform due diligence to assess the degree of protection that will be needed and to act accordingly."[1] Thus, a wise lawyer will create their own checklist of items that should be considered before using any cloud-based technology. That checklist would include the specific questions that ensure that our ethical obligations are addressed. We can't simply rely on the security measures that are proffered by the vendor because they don't understand the rules of attorney ethics. The Oregon State Bar said it best when they discussed the lawyer's obligation to ensure that vendors will protect client data when they stated, "Under certain circumstances, this may be satisfied through a third-party vendor's compliance with industry standards relating to confidentiality and security, provided that those industry standards meet the minimum requirements imposed on the Lawyer by

---

[1].0(e) http://courts.delaware.gov/rules/DLRPCFebruary2010.pdf. Pages last checked by the author August 13, 2013.

[2]New Hampshire Opinion #2012-13/4 at 2.

[3]Massachusetts Bar Association, Ethics Opinion 12-03 at 2.

[Section 8:11]

[1]Iowa Ethics Opinion 11-01, September 9, 2011.

§ 8:11   NAVIGATING LEGAL ETHICS

the Oregon RPC."[2] We need to make sure that we ask the right questions before using these technologies.

Below are a series of issues that were set forth in various advisory opinions from across the country. The issues raised below could be incorporated into your own checklist:[3]

From North Carolina 2011 Formal Opinion 6:

- Inclusion in the SaaS vendor's Terms of Service or Service Level Agreement, or in a separate agreement between the SaaS vendor and the lawyer or law firm, of an agreement on how the vendor will handle confidential client information in keeping with the lawyer's professional responsibilities.

- If the lawyer terminates use of the SaaS product, the SaaS vendor goes out of business, or the service otherwise has a break in continuity, the law firm will have a method for retrieving the data, the data will be available in a non-proprietary format that the law firm can access, or the firm will have access to the vendor's software or source code. The SaaS vendor is contractually required to return or destroy the hosted data promptly at the request of the law firm.

- Careful review of the terms of the law firm's user or license agreement with the SaaS vendor including the security policy.

- Evaluation of the SaaS vendor's (or any third party data hosting company's) measures for safeguarding the security and confidentiality of stored data including, but not limited to, firewalls, encryption techniques, socket security features, and intrusion-detection systems.

- Evaluation of the extent to which the SaaS vendor backs up hosted data.

From Iowa Ethics Opinion 11-02

We suggest that lawyers intending to use SaaS, or other information technology services that store the lawyer's work product and client information on servers that are not owned by the lawyer, should ask the following questions:

1. Access:

Will I have unrestricted access to the stored data? Have I stored the data elsewhere so that if access to my data is denied I can acquire the data via another source?

---
[2]Oregon State Bar, Formal Ethics Opinion 2011-188.
[3]All footnotes omitted.

2. Legal Issues:

Have I performed "due diligence" regarding the company that will be storing my data? Are they a solid company with a good operating record and is their service recommended by others in the field? What country and state are they located and do business in? Does their end user's licensing agreement (EULA) contain legal restrictions regarding their responsibility or liability, choice of law or forum, or limitation on damages? Likewise does their EULA grant them proprietary or user rights over my data?

3. Financial Obligation:

What is the cost of the service, how is it paid and what happens in the event of non-payment? In the event of a financial default will I lose access to the data, does it become the property of the SaaS company or is the data destroyed?

4. Termination:

How do I terminate the relationship with the SaaS company? What type of notice does the EULA require. How do I retrieve my data and does the SaaS company retain copies?

Data Protection

In addition to the concepts covered above, lawyers intending to use SaaS should also perform due diligence regarding the degree of protection that will be afforded the data:

1. Password Protection and Public Access:

Are passwords required to access the program that contains my data? Who has access to the passwords? Will the public have access to my data? If I allow non-clients access to a portion of the data will they have access to other data that I want protected?

2. Data Encryption:

Recognizing that some data will require a higher degree of protection than others, will I have the ability to encrypt certain data using higher level encryption tools of my choosing?

From Pennsylvania Formal Opinion 2011-200

Thus, the standard of reasonable care for "cloud computing" may include:

• Backing up data to allow the firm to restore data that has been lost, corrupted, or accidentally deleted;

• Installing a firewall to limit access to the firm's network;

- Limiting information that is provided to others to what is required, needed, or requested;
- Avoiding inadvertent disclosure of information;
- Verifying the identity of individuals to whom the attorney provides confidential information;
- Refusing to disclose confidential information to unauthorized individuals (including family members and friends) without client permission;
- Protecting electronic records containing confidential data, including backups, by encrypting the confidential data;
- Implementing electronic audit trail procedures to monitor who is accessing the data;
- Creating plans to address security breaches, including the identification of persons to be notified about any known or suspected security breach involving confidential data;
- Ensuring the provider:
  ◦ explicitly agrees that it has no ownership or security interest in the data;
  ◦ has an enforceable obligation to preserve security;
  ◦ will notify the lawyer if requested to produce data to a third party, and provide the lawyer with the ability to respond to the request before the provider produces the requested information;
  ◦ has technology built to withstand a reasonably foreseeable attempt to infiltrate data, including penetration testing;
  ◦ includes in its "Terms of Service" or "Service Level Agreement" an agreement about how confidential client information will be handled;
  ◦ provides the firm with right to audit the provider's security procedures and to obtain copies of any security audits performed;
  ◦ will host the firm's data only within a specified geographic area. If by agreement, the data are hosted outside of the United States, the law firm must determine that the hosting jurisdiction has privacy laws, data security laws, and protections against unlawful search and seizure that are as rigorous as those of the United States and Pennsylvania;
  ◦ provides a method of retrieving data if the lawyer terminates use of the SaaS product, the SaaS vendor goes out of business, or the service otherwise has a break in continuity; and,
  ◦ provides the ability for the law firm to get data "off" of the vendor's or third party data hosting company's servers for the firm's own use or in-house backup offline.

- Investigating the provider's:
  - security measures, policies and recovery methods;
  - system for backing up data;
  - security of data centers and whether the storage is in multiple centers;
  - safeguards against disasters, including different server locations;
  - history, including how long the provider has been in business;
  - funding and stability;
  - policies for data retrieval upon termination of the relationship and any related charges; and,
  - process to comply with data that is subject to a litigation hold.
- Determining whether:
  - data is in non-proprietary format;
  - the Service Level Agreement clearly states that the attorney owns the data;
  - there is a 3rd party audit of security; and,
  - there is an uptime guarantee and whether failure results in service credits.
- Employees of the firm who use the SaaS must receive training on and are required to abide by all end-user security measures, including, but not limited to, the creation of strong passwords and the regular replacement of passwords.
- Protecting the ability to represent the client reliably by ensuring that a copy of digital data is stored onsite.
- Having an alternate way to connect to the Internet, since cloud service is accessed through the Internet.

From New York State Bar Opinion #842

"Reasonable care" to protect a client's confidential information against unauthorized disclosure may include consideration of the following steps:

(1) Ensuring that the online data storage provider has an enforceable obligation to preserve confidentiality and security, and that the provider will notify the lawyer if served with process requiring the production of client information;

(2) Investigating the online data storage provider's security measures, policies, recoverability methods, and other procedures to determine if they are adequate under the circumstances;

(3) Employing available technology to guard against

§ 8:11 NAVIGATING LEGAL ETHICS

reasonably foreseeable attempts to infiltrate the data that is stored; and/or

(4) Investigating the storage provider's ability to purge and wipe any copies of the data, and to move the data to a different host, if the lawyer becomes dissatisfied with the storage provider or for other reasons changes storage providers.

From Massachusetts Opinion 12-03

"Reasonable efforts" by Lawyer with respect to such a provider would include, in the Committee's opinion:

(a) examining the provider's terms of use and written policies and procedures with respect to data privacy and the handling of confidential information;

(b) ensuring that the provider's terms of use and written policies and procedures prohibit unauthorized access to data stored on the provider's system, including access by the provider itself for any purpose other than conveying or displaying the data to authorized users;

(c) ensuring that the provider's terms of use and written policies and procedures, as well as its functional capabilities, give the Lawyer reasonable access to, and control over, the data stored on the provider's system in the event that the Lawyer's relationship with the provider is interrupted for any reason (e.g., if the storage provider ceases operations or shuts off the Lawyer's account, either temporarily or permanently);

(d) examining the provider's existing practices (including data encryption, password protection, and system backups) and available service history (including reports of known security breaches or "holes") to reasonably ensure that data stored on the provider's system actually will remain confidential, and will not be intentionally or inadvertently disclosed or lost; and

(e) periodically revisiting and reexamining the provider's policies, practices and procedures to ensure that they remain compatible with Lawyer's professional obligations to protect confidential client information reflected in Rule 1.6(a).

From New Hampshire Factors Opinion 2012-13/4

The issues which an attorney must consider before using a cloud computing service include the following:

Is the provider of cloud computing services a reputable organization?

Does the provider offer robust security measures? Such measures must include at a minimum password protections or other verification procedures limiting access to the data; safeguards such as data back-up and restoration, a firewall, or encryption; periodic audits by third parties of the provider's security; and notification procedures in case of a breach.

Is the data stored in a format that renders it retrievable as well as secure? Is it stored in a proprietary format and is it promptly and reasonably retrievable by the lawyer in a format acceptable to the client? See also PA Bar Ethics Op. 2011-200, p. 9. It bears repeating that, if a client requests a copy of her file, the lawyer has an obligation to provide all files pertinent to representation of that client. NH Bar Ethics Op. 2005-06/3; Averill, 145 N.H. at 339-40.

Does the provider commingle data belonging to different clients and/or different practitioners such that retrieval may result in inadvertent disclosure?

Do the terms of service state that the provider merely holds a license to the stored data, as for example Google's do? Some providers routinely inform those accessing their service that it is the provider-not the user -that "owns" the data. If the provider owns the stored data, the lawyer may run afoul of Rule 1.15, which requires that the client's property "be identified as property of the client." To comply with Rule 1.15, the provider may not "own" the data stored in the cloud.

Does the provider have an enforceable obligation to keep the data confidential?

Where are the provider's servers located and what are the privacy laws in effect at that location regarding unauthorized access, retrieval, and destruction of compromised data? If the servers are located in a foreign country, do the privacy laws of that country reasonably mirror those of the United States? If the servers are relocated, will the provider notify the lawyer in advance?

Will the provider retain the data — and, if so, for how long — when the representation ends or the agreement between the lawyer and provider is terminated for another reason? The data must not be destroyed immediately and without notice or compromised in case of nonpayment.

Do the terms of service obligate the provider to warn the lawyer if information is being subpoenaed by a third party, where the law permits such notice? Such a provision may be

§ 8:11

especially timely given that the Senate Judiciary Committee recently considered, but rejected legislation which would have expanded law enforcement agencies' access to privately stored data.

What is the provider's disaster recovery plan with respect stored data? Is a copy of the digital data stored on-site? *[footnotes omitted].*

§ 8:12 Texting

Many clients choose to keep in touch with their lawyer via text message. In fact, with the younger generations, texting is the preferred method of communication (any of us who have kids under 21 can attest to that). As lawyers, we need to consider whether texting complies with both the ethics rules and our concepts of professionalism.

One problem we have with texting is the short nature of the medium. Most texts are only a few words, a couple of sentences at most. The question we need to ask ourselves is, if we communicate with our clients primarily through texting, are we fulfilling our obligations under Rule 1.4,[1] "Communication"? That rule reads:

Rule 1.4. Communication

(a) A lawyer shall:

(1) promptly inform the client of any decision or circumstance with respect to which the client's informed consent, as defined in Rule 1.0(e), is required by these Rules;

(2) reasonably consult with the client about the means by which the client's objectives are to be accomplished;

(3) keep the client reasonably informed about the status of the matter;

(4) promptly comply with reasonable requests for information; and

(5) consult with the client about any relevant limitation on the lawyer's conduct when the lawyer knows that the client expects assistance not permitted by the Rules of Professional Conduct or other law.

[Section 8:12]

[1]Del. Prof. Conduct R. 1.4.
 1.4 http://courts.delaware.gov/rules/DLRPCFebruary2010.pdf. Pages last checked by the author August 13, 2013.

(b) A lawyer shall explain a matter to the extent reasonably necessary to permit the client to make informed decisions regarding the representation.

What amount of communication consists "reasonably consulting" with a client? If a client asks us a question via text, does shooting back a quick response that says, "Gotcha" mean we're consulting? How about "Yes" or something like, "That sounds good. I'll take care of it." It seems ridiculous, but this type of short phrase, or even one-word response is common in the world of text messaging. If we rely on texting as our primary method of communication, chances are we are not fulfilling our Rule 1.4 obligations. The key word in that last sentence was "primarily." Hopefully, many of us aren't primarily relying on texting to communicate. However, if texting is simply one facet of your overall communication portfolio, so to speak, then it's probably not going to create an ethical dilemma.

Speaking of pitfalls, this entire analysis brings up an interesting, related question. Is texting professional? Regardless of the ethical implications, should we be using texting in the practice of law, or is it too unprofessional? I heard bar counsel in a state-not-to-be-mentioned opine at a recent CLE program and he didn't think it was professional. He didn't give any particular ethical reason for the prohibition; rather, it was his opinion that using text messages to communicate with clients was not consistent with our professional ideals and should be avoided. I must respectfully disagree. There are two reasons I disagree: (1) I think the medium can be used responsibly and (2) I don't think many of us have a choice. Let's start with the latter.

I know that many of us don't want to use texting to communicate with clients, but the fact is that many of our clients are demanding that we communicate through texts. Why? Because that's simply how people roll these days (note the hip phraseology, clearly letting you know that I'm "with it" and therefore a viable authority on issues pertaining to popular culture). If we want to keep these clients we need to get with the program. But the question remains, how can we use the medium responsibly?

We can use texting responsibly if we just follow some common sense (easier said than done, I know). For instance, should we use text acronyms? Consider the following two phrases:

1-BTW, will u b at court 2morrow?

§ 8:12   NAVIGATING LEGAL ETHICS

2-That was cute. I'm LMFAO.

Is it professional to speak this way to a client? I believe example #1 would pass professional muster. Yes, it's ultra-casual to put it mildly. But it happens to be an accurate reflection of the way much of society is starting to communicate. Example #2 is another story. Not sure what it means? Go ask your teenager for the definition, but understand something—it's definitely NSFW (I'll be gracious and define that term for you—Not Safe For Work). Loosely translated and somewhat cleaned up, LMFAO means "Laughing My Freaking Butt Off." Incidentally, I'm not one who normally includes references to vulgarity in my ethics materials, but in this context it's important to hear about it. Let's face reality—we are communicating in text messages with our clients and that means that our associates are doing it too. And if the youngsters are using this type of language in their own texts, it's possible that our young-ish associates will use it in our communications with clients. As a result, we need to understand that these vulgar-oriented communications are part of the text-lexicon. However, I explain this to you so that you can make sure to tell your associates (and everyone else in your office for that matter) that this category of communication is not appropriate in the practice of law. To give you some further guidance in that regard, I offer the following "rule."

I believe that text acronyms can be used in the practice of law consistent with the professional ideals of the practice if, when you say the phrase out loud (instead of using the acronym), it's the type of phrase that you could you can say in the presence of a tribunal and not face any ethical or professional backlash. So using the text phrase, "BTW" would be okay, because that refers to the phrase, "By The Way." You could say that in a tribunal and not face any repercussions. LMFAO—not so much.

§ 8:13 Mega issues with metadata

1. What is Metadata?

The explanation of what constitutes metadata and why it's a concern for lawyers was best set forth in the New York State Bar Association Committee on Professional Ethics Opinion No. 782, issued in December of 2004. It's a long excerpt, but it's a great, complete description of the issue:

Word-processing software commonly used by lawyers, such as

Microsoft Word and Corel WordPerfect, include features that permit recipients of documents transmitted by e-mail to view "metadata," which may be loosely defined as data hidden in documents that is generated during the course of creating and editing such documents. It may include fragments of data from files that were previously deleted, overwritten or worked on simultaneously. [Footnote omitted] Metadata may reveal the persons who worked on a document, the name of the organization in which it was created or worked on, information concerning prior versions of the document, recent revisions of the document, and comments inserted in the document in the drafting or editing process. The hidden text may reflect editorial comments, strategy considerations, legal issues raised by the client or the lawyer, legal advice provided by the lawyer, and other information. [Footnote omitted] Not all of this information is a confidence or secret, but it may, in many circumstances, reveal information that is either privileged or the disclosure of which would be detrimental or embarrassing to the client . . . For example, a lawyer may transmit a document by e-mail to someone other than the client without realizing that the recipient is able to view prior edits and comments to the document that would be protected as privileged attorney-client communications. Or, more dramatically, a prosecutor using a cooperation agreement signed by one confidential witness may use the agreement as a template in drafting the agreement for another confidential witness. The second document's metadata could contain the name of the original cooperating witness, and if e-mailed, could expose that witness to extreme risks.[1]

2. The Two Issues in the Metadata Debate

The matter was taken up in West Virginia, and that opinion identified the two key issues that are implicated in the metadata topic. First, there are concerns on the part of the lawyer who *sends* documents because ". . . it is important to be familiar with the types of metadata contained in computer documents and to take steps to protect or remove it when necessary. Failure to do so could be viewed as a violation of the Rules . . ."[2] Second, the lawyer who *receives* metadata also must be careful because, ". . . searching for or viewing metadata in documents received from others after

---

[Section 8:13]
[1] New York State Bar Association Opinion 782 at 1–2.
[2] West Virginia LEO 2009-01 at 1–2.

§ 8:13   NAVIGATING LEGAL ETHICS

an attorney has taken steps to protect such (data)[3] could also be viewed as a violation of the Rules . . ."[4]

a. The Duties for Lawyers Who Send Metadata

Lawyers who send documents containing metadata are under an obligation to understand that such data exists and that it could reveal confidential information. Lawyers also must "take reasonable steps to protect the confidentiality of the documents in their possession."[5] The West Virginia opinion confirmed that lawyers have such obligations per Rule 1.1 (Competence) and Rule 1.6 (Confidentiality). That includes "taking care to avoid providing electronic documents that inadvertently contain accessible information that is either confidential or privileged, and to employ reasonable means to remove such metadata before sending the document."[6] The West Virginia decision confirmed that lawyers have an affirmative duty as lawyers to either personally understand the software they use or ensure that "their office employs safeguards to minimize the risk of inadvertent disclosures."[7] The opinion also mentions that such precautions aren't that tough to employ (such as sending PDFs or using metadata scrubbing programs).[8]

b. The Duties for Lawyers Who Receive Metadata

The ABA-style rules say that if you receive documents or electronically stored information that was sent inadvertently, you need to notify the sender. See Rule 4.4(b).[9] The rule doesn't say that you need to return the information, just that you need to notify the sender. According to the commentary of the most recent ABA version of Rule 4.4,[10]

---

[3]I added the word "data" because I think it was left out of the text in the opinion by accident. It seems like a typo.

[4]West Virginia LEO 2009-01 at 2.

[5]West Virginia LEO 2009-01 at 2.

[6]West Virginia LEO 2009-01 at 2.

[7]West Virginia LEO 2009-01 at 2, citing New York State Bar Association Opinion 782, D.C. Bar Op. 341.

[8]West Virginia LEO 2009-01 at 3.

[9]Del. Prof. Conduct R. 4.4(b).

  4.4(b) http://courts.delaware.gov/rules/DLRPCFebruary2010.pdf. Pages last checked by the author August 13, 2013.

[10]Del. Prof. Conduct R. 4.4.

  4.4 http://courts.delaware.gov/rules/DLRPCFebruary2010.pdf. Pages last checked by the author August 13, 2013.

electronically stored information includes metadata. But even though the rules only require you to notify the sender, various state advisory opinions forbid a lawyer from reviewing that metadata.

Consistent with Rule 4.4(b), some states say that metadata that is inadvertently sent is fair game to the receiver. Oregon, for instance, stated in its Formal Opinion 2011-187 that "if . . . the receiving lawyer knows or reasonably should know that metadata was inadvertently included in the document," the Oregon rule only requires notice to the Sender.[11] The rules don't require the document to be returned to the sender unread.[12] However, that's not accepted in every state.

The aforementioned West Virginia opinion, for instance, stated that where a lawyer knows that privileged information was inadvertently sent, it could be a violation of Rule 8.4(c)[13] if they review and use that information without consulting the sender.[14] You might recall that Rule 8.4 is the rule that prohibits misconduct and states, "It is professional misconduct for a lawyer to . . .(c) engage in conduct involving dishonesty, fraud, deceit or misrepresentation . . ." The opinion says that "the lawyer should not review the metadata before consulting with the sending lawyer to determine whether the metadata includes work-product or confidences."[15] Once you consult the sender about the inadvertently sent material and you confirm that the metadata has confidences contained in it, it appears that you can't review that metadata in West Virginia. I say "it appears" for a reason— the opinion isn't entirely clear (it's not artfully drafted, to say the least). It doesn't clearly proclaim that you can't view the inadvertently received material if it contains confidences, but in the very next sentence they cite the New York authorities, who held "Lawyer-recipients . . . have an obligation not to exploit an inadvertent or unauthorized transmission of client confidences or secrets."[16] Thus, it seems like a reasonable interpretation.

---

[11]Oregon State Bar Formal Opinion No. 2011-187 at 570.

[12]Oregon Op. 2011-187 at 570.

[13]Del. Prof. Conduct R. 8.4(c).
    8.4(c) http://courts.delaware.gov/rules/DLRPCFebruary2010.pdf. Pages last checked by the author August 13, 2013.

[14]West Virginia LEO 2009-01 at 3.

[15]West Virginia LEO 2009-01 at 3.

[16]New York State Bar Association Opinion 782 at 3.

§ 8:13   NAVIGATING LEGAL ETHICS

Although Oregon didn't completely agree with the West Virginia and New York positions regarding inadvertent releases of metadata, even that state drew a line in the sand when it came to searching with computer programs under certain situations. Thus, Oregon held that "Searching for metadata using special software when it is apparent that the sender has made reasonable efforts to remove the metadata may be analogous to surreptitiously entering the other lawyer's office to obtain client information and may constitute 'conduct involving dishonesty, fraud, deceit or misrepresentation' in violation of Oregon RPC 8.4(a)(3)."[17]

So, here's the recap regarding the receipt of metadata: Some states (like Oregon) say that if metadata is inadvertently sent, it's fair game. Others (like West Virginia and New York) say that it isn't. Trying to determine what your state will hold is tough because even many of the states that give greater protection to metadata still only have the loose ABA style language in Rule 4.4(b). It might help if you review previous advisory opinions on how your state dealt with inadvertently sent documents and a lawyer's obligations under Rule 4.4(b). It won't be a perfect guide to how they'll deal with metadata, but it might give you some valuable insight. If they are more stringent then maybe they will apply that approach to metadata as well. Regardless, my gut tells me that it will be universally accepted that using software to scour documents that were already scrubbed of metadata is off limits.

The West Virginia authorities gave a slight practical warning as well. They noted that "in many situations, it may not be clear whether the disclosure was inadvertent. In order to avoid misunderstanding, it is always safer to notify the sender before searching electronic documents for metadata. If attorneys cannot agree on how to handle the matter, either lawyer may seek a ruling from the court or other tribunal on the issue."[18]

§ 8:14 What everyone's missing in the virtual law office debate

The Internet allows us to have virtual friends and virtual second lives. It even allows lawyers to have virtual law offices (VLOs). The phrase virtual law office or virtual law firm

---

[17]Also see West Virginia LEO 2009-01 at 2.
[18]West Virginia LEO 2009-01 at 4.

(or whatever derivation you choose) could be defined several ways. It all depends upon the individual lawyer and how they choose to form their practice. What's consistent among the category is that virtual lawyers are using technology in a major way and they butt heads with the traditionalists of the practice.

The virtual lawyer is usually a solo attorney or small firm. They are mobile, using technology to operate out of courthouses, coffee houses, and their personal houses. They work on files wherever they desire, using Wi-Fi connections to access client files from cloud storage sites. They use cloud-based practice management software that can be accessed through their phones and tablets. They rarely have a conventional brick-and-mortar office and meet their clients by appointment only, often in shared conference rooms that are rented on an as-needed basis. Is this a good thing or a bad thing? It depends whom you ask.

The issue of whether virtual law offices should be permitted has emerged as a defining issue between two camps in the law: the protectionists/traditionalists vs. the technologists/progressives. If, by virtue of the labels themselves, I appear to have planted myself inside either camp, I apologize because I didn't mean to. As you'll see, I find merit in both positions. This is one of those issues, however, where the differences between the Hatfields and the McCoys become apparent and they're even fighting over the advisory opinions on the topic.

Several states have issued opinions about legal topics that impact virtual law offices. Many of them, however, haven't passed judgment on their permissibility directly. Instead, they address ethical issues in technology like cloud computing, safety of wireless networks, confidentiality, competence, and supervision. These apply to every technology-using lawyer, regardless of whether you're involved in a VLO. However, there are some issues that pertain specifically to the VLO, and they've been taken on in several jurisdictions.

States including New Jersey, Pennsylvania, and California, have dealt with VLOs and, in New Jersey's case, more than once. I'm not going to summarize them because the opinions are short and well written. They explain their reasoning in a clear, concise, and direct manner and it's a good idea to review them in their entirety. And I recommend that you actually read the opinion—be careful when you read the analyses on the blogosphere, because almost every blogger is

§ 8:14

motivated by some agenda. Some believe, "We should retain the traditional values of the practice" while others' mantra is, "We should redefine the modern practice." As a result, their analyses are littered with cheap attacks at the other side which, while sometimes quite pithy, blur the real issues. The feud between the traditionalists and the technologists is muddling some key issues with which we must all be concerned.

Proponents of VLOs set forth compelling reasons for embracing the technology in this manner. The benefits they cite include increasing availability of legal services for the client, how technology and VLOs can keep down the cost of legal services, etc. The advisory opinions from around the country don't take much issue with those items. The biggest variation of opinion and the defining sub-issue of the debate revolves around a lawyer's office.

Here's the issue: Do you need to have a brick-and-mortar office? Do the ethics rules require that you have an actual, physical office where you have secretaries and copy machines and the rest? The problem is that a hallmark of the virtual office is that there is no traditional office maintained by the lawyer. Instead, the lawyer conducts their business wherever they prefer—the coffee shop, their bedroom, a library, whatever. Indeed, in some instances the virtual lawyer doesn't want to reveal where they work, since that might be their place of residence. They might not want to publicize where they live because they're often home alone, or leave their children by themselves. That puts themselves and their families at potential risk from the crazies of the world. The problem is that the ethics rules as they are currently written don't make it clear whether it's acceptable to forgo having that physical space. In fact, some rules appear to require it.

There are two types of applicable rules. A clear bar to VLOs exists if a state has a rule that requires a bona fide office (like New Jersey had, pre-2013). In other states, a defacto prohibition exists if there is a rule that requires disclosure of one's physical office address whenever they advertise. Let's tackle the latter situation.

Many states have a derivation of Rule 7.2(c)[1] ("Advertising") which states, "Any communication made pursuant to

---

[Section 8:14]
[1] Del. Prof. Conduct R. 7.2(c).

this rule shall include the name and office address of at least one lawyer or law firm responsible for its content."[2]

This isn't necessarily a bar for VLOs. You just need to make sure that you never, ever advertise and you won't run afoul of this rule. Can you see the sarcasm dripping from my fingers as that's typed? Advertising is the lifeblood of a virtual law practice! Thus, it appears that there are two threshold questions we need to answer: (1) What is an advertisement, and (2) What is an office?

As we've seen elsewhere in this book, the term "advertising" is broadly defined. New York confirmed that for us in the New York State Bar Association Committee on Professional Ethics Opinion 964 (4/4/13). In that opinion, the Bar Association addressed the question of whether business cards were considered advertising. They stated, "When a business or professional card or letterhead is used in the ordinary course of professional practice or social intercourse without primary intent to secure retention—e.g., simply to identify the lawyer—it does not constitute advertising [citation omitted]"[3] However, the Committee stated that business cards could be ads when they opined, "If such cards or letterhead were given or sent to someone other than an existing client or another lawyer, and primarily in furtherance of an effort to secure retention of the lawyer or law firm, then the card or letterhead would constitute advertising. [citation omitted]."[4] The opinion made clear that in those cases, the rule "would require it to include a principal law office street address."[5]

Thus, at least in some instances, business cards are considered ads (the practical effect of that decision is that a New York lawyer must *always* treat their business cards as advertising). This is consistent with the broad view taken by

---

7.2(c) http://courts.delaware.gov/rules/DLRPCFebruary2010.pdf. Pages last checked by the author August 13, 2013.

[2]http://courts.delaware.gov/rules/DLRPCFebruary2010.pdf, last checked by the author on August 22, 2013.

[3]http://www.nysba.org/AM/Template.cfm?Section=Ethics_Opinions&template=/CM/ContentDisplay.cfm&ContentID=198038, last checked by the author August 22, 2013.

[4]http://www.nysba.org/AM/Template.cfm?Section=Ethics_Opinions&template=/CM/ContentDisplay.cfm&ContentID=198038, last checked by the author August 22, 2013.

[5]http://www.nysba.org/AM/Template.cfm?Section=Ethics_Opinions&template=/CM/ContentDisplay.cfm&ContentID=198038, last checked by the author August 22, 2013.

§ 8:14   NAVIGATING LEGAL ETHICS

other states when determining what is considered to be an ad.[6] This categorization has a significant effect—it means that New York lawyers always need to have a physical office address listed on their cards. And yes, the opinion makes it clear that when they state "office" they mean a physical office. Thus, it's impossible to maintain a virtual practice in New York without having a brick and mortar office that one calls home.

Decisions like this are met with horror by the technologists. They shout that rules like this are "antiquated," or evidence of the elitism of Big Law and perpetuation of the proverbial "Old Boys Club." But all they need to do is follow the turnpike out of New York, zip through New Jersey and head into Pennsylvania. They'll find that state far more hospitable because Pennsylvania views the address requirement differently.

The Pennsylvania Bar Association Committee on Legal Ethics and Professional Responsibility addressed the issue of virtual law offices directly in its Formal Opinion 2010-200. The Committee addressed a variety of concerns relevant to VLOs, like confidentiality and supervision, but it also tackled the office address issue. The Committee stated that Pennsylvania's rule doesn't require that an actual physical address be listed on advertisements; they simply require that the lawyer set forth the geographical location (by city or town) where the lawyer principally practices law.[7] The opinion notes that the "goal of the Rules is to assure that clients are informed about the locations where the firm operates and the jurisdictions in which the attorneys at the firm practice.[8] The opinion goes even further and states that it's even permissible for lawyers to use a post office box as the address where services are rendered, so long as the geographic area requirement is met.[9] Under the Pennsylvania interpretation, a VLO wouldn't be precluded by the advertising rules. In fact, the opinion specifically stated that for this reason,

---

[6]This would have been discussed elsewhere in the book already.

[7]http://lawyersusaonline.com/wp-files/pdfs-2/f2010-200.pdf, last checked by the author on August 22, 2013.

[8]http://lawyersusaonline.com/wp-files/pdfs-2/f2010-200.pdf, last checked by the author on August 22, 2013.

[9]http://lawyersusaonline.com/wp-files/pdfs-2/f2010-200.pdf, last checked by the author on August 22, 2013.

§ 8:14

and all of the others discussed therein, a virtual law office was permissible in the Keystone State.[10]

In order to get at the heart of the issue, however, one would need to backtrack in our travels and return to my home state of New Jersey. In my opinion, New Jersey's rules do the best job of framing the key issue of the VLO debate.

For years, New Jersey was famous (or notorious, depending upon your point of view) for having a "bona fide office rule." New Jersey's Court Rules contained provision 1:21-1(a), which required that a New Jersey attorney maintain a bona fide office for the practice of law. The rule stated,

> For the purpose of this section, a bona fide office is a place where clients are met, files are kept, the telephone is answered, mail is received and the attorney or a responsible person acting on the attorney's behalf can be reached in person and by telephone during normal business hours to answer questions posed by the courts, clients or adversaries and to ensure that competent advice from the attorney can be obtained within a reasonable period of time.[11]

In 2010, New Jersey issued an opinion that outlawed virtual offices specifically because the powers-that-be believed that the physical location requirement was a key component of a proper law practice. The Advisory Committee on Professional Ethics issued Joint Opinion 718 with the State's Committee on Attorney Advertising and stated that, "A virtual office" cannot be a bona fide office since the attorney generally is not present during normal business hours but will only be present when he or she has reserved the space."[12]

Later on, the opinion discusses the issue of listing offices on ads and it touched on the crux of the issue:

> An attorney must have at least one bona fide office but may also list satellite office locations on letterhead, websites, and other advertisements provided the listing of such office locations is accurate and not misleading . . . An attorney who has a bona fide office may also have a satellite office that is a "virtual office." The attorney may list that "virtual office" satel-

---

[10]Of course, the opinion is only advisory in nature and, therefore, not binding. See the full disclaimer set forth on the last page of the actual opinion.

[11]http://www.judiciary.state.nj.us/notices/2010/n100326a.pdf, last checked by the author on August 22, 2013.

[12]http://www.judiciary.state.nj.us/notices/2010/n100326a.pdf, last checked by the author on August 22, 2013.

§ 8:14

lite location on attorney or law firm letterhead, websites, or other advertisements, but the communication must state that the "virtual office" location is "by appointment only." A "virtual office" location is not a place where a client can meet with the attorney unannounced. An attorney is not routinely found at a "virtual office" location and would need to make arrangements to reserve the space. Accordingly, while "virtual office" locations may be listed on attorney or law firm letterhead, websites, or other advertisements, the communication must state that the location is "by appointment only."[13]

Why were they so insistent upon an actual office? Sure, it could be for nefarious reasons, like protectionism for elite lawyers. But I think there's another reason. The key phrase to focus on in the previous quote is, "A 'virtual office' location is not a place where a client can meet with the attorney unannounced."[14] I believe that that's what this issue is really about. The real disagreement isn't about misleading advertising or whether to use technology. Those are concerns that are relatively easy to resolve. The real divide revolves around communication and the allocation of power between the lawyer and client.

Permit me to illustrate with a personal anecdote.

I needed to hire a lawyer recently to deal with a personal legal problem, so I got the chance to see the system from the client's point of view. My lawyer was a solo attorney in my hometown. He has a typical small office in a local office condo development, two secretaries and some loose relationship with another local lawyer (I couldn't tell exactly, but it didn't look like they had a typical partner/associate thing going). Throughout the representation we communicated mostly through email. I tried to make phone calls, but he was only there sporadically, so email worked best. The problem was that many of the responses I got were single words or short phrases. Typical email exchanges resembled the following:

ME: "Did you hear from the other side about the stipulation yet?"
LAWYER: "Nope."
ME: "When do you want to broach the settlement with the other side?"
LAWYER: "Not yet."

---

[13]http://www.judiciary.state.nj.us/notices/2010/n100326a.pdf, last checked by the author on August 22, 2013.

[14]http://www.judiciary.state.nj.us/notices/2010/n100326a.pdf, last checked by the author on August 22, 2013.

I grew increasingly frustrated with the curt responses and at times I specifically asked for more detailed descriptions, but my pleas went unanswered. Responses continued to be short bursts like,

> ME: "Have we received a response to our offer yet? It's been a while—what do you think we should do if we don't get a response by the end of the week?"
> LAWYER: "Didn't get a response yet. I'll advise."

As time passed, I felt completely disconnected from my case. It made me very concerned and I wrote emails that said things like, "Please call me, I am really anxious and I'm in the dark." Usually these went without response. No matter what I said and no matter how much desperation I built into the language of my emails, I wasn't able to get any consistent or meaningful responses from the lawyer. My lawyer wasn't communicating with me consistent with Rule 1.4.

I was at my wits end and I felt like I was running out of options. I had no choice but to go to his office, plant myself in his waiting room, and confront him when he walked in the door. When I did that, I got the answers I needed.

Frequently, and unfortunately, that's the only way a client can get ahold of their lawyer. And the way I see it, it's among the biggest reasons for requiring a physical office location. If there isn't proper communication, the only weapon in the client's arsenal might be to make themselves a fixture in the lawyer's office. The concern is that the absence of an office denies the client that option. It makes the lawyer less accessible to the client.

Not every critic of VLOs is concerned with this ethical dilemma. Sure, there are protectionists whose motivation is to resist change. Yes, there are people in Big Law who want to use the rules to build a system that keeps the deck stacked in their favor. But set aside those motivations and review the matter free of any agenda and we can see that there are some respectable and important ethical motivations.

I think the disciplinary authorities believe that the client should have the ability to see their lawyer when the client wishes to do so. I'm sure that many diligent proprietors of VLOs bend over backward to accommodate clients' requests for meetings. But a system that provides for face-to-face meetings with a lawyer "by appointment only" doesn't afford the client the ability to see the lawyer at a time of the client's choosing. Restricting lawyer-client personal meetings to an appointment-only system puts the power in the hands of the

§ 8:14   NAVIGATING LEGAL ETHICS

lawyer and that's not consistent with the most basic values of attorney ethics. Remember, it's not about you; it's about the client. Thus, the major divide with virtual law offices isn't really about technology; rather, it's about empowering the client.

Some argue that the cure is to clearly set forth your policy. "If the client knows that you can be met by appointment only," the argument goes, "then they know what they're getting into." Yes . . . but. Sure, they are aware of the policy, but most clients don't really understand the impact of such a policy until the representation unfolds in real life. Then it's too late. Besides, the issue is not just about whether you've adequately put a client on notice; it's about giving your client the opportunity to find you when *they* want to find you.

Technologists also point out that the client could show up and the lawyer won't be there. But it's up to the client whether they want to stay there and wait—if it's the lawyer's office they could feel reasonably assured that the lawyer will eventually come back. Heck, nothing's perfect, but at least the client knows where home-base is.

Diligent virtual lawyers may take offense to the non-communication argument. After all, many are eager to meet their clients and keep them properly informed. But the disciplinary system isn't concerned about the diligent virtual lawyer—that lawyer who understands the importance of communication and would likely do it even in the absence of an ethics code. The disciplinary system needs to craft rules to ensure that those among us who would not voluntarily communicate with our clients continue to do so anyway.

A review of the recent New Jersey amendments to their court rules further illustrates this issue. Recently, New Jersey passed a major amendment to its bona fide office rule. It reads:

> (1) An attorney need not maintain a fixed physical location, but must structure his or her practice in such a manner as to assure, as set forth in RPC 1.4, prompt and reliable communication with and accessibility by clients, other counsel, and judicial and administrative tribunals before which the attorney may practice, provided that an attorney may designate one or more fixed physical locations where client files and the attorney's business and financial records many be inspected on short notice by duly authorized regulatory authorities, where mail or hand-deliveries may be made and promptly received, and where process may be served on the attorney for

all actions, including disciplinary actions, that may arise out of the practice of law and activities related thereto.[15]

The change to the NJ rule illustrates perfectly the tight rope that the ethics authorities must walk. The critical concepts that this new language addresses are "communication" and "accessibility." The drafters are clearly trying to find a balance—how do they allow the practice to use technology, while still protecting the public. We want virtual lawyers, not vanishing lawyers. We need to craft rules that allow a technology-savvy lawyer to flourish while ensuring that unprincipled lawyers don't use that technology to disappear.

How do the drafters permit lawyers to stay cutting edge while ensuring that the client retain some personal power in the attorney-client relationship? In the new rule, New Jersey appears to eliminate the need for a brick-and-mortar office, but continues to impose a requirement that the lawyer remain accessible. It's going to be interesting to see how proprietors of VLOs execute this directive. I'm sure many will adopt an "appointment only" policy and we won't know if that satisfies the rule until someone gets in trouble. But now we see that therein lies the hidden source of our undoing—communication and accessibility.

Some of you may be wondering: How do we reconcile the Pennsylvania opinion? If this is all about empowering the client, why did Pennsylvania go in the other direction? The answer is that I don't think they went in another direction. Pennsylvania seems to have simply made a policy decision.

Pennsylvania's requirement that a lawyer reveal the geographic location where they practice may be motivated by the desire to allow clients to choose a lawyer who is familiar with the practice in the area where the client's case is located. Presumably, the client will want to hire a lawyer who is familiar with local laws and customs. My reading of the opinion is that the authorities are more concerned about the client understanding that they are hiring a lawyer who is familiar with local practice.

When balancing conflicting policy considerations, the Pennsylvania drafters appear to be less concerned about lawyer accessibility and more concerned about the ability of the client to determine that the lawyer practices in a partic-

---

[15]http://op.bna.com/mopc.nsf/id/jros-94eh8t/$File/NJbonafideofficeamendments.pdf, last checked by the author on August 23, 2013.

§ 8:14   NAVIGATING LEGAL ETHICS

ular community. Notice, however, that even though Pennsylvania comes to a different conclusion from New Jersey, their thought process was still client-centered.

For the most part, the issue of virtual law practices isn't a battle between people who want to move forward and others stuck in the past. To a certain extent, it's a question about who's interests will dominate your thinking—the lawyer's or the client's? The technology-savvy lawyers who want to transform the practice see it from the lawyer's perspective, while the disciplinary authorities look at it from the client's. I'm not indicting the technologists. I'm not claiming that they don't want to protect the client. I'm just saying that they are more concerned with helping lawyers leverage technology and create a practice that affords a certain lifestyle to the lawyer. While that's a worthy goal, one must understand that it's not completely shared by the disciplinary authorities. The primary motivation of the disciplinary authorities is to protect the client. We need to understand that critical difference so that when we use these new technologies we can craft our own best practices after proper consideration of the dangers.

§ 8:15 The issues with wireless networks

Clearly, the use of wireless technology is on the rise. A laptop user who finds free Wi-Fi in a coffee shop is comparable to a deep sea diver who finds a tank of oxygen. The downside of many of those wireless networks, however, is that they are vulnerable to being compromised if they are unsecured. That poses a problem for attorneys because it means that if we use an unsecured wireless network to perform work on behalf of our clients, our confidential information may be exposed. The question then becomes, are lawyers permitted to use unsecured wireless networks to do client work?

The issue, of course, is confidentiality because an unsecured wireless network is easily accessed by hackers. The concept of competence is also in question because Comments [16] and [17] of Rule 1.1[1] (Competence) remind lawyers that we must, "act competently to safeguard information . . .

[Section 8:15]
[1]Del. Prof. Conduct R. 1.1.
   1.1 http://courts.delaware.gov/rules/DLRPCFebruary2010.pdf. Pages last checked by the author August 13, 2013.

against . . . unauthorized disclosure," and that when transmitting a communication we must, "take reasonable precautions to prevent the information from coming into the hands of unintended recipients."

The State Bar of California's Standing Committee on Professional Responsibility and Conduct tackled the question directly in Formal Opinion No. 2010-179. In particular, it considered whether a lawyer could work on client files while using an unsecured wireless router in a coffee shop. The Opinion stated that, "An attorney's duties of confidentiality and competence require the attorney to take appropriate steps to ensure that his or her use of technology in conjunction with a client's representation does not subject confidential client information to an undue risk of unauthorized disclosure."[2] The Committee further stated that it was their belief that lawyers should not use unsecured wireless connections when working on client matters. The opinion states,

> With regard to the use of a public wireless connection, the Committee believes that, due to the lack of security features provided in most public wireless access locations, Attorney risks violating his duties of confidentiality and competence in using the wireless connection at the coffee shop to work on Client's matter unless he takes appropriate precautions, such as using a combination of file encryption, encryption of wireless transmissions and a personal firewall. [FN omitted] Depending on the sensitivity of the matter, Attorney may need to avoid using the public wireless connection entirely or notify Client of possible risks attendant to his use of the public wireless connection, including potential disclosure of confidential information and possible waiver of attorney-client privilege or work product protections, and seek her informed consent to do so. [FN omitted][3]

The takeaway: If your jurisdiction agrees with California, you might not be able to use wireless networks for client matters. The only way you will know for sure is when the Bar finally acts, either because they were asked to opine on the subject or they are disciplining someone. The question I ask myself is . . . do I want to be that person who makes the law by being the first person to be disciplined?

Something else from that opinion should rattle your cage. The Committee went on to talk about the set up in our homes:

---

[2]California Formal Opinion 2010-179.
[3]California Formal Opinion 2010-179.

§ 8:15   NAVIGATING LEGAL ETHICS

Finally, if Attorney's personal wireless system has been configured with appropriate security features [FN omitted] the Committee does not believe that Attorney would violate his duties of confidentiality and competence by working on Client's matter at home. Otherwise, Attorney may need to notify Client of the risks and seek her informed consent, as with the public wireless connection.[4]

While I normally don't care for anyone peeking between my curtains and commenting on what I do in my home, I understand why the authorities are going there in this opinion. The fact is that many of us keep sensitive client information on computers in our homes. Even if the information isn't on our home computer, we often use the wireless routers in our home to do our client work on our laptops, or through remote connections to the office server. If that router is vulnerable, then our client information is exposed. Thus, this opinion isn't so much intrusive as it is cautionary.

§ 8:16   Implications for smart phones, iPads and other devices

Here's a scary extension of that wireless opinion. Let's say your jurisdiction agrees with the California rule and you are not permitted to connect your laptop to the internet through an unsecured wireless router and work on client matters. Then shouldn't you also be prohibited from connecting your iPad, Smartphone or other mobile device to an unsecured wireless router to work on client matters? It would seem that you are prohibited from connecting any mobile device in that manner. Take it one step further . . . while I'm not a technology expert, I've been told by people who claim to be experts that wireless cellular service is just as vulnerable as a wireless router. Experts say that a cellular network is the functional equivalent (from a hacking/security perspective) as an unsecured wireless network.

The takeaway: While there are no opinions on topic, logic seems to dictate that you are not permitted to utilize your device's cellular signal (i.e., 4G or LTE service) to access the internet and work on client matters. That means that you cannot use your iPad, Smartphone or other device to work on client matters unless it is using a secured Internet connection. Admittedly, this issue is in its infancy at the time of this writing, so it's going to need to be updated. But keep your eyes peeled for opinions on the topic. It's ripe for

---

[4]California Formal Opinion 2010-179.

review. Luckily, the California Opinion I referred to earlier provides some guidance. Read on . . . .

Chapter 9

Guidence For The Future

§ 9:1 Introduction
§ 9:2 Ability to assess the level of security afforded by the technology, including how the technology differs from other media use
§ 9:3 Ability to assess the level of security afforded by the technology, including whether reasonable restrictions may be taken when using the technology to increase the level of security
§ 9:4 Ability to assess the level of security afforded by the technology, including limitations on who is permitted to monitor the use of the technology to what extend and on what grounds
§ 9:5 Legal ramifications to third parties of intercepting the information
§ 9:6 The degree of sensitivity of the information
§ 9:7 Possible impact on the client of an inadvertent disclosure of privileged or confidential information or work product, including possible waiver of privileges.
§ 9:8 The urgency of the situation
§ 9:9 Client instructions and circumstances
§ 9:10 The takeaway on the technology permissibility factors

KeyCite®: Cases and other legal materials listed in KeyCite Scope can be researched through the KeyCite service on Westlaw®. Use KeyCite to check citations for form, parallel references, prior and later history, and comprehensive citator information, including citations to other decisions and secondary materials.

---

§ 9:1 Introduction

California Formal Opinion No. 2010-179 provided a bit more information than the few quotes about the coffee shop set forth in the previous chapter. They understood that the realities of work in the coffee shop meant that "without appropriate safeguards (such as firewalls, secure username/password combinations, and encryption), data transmitted

§ 9:1

wirelessly can be intercepted and read with increasing ease."[1] In making that statement, they clearly realized that the issue was bigger than just working in a coffee shop and that what they were really addressing was the appropriate use of technology, in general. The drafters knew that they were in a tough spot and they acknowledged that, "unfortunately, guidance to attorneys on this area has not kept pace with technology."[2] The opinion, therefore, attempts to provide broader direction for lawyer. Opinion 179 actually sets forth some general guidance that helps lawyers navigate both existing technologies, as well as those that may arise in the future.

The factors are critical guidance for the lawyer because the reality is that we are on our own when it comes to new technologies. We all know that the pace of technological innovation is much faster than the disciplinary authorities. As a result, we're not going to have much advance guidance about the appropriateness of new platforms/technologies. Thus, if we want to avail ourselves of new systems we're going to have to make individual judgments about the ethical permissibility of those systems. Basically, we need to act as our own little ethics board. While it can be said that we make personal calls on the ethical permissibility on lots of occasions, rarely do we find ourselves faced with the unique circumstances that we face in new technologies.

To assist lawyers in that regard, the opinion lists six factors (with some sub-categories) that an attorney should consider when evaluating new technologies. I call this list the "Technology Permissibility Factors." The factors could be helpful for all attorneys when evaluating the permissibility of new systems in the future. Here is a list of the factors, followed by a bit of insight. However, I strongly encourage you to read the actual opinion because they explain the factors more fully and it makes more sense after you read the text. The opinion states, ". . . an attorney should consider the following before using a specific technology [Footnote omitted]:

    1. An attorney's ability to assess the level of security afforded by the technology, including

        (i)   how the technology differs from other media use

        (ii) whether reasonable restrictions may be taken

[Section 9:1]

[1]California Opinion No. 2010-179 at 1.

[2]California Opinion No, 2010-179 at 1.

when using the technology to increase the level of security and

(iii) Limitations on who is permitted to monitor the use of the technology to what extend and on what grounds.

2. Legal ramifications to third parties of intercepting the information

3. The degree of sensitivity of the information

4. Possible impact on the client of an inadvertent disclosure of privileged or confidential information or work product, including possible waiver of privileges.

5. The urgency of the situation

6. Client instructions and circumstances."[3]

§ 9:2 Ability to assess the level of security afforded by the technology, including how the technology differs from other media use

Here's where understanding existing technologies becomes key. The only way to properly evaluate the risks of systems that have not yet been reviewed by disciplinary authorities is to compare them to the systems that have already been evaluated. Are the risks the same? How are they different? Do the issues that were raised when disciplinary authorities opined on the existing technologies apply to these new systems?

§ 9:3 Ability to assess the level of security afforded by the technology, including whether reasonable restrictions may be taken when using the technology to increase the level of security

Are there tools available to increase security, such as complicated password generators, remote wipe capabilities for cell phones, super-duper encryption techniques for websites?

§ 9:4 Ability to assess the level of security afforded by the technology, including limitations on who is permitted to monitor the use of the technology to what extend and on what grounds

This combines two questions: First, what third parties will

---

[3]California Formal Opinion No. 2010-179.

§ 9:4

have access to the technology? This implicates Rule 5.3[1] and the duty to supervise those nonlawyer personnel. Also, do you need any assistance from technologically knowledgeable individuals to help you operate/secure the systems? If so, they may be monitoring the technology and they should be watched as well.

§ 9:5 Legal ramifications to third parties of intercepting the information

This is a biggie. Remember that one of the main reasons that lawyers were ultimately permitted to use unencrypted email was because the interception of the information sought was criminalized. Only then was the lawyer considered to have a reasonable expectation of privacy in using the systems. If new systems arise and there are no legal ramifications to intercepting the information that travels through that system, then it's not likely to be ethically permissible.

§ 9:6 The degree of sensitivity of the information

The California opinion says it best. "The greater the sensitivity of the information, the less risk an attorney should take with technology."[1] Common sense.

§ 9:7 Possible impact on the client of an inadvertent disclosure of privileged or confidential information or work product, including possible waiver of privileges.

Here's an example of how we need to think outside of the proverbial box. Consider the issue of texting our clients and whether it would be a good idea from a privilege point of view. We need to make sure that we keep the advice we give our client confidential in order to claim and preserve the attorney-client privilege. If the statements are revealed to a third party we lose that protection. It seems like it would be safe to text information to a client, given that the informa-

---

[Section 9:4]

[1]Del. Prof. Conduct R. 5.3.

5.3 http://courts.delaware.gov/rules/DLRPCFebruary2010.pdf. Pages last checked by the author August 13, 2013.

[Section 9:6]

[1]California Formal Opinion No. 2010–179 at 5.

tion is going directly to the client's phone.[1] It's not like we're posting our messages on Facebook where all the world can see them. However, there could be a waiver issue nonetheless.

For instance, what if we know that the boyfriend of our unmarried client commonly reviews our client's text messages? If we are aware that the information we text to our client is likely to be viewed by a third party, then aren't we jeopardizing privilege? You could argue that it's no different from emails. Any message sent to the client's phone could be viewed by another party thereby blowing privilege. Of course, I don't see how that helps you—it just gives further credibility to the argument that maybe we shouldn't be using these technologies to send messages.

I'm not sure how this will play out, but these are the things we need to watch out for when it comes to evaluating new technologies.

§ 9:8 The urgency of the situation

The opinion gives concise and valuable guidance on this factor. "If the use of technology is necessary to address an imminent situation or exigent circumstances and other alternatives are not reasonably available, it may be reasonable in limited cases for the attorney to do so without taking additional precautions."[1]

§ 9:9 Client instructions and circumstances

The opinion states that if a client tells us not to use a certain technology, we can't use it. Got it.

§ 9:10 The takeaway on the technology permissibility factors

As time goes by, lawyers will find themselves asking new questions for technologies that are not yet even discovered. Whether it's new devices, new modes of communications, new cloud technologies, or anything else, California's Formal

---

[Section 9:7]

[1]There are a variety of other concerns that come up with texting clients, but I'm just focusing on privilege right now. I don't intend this line of reasoning to be dispositive about the permissibility of texting.

[Section 9:8]

[1]California Opinion 2010-179 at 6.

§ 9:10   Navigating Legal Ethics

Opinion 2010-179 is helpful in navigating the ethical permissibility of those systems.

Granted, the California Opinion 2010-179 may not be binding in your jurisdiction, but it wouldn't be such a bad idea to consider these factors when you find yourself in a pickle in the absence of a direct ruling from your home jurisdiction. Consider how a disciplinary board would react if you were faced with a new technology, but before using it you evaluated the California technology permissibility factor and wrote a memo inthe file detailing your analysis. I would expect that a disciplinary board would look favorably upon you in a hearing situation.

APPENDIX A

The Delaware Lawyers' Rules of Professional Conduct

(Effective July 1, 2003 and current through amendment to Rule 1.15 approved by the Court on Feb. 16, 2010, which appears in bold and becomes effective May 1, 2010)

Preamble: A lawyer's responsibilities

[1] A lawyer, as a member of the legal profession, is a representative of clients, an officer of the legal system and a public citizen having special responsibility for the quality of justice.

[2] As a representative of clients, a lawyer performs various functions. As advisor, a lawyer provides a client with an informed understanding of the client's legal rights and obligations and explains their practical implications. As advocate, a lawyer zealously asserts the client's position under the rules of the adversary system. As negotiator, a lawyer seeks a result advantageous to the client but consistent with requirements of honest dealings with others. As an evaluator, a lawyer acts by examining a client's legal affairs and reporting about them to the client or to others.

[3] In addition to these representational functions, a lawyer may serve as a third-party neutral, a nonrepresentational role helping the parties to resolve a dispute or other matter. Some of these Rules apply directly to lawyers who are or have served as third-party neutrals. See, e.g., Rules 1.12 and 2.4. In addition, there are Rules that apply to lawyers who are not active in the practice of law or to practicing lawyers even when they are acting in a nonprofessional capacity. For example, a lawyer who commits fraud in the conduct of a business is subject to discipline for engaging in conduct involving dishonesty, fraud, deceit or misrepresentation. See Rule 8.4.

[4] In all professional functions a lawyer should be competent, prompt and diligent. A lawyer should maintain communication with a client concerning the representation. A lawyer should keep in confidence information relating to representation of a client except so far as disclosure is required or permitted by the Rules of Professional Conduct or other law.

[5] A lawyer's conduct should conform to the requirements of the law, both in professional service to clients and in the lawyer's business and personal affairs. A lawyer should use the law's procedures only for legitimate purposes and not to harass or intimidate others. A lawyer should demonstrate respect for the legal system and for those who serve it, including judges, other lawyers and public officials. While it is a lawyer's duty, when necessary, to challenge the rectitude of official action, it is also a lawyer's duty to uphold legal process.

[6] As a public citizen, a lawyer should seek improvement of the law, access to the legal system, the administration of justice and the quality of service rendered by the legal profession. As a member of a learned profession, a lawyer should cultivate knowledge of the law beyond its use for clients, employ that knowledge in reform of the law and work to strengthen legal education. In addition, a lawyer should further the public's understanding of and confidence in the rule of law and the justice system because legal institutions in a constitutional democracy depend on popular participation and support to maintain their authority. A lawyer should be mindful of deficiencies in the administration of justice and of the fact that the poor, and sometimes persons who are not poor, cannot afford adequate legal assistance. There-fore, all lawyers should devote professional time and resources and use civic influence to ensure equal access to our system of justice for all those who because of economic or social barriers cannot afford or secure adequate legal counsel. A lawyer should aid the legal profession in pursuing these objectives and should help the bar regulate itself in the public interest.

[7] Many of a lawyer's professional responsibilities are prescribed in the Rules of Professional Conduct, as well as substantive and procedural law. However, a lawyer is also guided by personal conscience and the approbation of professional peers. A lawyer should strive to attain the highest level of skill, to improve the law and the legal profession and to exemplify the legal profession's ideals of public service.

[8] A lawyer's responsibilities as a representative of clients, an officer of the legal system and a public citizen are usually harmonious. Thus, when an opposing party is well represented, a lawyer can be a zealous advocate on behalf of a client and at the same time assume that justice is being done. So also, a lawyer can be sure that preserving client confidences ordinarily serves the public interest because people are more likely to seek legal advice, and thereby heed their legal obligations, when they know their communications will be private.

[9] In the nature of law practice, however, conflicting responsibilities are encountered. Virtually all difficult ethical problems arise from conflict between a lawyer's responsibilities to clients, to the legal system and to the lawyer's own interest in remaining an ethical person while earning a satisfactory living. The Rules of Professional conduct often prescribe terms for resolving such conflicts. Within the framework of these Rules, however, many difficult issues of professional discretion can arise. Such issues must be resolved through the exercise of sensitive professional and moral judgment guided by the basic principles underlying the Rules. These principles include the lawyer's obligation zealously to protect and pursue a client's legitimate interests, within the bounds of the law, while maintaining a professional, courteous and civil attitude toward all persons involved in the legal system.

[10] The legal profession is largely self-governing. Although other professions also have been granted powers of self-government, the legal profession is unique in this respect because of the close relationship between the profession and the processes of government and law enforcement. This connection is manifested in the fact that ultimate authority over the legal profession is vested largely in the courts.

[11] To the extent that lawyers meet the obligations of their professional calling, the occasion for government regulation is obviated. Self-regulation also helps maintain the legal profession's independence from government domination. An independent legal profession is an important force in preserving government under law, for abuse of legal authority is more readily challenged by a profession whose members are not dependent on government for the right to practice.

[12] The legal profession's relative autonomy carries with it special responsibilities of self-government. The profession has a responsibility to assure that its regulations are conceived in the public interest and not in furtherance of parochial or self interested concerns of the bar. Every lawyer is responsible for observance of the Rules of Professional Conduct. A lawyer should also aid in securing their observance by other lawyers. Neglect of these responsibilities compromises the independence of the profession and the public interest which it serves.

[13] Lawyers play a vital role in the preservation of society. The fulfillment of this role requires an understanding by lawyers of their relationship to our legal system. The Rules of Professional Conduct, when properly applied, serve

to define that relationship.

SCOPE

[14] The Rules of Professional Conduct are rules of reason. They should be interpreted with reference to the purposes of legal representation and of the law itself. Some of the Rules are imperatives, cast in the terms "shall" or "shall not." These define proper conduct for purposes of professional discipline. Others, generally cast in the term "may," are permissive and define areas under the Rules in which the lawyer has discretion to exercise professional judgment. No disciplinary action should be taken when the lawyer chooses not to act or acts within the bounds of such discretion. Other Rules define the nature of relationships between the lawyer and others. The Rules are thus partly obligatory and disciplinary and partly constitutive and descriptive in that they define a lawyer's professional role. Many of the Comments use the term "should." Comments do not add obligations to the Rules but provide guidance for practicing in compliance with the Rules.

[15] The Rules presuppose a larger legal context shaping the lawyer's role. That context includes court rules and statutes relating to matters of licensure, laws defining specific obligations of lawyers and substantive and procedural law in general. The Comments are sometimes used to alert lawyers to their responsibilities under such other law.

[16] Compliance with the Rules, as with all law in an open society, depends primarily upon understanding and voluntary compliance, secondarily upon reenforcement by peer and public opinion and finally, when necessary, upon enforcement through disciplinary proceedings. The Rules do not, however, exhaust the moral and ethical considerations that should inform a lawyer, for no worthwhile human activity can be completely defined by legal rules. The Rules simply provide a framework for the ethical practice of law.

[17] Furthermore, for purposes of determining the lawyer's authority and responsibility, principles of substantive law external to these Rules determine whether a client-lawyer relationship exists. Most of the duties flowing from the client-lawyer relationship attach only after the client has requested the lawyer to render legal services and the lawyer has agreed to do so. But there are some duties, such as that of confidentiality under Rule 1.6, that attach when the lawyer agrees to consider whether a client-lawyer relationship shall be established. See Rule 1.18. Whether a client-lawyer relationship exists for any specific purpose can depend on the circumstances and may be a question of fact.

[18] Under various legal provisions, including constitu-

tional, statutory and common law, the responsibilities of government lawyers may include authority concerning legal matters that ordinarily reposes in the client in private client-lawyer relationships. For example, a lawyer for a government agency may have authority on behalf of the government to decide upon settlement or whether to appeal from an adverse judgment. Such authority in various respects is generally vested in the attorney general and the state's attorney in state government, and their federal counterparts, and the same may be true of other government law officers. Also, lawyers under the supervision of these officers may be authorized to represent several government agencies in intragovernmental legal controversies in circumstances where a private lawyer could not represent multiple private clients. These Rules do not abrogate any such authority.

[19] Failure to comply with an obligation or prohibition imposed by a Rule is a basis for invoking the disciplinary process. The Rules presuppose that disciplinary assessment of a lawyer's conduct will be made on the basis of the facts and circumstances as they existed at the time of the conduct in question and in recognition of the fact that a lawyer of-ten has to act upon uncertain or incomplete evidence of the situation. Moreover, the Rules presuppose that whether or not discipline should be imposed for a violation, and the severity of a sanction, depend on all the circumstances, such as the willfulness and seriousness of the violation, extenuating factors and whether there have been previous violations.

[20] Violation of a Rule should not itself give rise to a cause of action against a lawyer nor should it create any presumption in such a case that a legal duty has been breached. In addition, violation of a Rule does not necessarily war-rant any other nondisciplinary remedy, such as disqualification of a lawyer in pending litigation. The rules are designed to provide guidance to lawyers and to provide a structure for regulating conduct through disciplinary agencies. They are not designed to be a basis for civil liability. Furthermore, the purpose of the Rules can be subverted when they are invoked by opposing parties as procedural weapons. The fact that a Rule is a just basis for a lawyer's self-assessment, or for sanctioning a lawyer under the administration of a disciplinary authority, does not imply that an antagonist in a collateral proceeding or transaction has standing to seek enforcement of the Rule.

[21] The Comment accompanying each Rule explains and illustrates the meaning and purpose of the Rule. The Preamble and this note on Scope provide general orientation. The Comments are intended as guides to interpretation, but the text of each rule is authoritative.

Rule 1.0. Terminology

(a) "Belief" or "believes" denotes that the person involved actually supposed the fact in question to be true. A person's belief may be inferred from circumstances.

(b) "Confirmed in writing," when used in reference to the informed consent of a person, denotes informed consent that is given in writing by the person or a writing that a lawyer promptly transmits to the person confirming an oral in-formed consent. See paragraph (e) for the definition of "informed consent." If it is not feasible to obtain or transmit the writing at the time the person gives informed consent, then the lawyer must obtain or transmit it within a reasonable time thereafter.

(c) "Firm" or "law firm" denotes a lawyer or lawyers in a law partnership, professional corporation, sole proprietor-ship or other association authorized to practice law; or lawyers employed in a legal services organization or the legal department of a corporation or other organization.

(d) "Fraud" or "fraudulent" denotes conduct that is fraudulent under the substantive or procedural law of the applicable jurisdiction and has a purpose to deceive.

(e) "Informed consent" denotes the agreement by a person to a proposed course of conduct after the lawyer has communicated adequate information and explanation about the material risks of and reasonably available alternatives to the proposed course of conduct.

(f) "Knowingly," "known," or "knows" denotes actual knowledge of the fact in question. A person's knowledge may be inferred from circumstances.

(g) "Partner" denotes a member of a partnership, a shareholder in a law firm organized as a professional corporation, or a member of an association authorized to practice law.

(h) "Reasonable" or "reasonably" when used in relation to conduct by a lawyer denotes the conduct of a reasonably prudent and competent lawyer.

(i) "Reasonable belief" or "reasonably believes" when used in reference to a lawyer denotes that the lawyer believes the matter in question and that the circumstances are such that the belief is reasonable.

(j) "Reasonably should know" when used in reference to a lawyer denotes that a lawyer of reasonable prudence and competence would ascertain the matter in question.

(k) "Screened" denotes the isolation of a lawyer from any participation in a matter through the timely imposition of procedures within a firm that are reasonably adequate under the circumstances to protect information that the isolated lawyer is obligated to protect under these Rules or other law.

(l) "Substantial" when used in reference to degree or extent denotes a material matter of clear and weighty importance.

(m) "Tribunal" denotes a court, an arbitrator in a binding arbitration proceeding or a legislative body, administrative agency or other body acting in an adjudicative capacity. A legislative body, administrative agency or other body acts in an adjudicative capacity when a neutral official, after the presentation of evidence or legal argument by a party or parties, will render a binding legal judgment directly affecting a party's interests in a particular matter.

(n) "Writing" or "written" denotes a tangible or electronic record of a communication or representation, including handwriting, typewriting, printing, photostating, photography, audio or video recording and e-mail. A "signed" writing includes an electronic sound, symbol or process attached to or logically associated with a writing and executed or adopted by a person with the intent to sign the writing.

Rule 1.1. Competence

A lawyer shall provide competent representation to a client. Competent representation requires the legal knowledge, skill, thoroughness and preparation reasonably necessary for the representation.

Rule 1.2. Scope of representation

(a) Subject to paragraphs (c) and (d), a lawyer shall abide by a client's decisions concerning the objectives of representation and, as required by Rule 1.4, shall consult with the client as to the means by which they are to be pursued. A lawyer may take such action on behalf of the client as is impliedly authorized to carry out the representation. A lawyer shall abide by a client's decision whether to settle a matter. In a criminal case, the lawyer shall abide by the client's decision, after consultation with the lawyer, as to a plea to be entered, whether to waive jury trial and whether the client will testify.

(b) A lawyer's representation of a client, including representation by appointment, does not constitute an endorsement of the client's political, economic, social or moral views or activities.

(c) A lawyer may limit the scope of the representation if the limitation is reasonable under the circumstances and the client gives informed consent.

(d) A lawyer shall not counsel a client to engage, or assist a client, in conduct that the lawyer knows is criminal or fraudulent, but a lawyer may discuss the legal consequences of any proposed course of conduct with a client and may counsel or assist a client to make a good faith effort to determine the validity, scope, meaning or application of the law.

Rule 1.3. Diligence

A lawyer shall act with reasonable diligence and promptness in representing a client.

Rule 1.4. Communication

(a) A lawyer shall:

(1) promptly inform the client of any decision or circumstance with respect to which the client's informed consent, as defined in Rule 1.0(e), is required by these Rules;

(2) reasonably consult with the client about the means by which the client's objectives are to be accomplished;

(3) keep the client reasonably informed about the status of the matter;

(4) promptly comply with reasonable requests for information; and

(5) consult with the client about any relevant limitation on the lawyer's conduct when the lawyer knows that the client expects assistance not permitted by the Rules of Professional Conduct or other law.

(b) A lawyer shall explain a matter to the extent reasonably necessary to permit the client to make informed decisions regarding the representation.

Rule 1.5. Fees

(a) A lawyer shall not make an agreement for, charge, or collect an unreasonable fee or an unreasonable amount for expenses. The factors to be considered in determining the reasonableness of a fee include the following:

(1) the time and labor required, the novelty and dif-

ficulty of the questions involved, and the skill requisite to per-form the legal service properly;

(2) the likelihood, if apparent to the client, that the acceptance of the particular employment will preclude other employment by the lawyer;

(3) the fee customarily charged in the locality for similar legal services;

(4) the amount involved and the results obtained;

(5) the time limitations imposed by the client or by the circumstances;

(6) the nature and length of the professional relationship with the client;

(7) the experience, reputation, and ability of the lawyer or lawyers performing the services; and

(8) whether the fee is fixed or contingent.

(b) The scope of the representation and the basis or rate of the fee and expenses for which the client will be responsible shall be communicated to the client, preferably in writing, before or within a reasonable time after commencing the representation, except when the lawyer will charge a regularly represented client on the same basis or rate. Any changes in the basis or rate of the fee or expenses shall also be communicated to the client.

(c) A fee may be contingent on the outcome of the matter for which the service is rendered, except in a matter in which a contingent fee is prohibited by paragraph (d) or other law. A contingent fee agreement shall be in a writing signed by the client and shall state the method by which the fee is to be determined, including the percentage or percentages that shall accrue to the lawyer in the event of settlement, trial or appeal; litigation and other expenses to be deducted from the recovery; and whether such expenses are to be deducted before or after the contingent fee is calculated. The agreement must clearly notify the client of any expenses for which the client will be liable whether or not the client is the prevailing party. Upon conclusion of a contingent fee matter, the lawyer shall provide the client with a written statement stating the outcome of the matter and, if there is a recovery, showing the remittance to the client and the method of its determination.

(d) A lawyer shall not enter into an arrangement for, charge, or collect:

(1) any fee in a domestic relations matter, the payment or amount of which is contingent upon the securing of a divorce or upon the amount of alimony or support, or property settlement in lieu thereof; or

(2) a contingent fee for representing a defendant in a criminal case.

(e) A division of fee between lawyers who are not in the same firm may be made only if:

(1) the client is advised in writing of and does not object to the participation of all the lawyers involved; and

(2) the total fee is reasonable.

(f) A lawyer may require the client to pay some or all of the fee in advance of the lawyer undertaking the representation, provided that:

(1) The lawyer shall provide the client with a written statement that the fee is refundable if it is not earned,

(2) The written statement shall state the basis under which the fees shall be considered to have been earned, whether in whole or in part, and

(3) All unearned fees shall be retained in the lawyer's trust account, with statement of the fees earned provided to the client at the time such funds are withdrawn from the trust account.

Rule 1.6. Confidentiality of information

(a) A lawyer shall not reveal information relating to the representation of a client unless the client gives informed consent, the disclosure is impliedly authorized in order to carry out the representation, or the disclosure is permitted by paragraph (b).

(b) A lawyer may reveal information relating to the representation of a client to the extent the lawyer reasonably believes necessary:

(1) to prevent reasonably certain death or substantial bodily harm;

(2) to prevent the client from committing a crime or fraud that is reasonably certain to result in substantial injury to the financial interests or property of another and in furtherance of which the client has used or is using the lawyer's ser-vices;

(3) to prevent, mitigate, or rectify substantial injury

to the financial interests or property of another that is reasonably certain to result or has resulted from the client's commission of a crime or fraud in furtherance of which the client has used the lawyer's services;

(4) to secure legal advice about the lawyer's compliance with these Rules;

(5) to establish a claim or defense on behalf of the lawyer in a controversy between the lawyer and the client, to establish a defense to a criminal charge or civil claim against the lawyer based upon conduct in which the client was involved, or to respond to allegations in any proceeding concerning the lawyer's representation of the client; or

(6) to comply with other law or a court order.

Rule 1.7. Conflict of interest: Current clients

(a) Except as provided in paragraph (b), a lawyer shall not represent a client if the representation involves a concur-rent conflict of interest. A concurrent conflict of interest exists if:

(1) the representation of one client will be directly adverse to another client; or

(2) there is a significant risk that the representation of one or more clients will be materially limited by the lawyer's responsibilities to another client, a former client or a third person or by a personal interest of the lawyer.

(b) Notwithstanding the existence of a concurrent conflict of interest under paragraph (a), a lawyer may represent a client if:

(1) the lawyer reasonably believes that the lawyer will be able to provide competent and diligent representation to each affected client;

(2) the representation is not prohibited by law;

(3) the representation does not involve the assertion of a claim by one client against another client represented by the lawyer in the same litigation or other proceeding before a tribunal; and

(4) each affected client gives informed consent, confirmed in writing.

Rule 1.8. Conflict of interest: Current clients: Specific rules

(a) A lawyer shall not enter into a business transaction with a client or knowingly acquire an ownership, possessory, security or other pecuniary interest adverse to a client unless:

(1) the transaction and terms on which the lawyer acquires the interest are fair and reasonable to the client and are fully disclosed and transmitted in writing to the client in a manner that can be reasonably understood by the client;

(2) the client is advised in writing of the desirability of seeking and is given a reasonable opportunity to seek the advice of independent legal counsel on the transaction; and

(3) the client gives informed consent, in a writing signed by the client, to the essential terms of the transaction and the lawyer's role in the transaction, including whether the lawyer is representing the client in the transaction.

(b) A lawyer shall not use information relating to representation of a client to the disadvantage of the client unless the client gives informed consent, except as permitted or required by these Rules.

(c) A lawyer shall not solicit any substantial gift from a client, including a testamentary gift, or prepare on behalf of a client an instrument giving the lawyer or a person related to the lawyer any substantial gift unless the lawyer or other recipient of the gift is related to the client. For purposes of this paragraph, related persons include a spouse, child, grandchild, parent, grandparent or other relative or individual with whom the lawyer or the client maintains a close, familial relationship.

(d) Prior to the conclusion of representation of a client, a lawyer shall not make or negotiate an agreement giving the lawyer literary or media rights to a portrayal or account based in substantial part on information relating to the representation.

(e) A lawyer shall not provide financial assistance to a client in connection with pending or contemplated litigation, except that:

(1) a lawyer may advance court costs and expenses of litigations, the repayment of which may be contingent on the outcome of the matter; and

(2) a lawyer representing an indigent client may pay court costs and expenses of litigation on behalf of the client.

(f) A lawyer shall not accept compensation for representing a client from one other than the client unless:

(1) the client gives informed consent;

(2) there is no interference with the lawyer's independence of professional judgment or with the client-lawyer relationship; and

(3) information relating to representation of a client is protected as required by Rule 1.6.

(g) A lawyer who represents two or more clients shall not participate in making an aggregate settlement of the claims of or against the clients, or in a criminal case an aggregated agreement as to guilty or nolo contendere pleas, unless each client gives informed consent, in a writing signed by the client. The lawyer's disclosure shall include the existence and nature of all the claims or pleas involved and of the participation of each person in the settlement.

(h) A lawyer shall not:

(1) make an agreement prospectively limiting the lawyer's liability to a client for malpractice unless the client is in-dependently represented in making the agreement; or

(2) settle a claim or potential claim for such liability with an unrepresented client or former client unless that per-son is advised in writing of the desirability of seeking and is given a reasonable opportunity to seek the advice of independent legal counsel in connection therewith.

(i) A lawyer shall not acquire a proprietary interest in the cause of action or subject matter of litigation the lawyer is conducting for a client, except that the lawyer may:

(1) acquire a lien authorized by law to secure the lawyer's fee or expenses; and

(2) contract with a client for a reasonable contingent fee in a civil case.

(j) A lawyer shall not have sexual relations with a client unless a consensual sexual relationship existed between them when the client-lawyer relationship commenced.

(k) While lawyers are associated in a firm, a prohibition in the foregoing paragraphs (a) through (i) that applies to any one of them shall apply to all of them.

Rule 1.9. Duties to former clients

(a) A lawyer who has formerly represented a client in a matter shall not thereafter represent another person in the same or a substantially related matter in which that person's interests are materially adverse to the interests of the former client unless the former client gives informed consent, confirmed in writing.

(b) A lawyer shall not knowingly represent a person in the same or a substantially related matter in which a firm with which the lawyer formerly was associated had previously represented a client:

(1) whose interests are materially adverse to that person; and

(2) about whom the lawyer had acquired information protected by Rules 1.6 and 1.9(c) that is material to the matter;

unless the former client gives informed consent, confirmed in writing.

(c) A lawyer who has formerly represented a client in a matter or whose present or former firm has formerly represented a client in a matter shall not thereafter:

(1) use information relating to the representation to the disadvantage of the former client except as these Rules would permit or require with respect to a client, or when the information has become generally known; or

(2) reveal information relating to the representation except as these Rules would permit or require with respect to a client.

Rule 1.10. Imputation of conflicts of interest: General rule

(a) Except as otherwise provided in this rule, while lawyers are associated in a firm, none of them shall knowingly represent a client when any one of them practicing alone would be prohibited from doing so by Rules 1.7 or 1.9, unless the prohibition is based on a personal interest of the prohibited lawyer and does not present a significant risk of materially limiting the representation of the client by the remaining lawyers in the firm.

(b) When a lawyer has terminated an association with a firm, the firm is not prohibited from thereafter representing a person with interests materially adverse to those of a client represented by the formerly associated lawyer and not currently represented by the firm, unless:

(1) the matter is the same or substantially related to that in which the formerly associated lawyer represented the client; and

(2) any lawyer remaining in the firm has information protected by Rules 1.6 and 1.9(c) that is material to the mat-ter.

(c) When a lawyer becomes associated with a firm, no lawyer associated in the firm shall knowingly represent a client in a matter in which that lawyer is disqualified under Rule 1.9 unless:

(1) the personally disqualified lawyer is timely screened from any participation in the matter and is apportioned no part of the fee therefrom; and

(2) written notice is promptly given to the affected former client.

(d) A disqualification prescribed by this rule may be waived by the affected client under the conditions stated in Rule 1.7.

(e) The disqualification of lawyers associated in a firm with former or current government lawyers is governed by Rule 1.11.

Rule 1.11. Special conflicts of interest for former and current government officers and employees

(a) Except as law may otherwise expressly permit, a lawyer who has formerly served as a public officer or employee of the government:

(1) is subject to Rule 1.9(c); and

(2) shall not otherwise represent a client in connection with a matter in which the lawyer participated personally and substantially as a public officer or employee, unless the appropriate government agency gives its informed consent, confirmed in writing, to the representation.

(b) When a lawyer is disqualified from representation under paragraph (a), no lawyer in a firm with which that lawyer is associated may knowingly undertake or continue representation in such a matter unless:

(1) the disqualified lawyer is timely screened from any participation in the matter and is apportioned no part of the fee therefrom; and

(2) written notice is promptly given to the appropriate government agency to enable it to ascertain compliance with the provisions of this rule.

(c) Except as law may otherwise expressly permit, a lawyer having information that the lawyer knows is confidential government information about a person acquired when the lawyer was a public officer or employee, may not represent a private client whose interests are adverse to that person in a matter in which the information could be used to the material disadvantage of that person. As used in this Rule, the term "confidential government information" means in-formation that has been obtained under governmental authority and which, at the time this Rule is applied, the government is prohibited by law from disclosing to the public or has a legal privilege not to disclose and which is not other-wise available to the public. A firm with which that lawyer is associated may undertake or continue representation in the matter only if the disqualified lawyer is timely screened from any participation in the matter and is apportioned no part of the fee therefrom.

(d) Except as law may otherwise expressly permit, a lawyer currently serving as a public officer or employee:

(1) is subject to Rules 1.7 and 1.9; and

(2) shall not:

(i) participate in a matter in which the lawyer participated personally and substantially while in private practice or nongovernmental employment, unless the appropriate government agency gives its informed consent, confirmed in writing; or

(ii) negotiate for private employment with any person who is involved as a party or as lawyer for a party in a matter in which the lawyer is participating personally and substantially, except that a lawyer serving as a law clerk to a judge, other adjudicative officer or arbitrator may negotiate for private employment as permitted by Rule 1.12(b) and subject to the conditions stated in Rule 1.12(b).

(e) As used in this Rule, the term "matter" includes:

(1) any judicial or other proceeding, application, request for a ruling or other determination, contract, claim, controversy, investigation, charge, accusation, arrest or other particular matter involving a specific party or parties, and

(2) any other matter covered by the conflict of interest rules of the appropriate government agency.

Rule 1.12. Former judge, arbitrator, mediator or other third-party neutral

(a) Except as stated in paragraph (d), a lawyer shall not represent anyone in connection with a matter in which the lawyer participated personally and substantially as a judge or other adjudicative officer or law clerk to such a person or as an arbitrator, mediator or other third-party neutral, unless all parties to the proceeding give informed consent, con-firmed in writing.

(b) A lawyer shall not negotiate for employment with any person who is involved as a party or as lawyer for a party in a matter in which the lawyer is participating personally and substantially as a judge or other adjudicative officer or as an arbitrator, mediator or other third-party neutral. A lawyer serving as a law clerk to a judge or other adjudicative officer may negotiate for employment with a party or lawyer involved in a matter in which the clerk is participating personally and substantially, but only after the lawyer has notified the judge or other adjudicative officer.

(c) If a lawyer is disqualified by paragraph (a), no lawyer in a firm with which that lawyer is associated may knowingly undertake or continue representation in the matter unless:

(1) the disqualified lawyer is timely screened from any participation in the matter and is apportioned no part of the fee therefrom; and

(2) written notice is promptly given to the parties and any appropriate tribunal to enable them to ascertain compliance with the provisions of this rule.

(d) An arbitrator selected as a partisan of a party in a multimember arbitration panel is not prohibited from subsequently representing that party.

Rule 1.13. Organization as client

(a) A lawyer employed or retained by an organization represents the organization acting through its duly authorized constituents.

(b) If a lawyer for an organization knows that an officer, employee or other person associated with the organization is engaged in action, intends to act or refuses to act in a matter related to the representation that is a violation of a legal obligation to the organization, or a violation of law which reasonably might be imputed to the organization, and is likely to result in substantial injury to the organization, the lawyer shall proceed as is reasonably necessary in the best interest of the organization. In determining how to proceed, the lawyer shall give due consideration to the seriousness of the violation and its consequences, the scope and nature of the lawyer's representation, the responsibility in the organization and the apparent motivation of the person involved, the policies of the organization concerning such matters and any other relevant considerations. Any measures taken shall be designed to minimize disruption of the organization and the risk of revealing information relating to the representation to persons outside the organization. Such measures may include among others:

(1) asking for reconsideration of the matter;

(2) advising that a separate legal opinion on the matter be sought for presentation to appropriate authority in the organization; and

(3) referring the matter to higher authority in the organization, including, if warranted by the seriousness of the matter, referral to the highest authority that can act on behalf of the organization as determined by applicable law.

(c) If, despite the lawyer's efforts in accordance with paragraph (b), the highest authority that can act on behalf of the organization insists upon action, or a refusal to act, that is clearly a violation of law and is likely to result in substantial injury to the organization, the lawyer may resign in accordance with Rule 1.16.

(d) In dealing with an organization's directors, officers, employees, members, shareholders or other constituents, a lawyer shall explain the identity of the client when the lawyer knows or reasonably should know that the organization's interests are adverse to those of the constituents with whom the lawyer is dealing.

(e) A lawyer representing an organization may also represent any of its directors, officers, employees, members, shareholders or other constituents, subject to the provisions of Rule 1.7. If the organization's consent to the dual representation is required by Rule 1.7, the consent shall be given by an appropriate official of the organization other than the individual who is to be represented, or by the shareholders.

Rule 1.14. Client with diminished capacity

(a) When a client's capacity to make adequately considered decisions in connection with a representation is diminished, whether because of minority, mental impairment or for some other reason, the lawyer shall, as far as reasonably possible, maintain a normal client-lawyer relationship with the client.

(b) When the lawyer reasonably believes that the client has diminished capacity, is at risk of substantial physical, financial or other harm unless action is taken and cannot adequately act in the client's own interest, the lawyer may take reasonably necessary protective action, including consulting with individuals or entities that have the ability to take action to protect the client and, in appropriate cases, seeking the appointment of a guardian ad litem, conservator or guardian.

(c) Information relating to the representation of a client with diminished capacity is protected by Rule 1.6. When taking protective action pursuant to paragraph (b), the lawyer is impliedly authorized under Rule 1.6(a) to reveal information about the client, but only to the extent reasonably necessary to protect the client's interests.

Rule 1.15. Safekeeping property

(a) A lawyer shall hold property of clients or third persons that is in a lawyer's possession in connection with a representation separate from the lawyer's own property. Funds shall be kept in a separate account designated solely for funds held in connection with the practice of law in this jurisdiction. Such funds shall be maintained in the state in which the lawyer's office is situated, or elsewhere with the consent of the client or third person. Funds of the lawyer that are reasonably sufficient to pay bank charges may be deposited therein; however, such amount may not exceed $1,000 and must be separately stated and accounted for in the same manner as clients' funds deposited therein. Other property shall be identified as such and appropriately safeguarded. Complete records of such account funds and other property shall be kept by the lawyer and shall be preserved for a period of five years after the completion of the events that they re-cord.

(b) Upon receiving funds or other property in which a client or third person has an interest, a lawyer shall promptly notify the client or third person. Except as stated in this Rule or otherwise permitted by law or by agreement with the client, a lawyer shall promptly deliver to the client or third person any funds or other property that the client or third person is entitled to receive and, upon request by the client or third person, shall promptly render a full accounting regarding such property.

(c) When in the course of representation a lawyer is in possession of property in which both the lawyer and another person claim interests, the property shall be kept separate by the lawyer until there is an accounting and severance of their interests. If a dispute arises concerning their respective interests, the portion in dispute shall be kept separate by the lawyer until the dispute is resolved.

(d) A lawyer engaged in the private practice of law must maintain financial books and records on a current basis, and shall preserve the books and records for at least five years following the completion of the year to which they re-late, or, as to fiduciary books and records, five years following the completion of that fiduciary obligation. The maintenance of books and records must conform with the following provisions:

(1) All bank statements, cancelled checks (or images and/or copies thereof as provided by the bank), records of electronic transfers, and duplicate deposit slips relating to fiduciary and non-fiduciary accounts must be preserved. Records of all electronic transfers from fiduciary accounts shall include the name of the person authorizing transfer, the date of transfer, the name of recipient and confirmation from the banking institution confirming the number of the fiduciary account from which the funds are withdrawn and the date and time the request for transfer was completed.

(2) Bank accounts maintained for fiduciary funds must be specifically designated as "Rule 1.15A Attorney Trust Account" or "1.15A Trust Account" or "Rule 1.15A Attorney Escrow Account" or "1.15A Escrow Account," and must be used only for funds held in a fiduciary capacity. A designation of the account as a "Rule 1.15A Attorney Trust Ac-count" or "1.15A Trust Account" or "Rule 1.15A Attorney Escrow Account" or "1.15A Escrow Account," must appear in the account title on the bank statement. Other related statements, checks, deposit slips, and other documents maintained for fiduciary funds, must contain, at a minimum, a designation of the account as "Attorney Trust Account" or "Attorney Escrow Account."

(3) Bank accounts and related statements, checks, deposit slips, and other documents maintained for non-fiduciary funds must be specifically designated as "Attorney Business Account" or "Attorney Operating Account," and must be used only for funds held in a non-fiduciary capacity. A lawyer in the private practice of law shall maintain a non-fiduciary account for general operating purposes, and the account shall be separate from any of the lawyer's personal or other accounts.

(4) All records relating to property other than cash received by a lawyer in a fiduciary capacity shall be maintained and preserved. The records must describe with specificity the identity and location of such property.

(5) All billing records reflecting fees charged and other billings to clients or other parties must be maintained and preserved.

(6) Cash receipts and cash disbursement journals must be maintained and preserved for each bank account for the purpose of recording fiduciary and non-fiduciary transactions. A lawyer using a manual system for such purposes must total and balance the transaction columns on a monthly basis.

(7) A monthly reconciliation for each bank account, matching totals from the cash receipts and cash disbursement journals with the ending check register balance, must be performed. The reconciliation procedures, however, shall not be required for lawyers using a computer accounting system or a general ledger.

(8) The check register balance for each bank account must be reconciled monthly to the bank statement balance.

(9) With respect to all fiduciary accounts:

(A) A subsidiary ledger must be maintained and preserved with a separate account for each client or third party in which cash receipts and cash disbursement transactions and monthly balances are recorded.

(B) Monthly listings of client or third party balances must be prepared showing the name and balance of each client or third party, and the total of all balances.

(C) No funds disbursed for a client or third party must be in excess of funds received from that client or third party. If, however, through error funds disbursed for a client or third party exceed funds received from that client or third party, the lawyer shall transfer funds from the non-fiduciary account in a timely manner to cover the excess disbursement.

(D) The reconciled total cash balance must agree with the total of the client or third party balance listing. There shall be no unidentified client or third party funds. The bank reconciliation for a fiduciary account is not complete unless there is agreement with the total of client or third party accounts.

(E) If a check has been issued in an attempt to disburse funds, but remains outstanding (that is, the check has not cleared the trust or escrow bank account) six months or more from the date it was issued, a lawyer shall promptly take steps to contact the payee to determine the reason the check was not deposited by the payee, and shall issue a replacement check, as necessary and appropriate. With regard to abandoned or unclaimed trust funds, a lawyer shall comply with requirements of Supreme Court Rule 73.

(F) No funds of the lawyer shall be placed in or left in the account except as provided in Rule 1.15(a).

(G) No funds which should have been disbursed shall remain in the account, including, but not limited to, earned legal fees, which must be transferred to the lawyer's non-fiduciary account on a prompt and timely basis when earned.

(H) When a separate real estate bank account is maintained for settlement transactions, and when client or third party funds are received but not yet disbursed, a listing must be prepared on a monthly basis showing the name of the client or third party, the balance due to each client or third party, and the total of all such balances. The total must agree with the reconciled cash balance.

(10) If a lawyer maintains financial books and records using a computer system, the lawyer must cause to be printed each month a hard copy of all monthly journals, ledgers, reports, and reconciliations, and/or cause to be created each month an electronic backup of these documents to be stored in such a manner as to make them accessible for re-view by the lawyer and/or the auditor for the Lawyers' Fund for Client Protection.

(e) A lawyer's financial books and records must be subject to examination by the auditor for the Lawyers'

Fund for Client Protection, for the purpose of verifying the accuracy of a certificate of compliance filed each year by the lawyer pursuant to Supreme Court Rule 69. The examination must be conducted so as to preserve, insofar as is consistent with these Rules, the confidential nature of the lawyer's books and records. If the lawyer's books and records are not located in Delaware, the lawyer may have the option either to produce the books and records at the lawyer's office in Delaware or to produce the books and records at the location outside of Delaware where they are ordinarily located. If the production occurs outside of Delaware, the lawyer shall pay any additional expenses incurred by the auditor for the purposes of an examination.

(f) A lawyer holding client funds must initially and reasonably determine whether the funds should or should not be placed in an interest-bearing depository account for the benefit of the client. In making such a determination, the lawyer must consider the financial interests of the client, the costs of establishing and maintaining the account, any tax reporting procedures or requirements, the nature of the transaction involved, the likelihood of delay in the relevant proceedings, whether the funds are of a nominal amount, and whether the funds are expected to be held by the lawyer for a short period of time. A lawyer must at reasonable intervals consider whether changed circumstances would warrant a different determination with respect to the deposit of client funds. Except as provided in these Rules, interest earned on client funds placed into an interest-bearing depository account for the benefit of the client (less any deductions for ser-vice charges or other fees of the depository institution) shall belong to the client whose funds are deposited, and the lawyer shall have no right or claim to such interest.

(g) A lawyer holding client funds who has reasonably determined, pursuant to subsection (f) of this Rule, that such funds need not be deposited into an interest-bearing depository account for the benefit of the client must maintain a pooled interest-bearing depository account for the deposit of the funds; provided, however, that this requirement shall not apply to a lawyer who either has obtained inactive status pursuant to Supreme Court Rule 69(d), or has obtained a Certificate of Retirement pursuant to Supreme Court Rule 69(f), or has formally elected to opt out of this requirement in accordance with the procedure set forth below in subparagraph (k).

(h) A lawyer who maintains such a pooled account shall comply with the following:

(1) The account shall include only client's funds which are nominal amount or are expected to be held for a short period of time.

(2) No interest from such an account shall be made available to a lawyer or law firm.

(3) Lawyers or law firms depositing client funds in a pooled interest-bearing account under this paragraph (h) [(g)] shall direct the depository institution:

(a) To remit interest, net any service charges or fees, as computed in accordance with the institution's standard ac-counting practice, at least quarterly, to the Delaware Bar Foundation; and

(b) To transmit with each remittance to the Delaware Bar Foundation a statement showing the name of the lawyer or law firm on whose accounting remittance is sent and the rate of interest applied; with a copy of statement to be transmitted to the lawyer or law firm by the Delaware Bar Foundation.

(i) The funds transmitted to the Delaware Bar Foundation shall be available for distribution for the following purposes:

(1) To improve the administration of justice;

(2) To provide and to enhance the delivery of legal services to the poor;

(3) To support law related education;

(4) For each other purposes that serve the public interest.

The Delaware Bar Foundation shall recommend for the approval of the Supreme Court of the State of Delaware, such distributions as it may deem appropriate. Distributions shall be made only upon the Court's approval.

(j) Lawyers or law firms, depositing client funds in a pooled interest-bearing depository account under this paragraph shall not be required to advise the client of such deposit or of the purposes to which the interest accumulated by reason of such deposits is to be directed.

(k) The procedure available for opting out of the requirement to maintain pooled interest-bearing accounts are as follows:

(1) Prior to December 15, 1983, a lawyer wishing to

decline to maintain a pooled interest-bearing account[s] de-scribed in this paragraph for any calendar year may do so by submitting a Notice of Declination in writing to the Clerk of the Supreme Court ab initio or before December 15 of the preceding calendar year. Any such submission shall re-main effective, unless revoked and need not be renewed for any ensuing year.

(2) Any lawyer who has not filed a Notice of Declination on or before December 15, 1983, may elect not to maintain a pooled interest-bearing depository account for client funds as required and instead to maintain a pooled depository account for such funds that does not bear interest or that bears interest solely for the benefit of the clients who de-posited the funds by certifying that the lawyer or law firm opts out of the obligation to comply with the requirements by timely submission of the Annual Registration Statement required by Supreme Court Rule 69(b)(i). Any such certification shall release the lawyer or law firm submitting it from participation effective as of the date that the certification is submitted and it shall remain effective until revoked as set forth below without need for renewal for any ensuing year.

(3) Notwithstanding the foregoing provisions of this subparagraph, any lawyer or law firm may petition the Court at any time and, for good cause shown, may be granted leave to opt out of the obligation to comply with the mandatory requirements of this paragraph.

(l) An election to opt out of the obligation to comply with paragraph (h) hereof may be revoked at any time upon the opening by a non-participating lawyer or law firm of a pooled interest-bearing account as previously described and due notification thereof to the Court Administrator of the Supreme Court pursuant to Supreme Court Rule 69(g).

(m) A lawyer shall not disburse fiduciary funds from a bank account unless the funds deposited in the lawyer's fi-duciary account to be disbursed, or the funds which are in the lawyer's unrestricted possession and control and are or will be timely deposited, are good funds as hereinafter defined. "Good funds" shall mean:

(1) cash;

(2) electronic fund ("wire") transfer;

(3) certified check;

(4) bank cashier's check or treasurer's check;

(5) U.S. Treasury or State of Delaware Treasury check;

(6) Check drawn on a separate trust or escrow account of an attorney engaged in the private practice of law in the State of Delaware held in a fiduciary capacity, including his or her client's funds;

(7) Check of an insurance company that is authorized by the Insurance Commissioner of Delaware to transact insurance business in Delaware;

(8) Check in an amount no greater than $10,000.00;

(9) Check greater than $10,000.00, which has been actually and finally collected and may be drawn against under federal or state banking regulations then in effect;

(10) Check drawn on an escrow account of a real estate broker licensed by the state of Delaware up to the limit of guarantee provided per transaction by statute.

Rule 1.15A. Trust account overdraft notification

(a) Every attorney practicing or admitted to practice in this jurisdiction shall designate every account into which attorney trust or escrow funds are deposited either as 'Rule 1.15A Attorney Trust Account' or '1.15A Trust Account' or 'Rule 1.15A Attorney Escrow Account' or '1.15A Escrow Account,' pursuant to Rule 1.15(d)(2).

(b) Bank accounts designated as 'Rule 1.15A Attorney Trust Account' or '1.15A Trust Account' or 'Rule 1.15A Attorney Escrow Account' or '1.15A Escrow Account,' pursuant to Rule 1.15(d)(2) shall be maintained only in financial institutions approved by the Lawyers' Fund for Client Protection (the "Fund").

(c) The Supreme Court may establish rules governing approval and termination of approved status for financial institutions and the Fund shall annually publish a list of approved financial institutions. No trust or escrow account shall be maintained in any financial institution that does not agree to make such reports. Any such agreement shall apply to all branches of the financial institution and shall not be canceled except upon thirty (30) days notice in writing to the Fund.

(d) The overdraft notification agreement shall provide that all reports made by the financial institution shall be in the following format:

(1) In the case of a dishonored instrument, the report shall be identical to the overdraft notice customarily forwarded to the depositor, and shall include a copy of the dishonored instrument to the ODC no later than seven (7) calendar days following a request for the copy by the ODC.

(2) In the case of instruments that are presented against insufficient funds, but which instruments are honored, the report shall identify the financial institution, the attorney or law firm, the account number, the date of presentation for payment, and the date paid, as well as the amount of the overdraft created thereby.

(e) Reports shall be made simultaneously with, and within the time provided by law for, notice of dishonor. If an instrument presented against insufficient funds is honored, then the report shall be made within seven (7) calendar days of the date of presentation for payment against insufficient funds.

(f) Every attorney practicing or admitted to practice in this jurisdiction shall, as a condition thereof, be conclusively deemed to have consented to the reporting and production requirements mandated by this rule.

(g) Nothing herein shall preclude a financial institution from charging a particular attorney or law firm for the reasonable costs of producing the reports and records required by this rule.

(h) The terms used in this section are defined as follows:

(1) "Financial institution" includes banks, savings and loan associations, credit unions, savings banks and any other business or persons which accept for deposit funds held in trust by attorneys.

(2) "Properly payable" refers to an instrument which, if presented in the normal course of business, is in a form requiring payment under the laws of Delaware.

(3) "Notice of dishonor" refers to the notice which a financial institution is required to give, under the laws of Delaware, upon presentation of an instrument which the institution dishonors.

Rule 1.16. Declining or terminating representation

(a) Except as stated in paragraph (c), a lawyer shall not represent a client or, where representation has commenced, shall withdraw from the representation of a client if:

(1) the representation will result in violation of the rules of professional conduct or other law;

(2) the lawyer's physical or mental condition materially impairs the lawyer's ability to represent the client; or

(3) the lawyer is discharged.

(b) Except as stated in paragraph (c), a lawyer may withdraw from representing a client if:

(1) withdrawal can be accomplished without material adverse effect on the interests of the client;

(2) the client persists in a course of action involving the lawyer's services that the lawyer reasonably believes is criminal or fraudulent;

(3) the client has used the lawyer's service to perpetrate a crime or fraud;

(4) a client insists upon taking action that the lawyer considers repugnant or with which the lawyer has a fundamental disagreement;

(5) the client fails substantially to fulfill an obligation to the lawyer regarding the lawyer's services and has been given reasonable warning that the lawyer will withdraw unless the obligation is fulfilled;

(6) the representation will result in an unreasonable financial burden on the lawyer or has been rendered unreasonably difficult by the client; or

(7) other good cause for withdrawal exists.

(c) A lawyer must comply with applicable law requiring notice to or permission of a tribunal when terminating a representation. When ordered to do so by a tribunal, a lawyer shall continue representation notwithstanding good cause for terminating the representation.

(d) Upon termination of representation, a lawyer shall take steps to the extent reasonably practicable to protect a client's interests, such as giving reasonable notice to the client, allowing time for employment of other counsel, surrendering papers and property to which the client is entitled and refunding any advance payment of fee or expense that has not been earned or incurred. The lawyer may retain papers relating to the client to the extent permitted by other law.

Rule 1.17. Sale of law practice

A lawyer or a law firm may sell or purchase a law practice, or an area of law practice, including good will, if the following conditions are satisfied:

(a) The seller ceases to engage in the private practice of law, or in the area of practice that has been sold in the jurisdiction in which the practice has been conducted;

(b) The entire practice, or the entire area of practice, is sold to one or more lawyers or law firms;

(c) The seller gives written notice to each of the seller's clients regarding:

(1) the proposed sale;

(2) the client's right to retain other counsel or to take possession of the file; and

(3) the client's consent to the transfer of the client's files will be presumed if the client does not take any action or does not otherwise object within ninety (90) days of receipt of the notice.

In a matter of pending litigation, if a client cannot be given notice, the representation of that client may be transferred to the purchaser only upon entry of an order so authorizing by a court having jurisdiction. The seller may disclose to the court in camera information relating to the representation only to the extent necessary to obtain an order authorizing the transfer of a file. If approval of the substitution of the purchasing lawyer for the selling lawyer is required by the rules of any tribunal in which a matter is pending, such approval must be obtained before the matter can be included in the sale.

(d) The fees charged clients shall not be increased by reason of the sale.

Rule 1.18. Duties to prospective client

(a) A person who discusses with a lawyer the possibility of forming a client-lawyer relationship with respect to a matter is a prospective client.

(b) Even when no client-lawyer relationship ensues, a lawyer who has had discussions with a prospective client shall not use or reveal information learned in the consultation, except as Rule 1.9 would permit with respect to information of a former client.

(c) A lawyer subject to paragraph (b) shall not represent a client with interests materially adverse to those of a prospective client in the same or a substantially related matter if the lawyer received information from the prospective client that could be significantly harmful to that person in the matter, except as provided in paragraph (d). If a lawyer is disqualified from representation under this paragraph, no lawyer in a firm with which that lawyer is associated may knowingly undertake or continue representation in such a matter, except as provided in paragraph (d).

(d) When the lawyer has received disqualifying information as defined in paragraph (c), representation is permissible if:

(1) both the affected client and the prospective client have given informed consent, confirmed in writing, or:

(2) the lawyer who received the information took reasonable measures to avoid exposure to more disqualifying in-formation than was reasonably necessary to determine whether to represent the prospective client; and

(i) the disqualified lawyer is timely screened from any participation in the matter and is apportioned no part of the fee therefrom; and

(ii) written notice is promptly given to the prospective client.

Rule 2.1. Advisor

In representing a client, a lawyer shall exercise independent professional judgment and render candid advice. In rendering advice, a lawyer may refer not only to law but to other considerations, such as moral, economic, social and political factors, that may be relevant to the client's situation.

Rule 2.2. Intermediary (Deleted)

Rule 2.3. Evaluation for use by third persons

(a) A lawyer may provide an evaluation of a matter affecting a client for the use of someone other than the client if the lawyer reasonably believes that making the evaluation is compatible with other aspects of the lawyer's relationship with the client.

(b) When the lawyer knows or reasonably should know that the evaluation is likely to affect the client's interests materially and adversely, the lawyer shall not provide the evaluation unless the client gives informed consent.

(c) Except as disclosure is authorized in connection

with a report of an evaluation, information relating to the evaluation is otherwise protected by Rule 1.6.

Rule 2.4. Lawyer serving as third-party neutral

(a) A lawyer serves as a third-party neutral when the lawyer assists two or more persons who are not clients of the lawyer to reach a resolution of a dispute or other matter that has arisen between them. Service as a third-party neutral may include service as an arbitrator, a mediator or in such other capacity as will enable the lawyer to assist the parties to resolve the matter.

(b) A lawyer serving as a third-party neutral shall inform unrepresented parties that the lawyer is not representing them. When the lawyer knows or reasonably should know that a party does not understand the lawyer's role in the matter, the lawyer shall explain the difference between the lawyer's role as a third-party neutral and a lawyer's role as one who represents a client.

Rule 3.1. Meritorious claims and contentions

A lawyer shall not bring or defend a proceeding, or assert or controvert an issue therein, unless there is a basis in law and fact for doing so that is not frivolous, which includes a good faith argument for an extension, modification or reversal of existing law. A lawyer for the defendant in a criminal proceeding, or the respondent in a proceeding that could result in incarceration, may nevertheless so defend the proceeding as to require that every element of the case be established.

Rule 3.2. Expediting litigation

A lawyer shall make reasonable efforts to expedite litigation consistent with the interests of the client.

Rule 3.3. Candor toward the tribunal

(a) A lawyer shall not knowingly:

(1) make a false statement of fact or law to a tribunal or fail to correct a false statement of material fact or law previously made to the tribunal by the lawyer;

(2) fail to disclose to the tribunal legal authority in the controlling jurisdiction known to the lawyer to be directly adverse to the position of the client and not disclosed by opposing counsel; or

(3) offer evidence that the lawyer knows to be false. If a lawyer, the lawyer's client, or a witness called by the lawyer, has offered material evidence and the lawyer

comes to know of its falsity, the lawyer shall take reasonable remedial measures, including, if necessary, disclosure to the tribunal. A lawyer may refuse to offer evidence, other than the testimony of a defendant in a criminal matter, that the lawyer reasonably believes is false.

(b) A lawyer who represents a client in an adjudicative proceeding and who knows that a person intends to engage, is engaging or has engaged in criminal or fraudulent conduct related to the proceeding shall take reasonable remedial measures, including, if necessary, disclosure to the tribunal.

(c) The duties stated in paragraph (a) and (b) continue to the conclusion of the proceeding, and apply even if compliance requires disclosure of information otherwise protected by Rule 1.6.

(d) In an ex parte proceeding, a lawyer shall inform the tribunal of all material facts known to the lawyer which will enable the tribunal to make an informed decision, whether or not the facts are adverse.

Rule 3.4. Fairness to opposing party and counsel

A lawyer shall not:

(a) unlawfully obstruct another party's access to evidence or unlawfully alter, destroy or conceal a document or other material having potential evidentiary value. A lawyer shall not counsel or assist another person to do any such act;

(b) falsify evidence, counsel or assist a witness to testify falsely, or offer an inducement to a witness that is prohibited by law.

(c) knowingly disobey an obligation under the rules of a tribunal, except for an open refusal based on an assertion that no valid obligation exists;

(d) in pretrial procedure, make a frivolous discovery request or fail to make reasonably diligent efforts to comply with a legally proper discovery request by an opposing party;

(e) in trial, allude to any matter that the lawyer does not reasonably believe is relevant or that will not be supported by admissible evidence, assert personal knowledge of facts in issue except when testifying as a witness, or state a personal opinion as to the justness of a cause, the credibility of a witness, the culpability of a civil litigant or the guilt or innocence of an accused; or

(f) request a person other than a client to refrain from voluntarily giving relevant information to another party unless:

(1) the person is a relative or an employee or other agent of a client; and

(2) the lawyer reasonably believes that the person's interests will not be adversely affected by refraining from giving such information.

Rule 3.5. Impartiality and decorum of the tribunal

A lawyer shall not:

(a) seek to influence a judge, juror, prospective juror or other official by means prohibited by law;

(b) communicate or cause another to communicate ex parte with such a person or members of such person's family during the proceeding unless authorized to do so by law or court order; or

(c) communicate with a juror or prospective juror after discharge of the jury unless the communication is permitted by court rule;

(d) engage in conduct intended to disrupt a tribunal or engage in undignified or discourteous conduct that is de-grading to a tribunal.

Rule 3.6. Trial publicity

(a) A lawyer who is participating or has participated in the investigation or litigation of a matter shall not make an extrajudicial statement that the lawyer knows or reasonably should know will be disseminated by means of public communication and will have a substantial likelihood of materially prejudicing an adjudicative proceeding in the matter.

(b) Notwithstanding paragraph (a), a lawyer may state:

(1) the claim, offense or defense involved and, except when prohibited by law, the identity of the persons involved;

(2) information contained in a public record;

(3) that an investigation of a matter is in progress;

(4) the scheduling or result of any step in litigation;

(5) a request for assistance in obtaining evidence and information necessary thereto;

(6) a warning of danger concerning the behavior of a person involved, when there is reason to believe that

there exists the likelihood of substantial harm to an individual or to the public interest; and

(7) in a criminal case, in addition to subparagraphs (1) through (6):

(i) the identity, residence, occupation and family status of the accused;

(ii) if the accused has not been apprehended, information necessary to aid in apprehension of that person;

(iii) the fact, time and place of arrest; and

(iv) the identity of investigating and arresting officers or agencies and the length of the investigation.

(c) Notwithstanding paragraph (a), a lawyer may make a statement that a reasonable lawyer would believe is required to protect a client from the substantial undue prejudicial effect of recent publicity not initiated by the lawyer or the lawyer's client. A statement made pursuant to this paragraph shall be limited to such information as is necessary to mitigate the recent adverse publicity.

(d) No lawyer associated in a firm or government agency with a lawyer subject to paragraph (a) shall make a statement prohibited by paragraph (a).

Rule 3.7. Lawyer as witness

(a) A lawyer shall not act as advocate at a trial in which the lawyer is likely to be a necessary witness unless:

(1) the testimony relates to an uncontested issue;

(2) the testimony relates to the nature and value of legal services rendered in the case; or

(3) disqualification of the lawyer would work substantial hardship on the client.

(b) A lawyer may act as advocate in a trial in which another lawyer in the lawyer's firm is likely to be called as a witness unless precluded from doing so by Rule 1.7 or Rule 1.9.

Rule 3.8. Special responsibilities of a prosecutor

The prosecutor in a criminal case shall:

(a) refrain from prosecuting a charge that the prosecutor knows is not supported by probable cause;

(b) make reasonable efforts to assure that the accused has been advised of the right to, and the procedure for obtaining, counsel and has been given reasonable opportunity to obtain counsel;

(c) not seek to obtain from an unrepresented accused a waiver of important pretrial rights, such as the right to a preliminary hearing;

(d) (1) make timely disclosure to the defense of all evidence or information known to the prosecutor that tends to negate the guilt of the accused or mitigates the offense, and, in connection with sentencing, disclose to the defense and to the tribunal all unprivileged mitigating information known to the prosecutor, except when the prosecutor is relieved of this responsibility by a protective order of the tribunal;

(2) when the prosecutor comes to know of new, credible and material evidence establishing that a convicted defendant did not commit the offense for which the defendant was convicted, the prosecutor shall, unless a court authorizes delay, make timely disclosure of that evidence to the convicted defendant and any appropriate court, or, where the conviction was obtained outside the prosecutor's jurisdiction, to the chief prosecutor of the jurisdiction where the conviction occurred;

(e) not subpoena a lawyer in a grand jury or other criminal proceeding to present evidence about a past or present client unless the prosecutor reasonably believes:

(1) the information sought is not protected from disclosure by any applicable privilege;

(2) the evidence sought is essential to the successful completion of an ongoing investigation or prosecution; and

(3) there is no other feasible alternative to obtain the information;

(f) except for statements that are necessary to inform the public of the nature and extent of the prosecutor's action and that serve a legitimate law enforcement purpose, refrain from making extrajudicial comments that have a substantial likelihood of heightening public condemnation of the accused and exercise reasonable care to prevent investigators, law enforcement personnel, employees or other persons assisting or associated with the prosecutor in a criminal case from making an extrajudicial statement that the prosecutor would be prohibited from making under Rule 3.6 or this Rule.

Rule 3.9. Advocate in nonadjudicative proceedings

A lawyer representing a client before a legislative body or administrative agency in a nonadjudicative proceeding shall disclose that the appearance is in a representative capacity and shall conform to the provisions of Rules 3.3(a) through (c), 3.4(a) through(c) and 3.5(a) and (c).

Rule 3.10. Communication with or investigation of jurors (Deleted)

Rule 4.1. Truthfulness in statements to others

In the course of representing a client a lawyer shall not knowingly:

(a) make a false statement of material fact or law to a third person; or

(b) fail to disclose a material fact when disclosure is necessary to avoid assisting a criminal or fraudulent act by a client, unless disclosure is prohibited by Rule 1.6.

Rule 4.2. Communication with person represented by counsel

In representing a client, a lawyer shall not communicate about the subject of the representation with a person the lawyer knows to be represented by another lawyer in the matter, unless the lawyer has the consent of the other lawyer or is authorized to do so by law or a court order.

Rule 4.3. Dealing with unrepresented person

In dealing on behalf of a client with a person who is not represented by counsel, a lawyer shall not state or imply that the lawyer is disinterested. When the lawyer knows or reasonably should know that the unrepresented person misunderstands the lawyer's role in the matter, the lawyer shall make reasonable efforts to correct the misunderstanding. The lawyer shall not give legal advice to an unrepresented person, other than the advice to secure counsel, if the lawyer knows or reasonably should know that the interests of such a person are or have a reasonable possibility of being in conflict with the interests of the client.

Rule 4.4. Respect for rights of third persons

(a) In representing a client, a lawyer shall not use means that have no substantial purpose other than to embarrass, delay or burden a third person, or use methods of obtaining evidence that violate the legal rights of such a person.

(b) A lawyer who receives a document relating to the representation of the lawyer's client and knows or reasonably should know that the document was inadvertently sent shall promptly notify the sender.

Rule 5.1. Responsibilities of partners, managers, and supervisory lawyers

(a) A partner in a law firm, and a lawyer who individually or together with other lawyers possesses comparable managerial authority in a law firm, shall make reasonable efforts to ensure that the firm has in effect measures giving reason-able assurance that all lawyers in the firm conform to the Rules of Professional Conduct.

(b) A lawyer having direct supervisory authority over another lawyer shall make reasonable efforts to ensure that the other lawyer conforms to the Rules of Professional Conduct.

(c) A lawyer shall be responsible for another lawyer's violation of the Rules of Professional Conduct if:

(1) the lawyer orders or, with knowledge of the specific conduct, ratifies the conduct involved; or

(2) the lawyer is a partner or has comparable managerial authority in the law firm in which the other lawyer practices, or has direct supervisory authority over the other lawyer, and knows of the conduct at a time when its consequences can be avoided or mitigated but fails to take reasonable remedial action.

Rule 5.2. Responsibilities of a subordinate lawyer

(a) A lawyer is bound by the Rules of Professional Conduct notwithstanding that the lawyer acted at the direction of another person.

(b) A subordinate lawyer does not violate the Rules of Professional Conduct if that lawyer acts in accordance with a supervisory lawyer's reasonable resolution of an arguable question of professional duty.

Rule 5.3. Responsibilities regarding non-lawyer assistants

With respect to a nonlawyer employed or retained by or associated with a lawyer:

(a) a partner in a law firm, and a lawyer who individually or together with other lawyers possesses comparable managerial authority in a law firm, shall make reasonable efforts to ensure that the firm has in effect measures giving reasonable assurance that the person's conduct is compatible with the professional obligations of the lawyer;

(b) a lawyer having direct supervisory authority over

the nonlawyer shall make reasonable efforts to ensure that the person's conduct is compatible with the professional obligations of the lawyer; and

(c) a lawyer shall be responsible for conduct of such a person that would be a violation of the Rules of Professional Conduct if engaged in by a lawyer if:

(1) the lawyer orders or, with the knowledge of the specific conduct, ratifies the conduct involved; or

(2) the lawyer is a partner or has comparable managerial authority in the law firm in which the person is employed, or has direct supervisory authority over the person, and knows of the conduct at a time when its consequences can be avoided or mitigated but fails to take reasonable remedial action.

Rule 5.4. Professional independence of a lawyer

(a) A lawyer or law firm shall not share legal fees with a nonlawyer, except that:

(1) an agreement by a lawyer with the lawyer's firm, partner, or associate may provide for the payment of money, over a reasonable period of time after the lawyer's death, to the lawyer's estate or to one or more specified persons;

(2) a lawyer who undertakes to complete unfinished legal business of a deceased lawyer may pay to the estate of the deceased lawyer that proportion of the total compensation which fairly represents the services rendered by the de-ceased lawyer;

(3) a lawyer who purchases the practice of a deceased, disabled, or disappeared lawyer may, pursuant to the provisions of Rule 1.17, pay to the estate or other representative of that lawyer the agreed-upon purchase price;

(4) a lawyer or law firm may include nonlawyer employees in a compensation or retirement plan, even though the plan is based in whole or in part on a profit-sharing arrangement; and

(5) a lawyer may share court-awarded legal fees with a nonprofit organization that employed, retained or recommended employment of the lawyer in the matter.

(b) A lawyer shall not form a partnership with a nonlawyer if any of the activities of the partnership consist of the practice of law.

(c) A lawyer shall not permit a person who recommends,

employs, or pays the lawyer to render legal services for another to direct or regulate the lawyer's professional judgment in rendering such legal services.

(d) A lawyer shall not practice with or in the form of a professional corporation or association authorized to practice law for a profit, if:

(1) a nonlawyer owns any interest therein, except that a fiduciary representative of the estate of a lawyer may hold the stock or interest of the lawyer for a reasonable time during administration;

(2) a nonlawyer is a corporate director or officer thereof or occupies the position of similar responsibility in any form of association other than a corporation; or

(3) a nonlawyer has the right to direct or control the professional judgment of a lawyer.

Rule 5.5. Unauthorized practice of law; multijurisdictional practice of law

(a) A lawyer shall not practice law in a jurisdiction in violation of the regulation of the legal profession in that jurisdiction, or assist another in doing so.

(b) A lawyer who is not admitted to practice in this jurisdiction shall not:

(1) except as authorized by these Rules or other law, establish an office or other systematic and continuous presence in this jurisdiction for the practice of law; or

(2) hold out to the public or otherwise represent that the lawyer is admitted to practice law in this jurisdiction.

(c) A lawyer admitted in another United States jurisdiction or in a foreign jurisdiction, and not disbarred or suspended from practice in any jurisdiction, may provide legal services on a temporary basis in this jurisdiction that:

(1) are undertaken in association with a lawyer who is admitted to practice in this jurisdiction and who actively participates in the matter;

(2) are in or reasonably related to a pending or potential proceeding before a tribunal in this or another jurisdiction, if the lawyer, or a person the lawyer is assisting, is authorized by law or order to appear in such proceeding or reasonably expects to be so authorized;

(3) are in or reasonably related to a pending or potential arbitration, mediation, or other alternative

dispute resolution proceeding in this or another jurisdiction, if the services arise out of or are reasonably related to the lawyer's practice in a jurisdiction in which the lawyer is admitted to practice and are not services for which the forum requires pro hac vice admission; or

(4) are not within paragraphs (c)(2) or (c)(3) and arise out of or are reasonably related to the lawyer's practice in a jurisdiction in which the lawyer is admitted to practice.

(d) A lawyer admitted in another United States jurisdiction, or in a foreign jurisdiction, and not disbarred or suspended from practice in any jurisdiction, may provide legal services in this jurisdiction that:

(1) are provided to the lawyer's employer or its organizational affiliates after compliance with Supreme Court Rule 55.1(a)(1) and are not services for which the forum requires pro hac vice admission; or

(2) are services that the lawyer is authorized to provide by federal law or other law of this jurisdiction.

Rule 5.6. Restrictions on right to practice

A lawyer shall not participate in offering or making:

(a) a partnership, shareholders, operating, employment, or other similar type of agreement that restricts the rights of a lawyer to practice after termination of the relationship, except an agreement concerning benefits upon retirement; or

(b) an agreement in which a restriction on the lawyer's right to practice is part of the settlement of a client controversy.

Rule 5.7. Responsibilities regarding law-related services

(a) A lawyer shall be subject to the Rules of Professional Conduct with respect to the provision of law-related ser-vices, as defined in paragraph (b), if the law-related services are provided:

(1) by the lawyer in circumstances that are not distinct from the lawyer's provision of legal services to clients; or

(2) in other circumstances by an entity controlled by the lawyer individually or with others if the lawyer fails to take reasonable measures to assure that a person obtaining the law-related services knows that the ser-

vices are not legal services and that the protections of the client-lawyer relationship do not exist.

(b) The term "law-related services" denotes services that might reasonably be performed in conjunction with and in substance are related to the provision of legal services, and that are not prohibited as unauthorized practice of law when provided by a nonlawyer.

Rule 6.1. Voluntary pro bono publico service

A lawyer should render public interest legal service. A lawyer may discharge this responsibility by providing professional services at no fee or a reduced fee to persons of limited means or to public service or charitable groups or organizations, by service in activities for improving the law, the legal system or the legal profession, and by financial support for organizations that provide legal services to persons of limited means.

Rule 6.2. Accepting appointments

A lawyer shall not seek to avoid appointment by a tribunal to represent a person except for good cause, such as:

(a) representing the client is likely to result in violation of the Rules of Professional Conduct or other law;

(b) representing the client is likely to result in an unreasonable financial burden on the lawyer; or

(c) the client or the cause is so repugnant to the lawyer as to be likely to impair the client-lawyer relationship or the lawyer's ability to represent the client.

Rule 6.3. Membership in legal services organization

A lawyer may serve as a director, officer or member of a legal services organization, apart from the law firm in which the lawyer practices, notwithstanding that the organization serves persons having interests adverse to a client of the lawyer. The lawyer shall not knowingly participate in a decision or action of the organization:

(a) if participating in the decision or action would be incompatible with the lawyer's obligations to a client under Rule 1.7; or

(b) where the decision or action could have a material adverse effect on the representation of a client of the organization whose interests are adverse to a client of the lawyer.

Rule 6.4. Law reform activities affecting client interests

A lawyer may serve as a director, officer or member of an organization involved in reform of the law or its administration notwithstanding that the reform may affect the interests of a client of the lawyer. When the lawyer knows that the interests of a client may be materially benefitted by a decision in which the lawyer participates, the lawyer shall disclose that fact but need not identify the client.

Rule 6.5. Non-profit and court-annexed limited legal-service programs

(a) A lawyer who, under the auspices of a program sponsored by a nonprofit organization or court, provides short-term limited legal services to a client without expectation by either the lawyer or the client that the lawyer will provide continuing representation in the matter:

(1) is subject to Rules 1.7 and 1.9(a) only if the lawyer knows that the representation of the client involves a conflict of interest; and

(2) is subject to Rule 1.10 only if the lawyer knows that another lawyer associated with the lawyer in a law firm is disqualified by Rule 1.7 or 1.9(a) with respect to the matter.

(b) Except as provided in paragraph (a)(2), Rule 1.10 is inapplicable to a representation governed by this Rule.

Rule 7.1. Communications concerning a lawyer's services

A lawyer shall not make a false or misleading communication about the lawyer or the lawyer's services. A communication is false or misleading if it contains a material misrepresentation of fact or law, or omits a fact necessary to make the statement considered as a whole not materially misleading.

Rule 7.2. Advertising

(a) Subject to the requirements of Rules 7.1 and 7.3, a lawyer may advertise services through written, recorded or electronic communication, including public media.

(b) Except as permitted by Rule 1.5(e), a lawyer shall not give anything of value to a person for recommending the lawyer's services except that a lawyer may

(1) pay the reasonable costs of advertisements or communications permitted by this Rule;

(2) pay the usual charges of a legal service plan or a not-for-profit or qualified lawyer referral service. A qualified lawyer referral service is a lawyer referral service that has been approved by an appropriate regulatory authority; and

(3) pay for a law practice in accordance with Rule 1.17.

(c) Any communication made pursuant to this rule shall include the name and office address of at least one lawyer or law firm responsible for its content.

Rule 7.3. Direct contact with prospective clients

(a) A lawyer shall not by in-person, live telephone or real-time electronic contact solicit professional employment from a prospective client when a significant motive for the lawyer's doing so is the lawyer's pecuniary gain, unless the person contacted:

(1) is a lawyer; or

(2) has a family, close personal, or prior professional relationship with the lawyer.

(b) A lawyer shall not solicit professional employment from a prospective client by written, recorded or electronic communication or by in-person, telephone or real-time electronic contact even when not otherwise prohibited by paragraph (a), if:

(1) the prospective client has made known to the lawyer a desire not to be solicited by the lawyer; or

(2) the solicitation involves coercion, duress or harassment.

(c) Every written, recorded or electronic communication from a lawyer soliciting professional employment from a prospective client known to be in need of legal services in a particular matter shall include the words "Advertising Material" on the outside envelope, if any, and at the beginning and ending of any recorded or electronic communication, unless the recipient of the communication is a person specified in paragraphs (a)(1) or (a)(2).

(d) Notwithstanding the prohibitions in paragraph (a), a lawyer may participate with a prepaid or group legal ser-vice plan operated by an organization not owned or directed by the lawyer that uses in-person or telephone contact to solicit memberships or subscriptions for the plan from persons who are not known to need legal services in a particular matter covered by the plan.

Rule 7.4. Communication of fields of practice and specialization

(a) A lawyer may communicate the fact that the lawyer does or does not practice in particular fields of law.

(b) A lawyer admitted to engage in patent practice before the United States Patent and Trademark Office may use the designation "Patent Attorney" or a substantially similar designation;

(c) A lawyer engaged in Admiralty practice may use the designation "Admiralty," "Proctor in Admiralty" or a substantially similar designation.

(d) A lawyer shall not state or imply that a lawyer is certified as a specialist in a particular field of law, unless:

(1) the lawyer has been certified as a specialist by an organization that has been approved by an appropriate state authority or that has been accredited by the American Bar Association; and

(2) the name of the certifying organization is clearly identified in the communication.

Rule 7.5. Firm names and letterheads

(a) A lawyer shall not use a firm name, letterhead or other professional designation that violates Rule 7.1. A trade name may be used by a lawyer in private practice if it does not imply a connection with a government agency or with a public or charitable legal services organization and is not otherwise in violation of Rule 7.1.

(b) A law firm with offices in more than one jurisdiction may use the same name or other professional designation in each jurisdiction, but identification of the lawyers in an office of the firm shall indicate the jurisdictional limitations on those not licensed to practice in the jurisdiction where the office is located.

(c) The name of a lawyer holding a public office shall not be used in the name of a law firm, or in communications on its behalf, during any substantial period in which the lawyer is not actively and regularly practicing with the firm.

(d) Lawyers may state or imply that they practice in a partnership or other organization only when that is the fact.

Rule 7.6. Political contributions to obtain government legal engagements or appointments by judges

A lawyer or law firm shall not accept a government legal engagement or an appointment by a judge if the lawyer or law firm makes a political contribution or solicits political contributions for the purpose of obtaining or being considered for that type of legal engagement or appointment.

Rule 8.1. Bar admission and disciplinary matters

An applicant for admission to the bar, or a lawyer in connection with a bar admission application or in connection with a disciplinary matter, shall not:

(a) knowingly make a false statement of material fact; or

(b) fail to disclose a fact necessary to correct a misapprehension known by the person to have arisen in the matter, or knowingly fail to respond to a lawful demand for information from an admission or disciplinary authority, except that this rule does not require disclosure of information otherwise protected by Rule 1.6.

Rule 8.2. Judicial and legal officials

(a) A lawyer shall not make a statement that the lawyer knows to be false or with reckless disregard as to its truth or falsity concerning the qualifications or integrity of a judge, adjudicatory officer or public legal officer, or a candidate for election or appointment to judicial or legal office.

(b) A lawyer who is a candidate for judicial office shall comply with the applicable provisions of the Code of Judicial Conduct.

Rule 8.3. Reporting professional misconduct

(a) A lawyer who knows that another lawyer has committed a violation of the rules of Professional Conduct that raises a substantial question as to that lawyer's honesty, trustworthiness or fitness as a lawyer in other respects, shall inform the appropriate professional authority.

(b) A lawyer who knows that a judge has committed a violation of applicable rules of judicial conduct that raises a substantial question as to the judge's fitness for office shall inform the appropriate authority.

(c) This Rule does not require disclosure of information otherwise protected by rule 1.6.

(d) Notwithstanding anything in this or other of the rules to the contrary, the relationship between members of either (i) the Lawyers Assistance Committee of the Delaware State Bar Association and counselors retained by the Bar Association, or (ii) the Professional Ethics Committee of the Delaware State Bar Association, or (iii) the Fee dispute Conciliation and Mediation Committee of the Delaware State Bar Association, or (iv) the Professional Guidance Committee of the Delaware State Bar Association, and a lawyer or a judge shall be the same as that of attorney and client.

Rule 8.4. Misconduct

It is professional misconduct for a lawyer to:

(a) violate or attempt to violate the Rules of Professional Conduct, knowingly assist or induce another to do so or do so through the acts of another;

(b) commit a criminal act that reflects adversely on the lawyer's honesty, trustworthiness or fitness as a lawyer in other respects;

(c) engage in conduct involving dishonesty, fraud, deceit or misrepresentation;

(d) engage in conduct that is prejudicial to the administration of justice;

(e) state or imply an ability to influence improperly a government agency or official or to achieve results by means that violate the Rules of Professional Conduct or other law; or

(f) knowingly assist a judge or judicial officer in conduct that is a violation of applicable rules of judicial conduct or other law.

Rule 8.5. Disciplinary authority; choice of law

(a) Disciplinary Authority. A lawyer admitted to practice in this jurisdiction is subject to the disciplinary authority of this jurisdiction, regardless of where the lawyer's conduct occurs. A lawyer not admitted in this jurisdiction is also subject to the disciplinary authority of this jurisdiction if the lawyer provides or offers to provide any legal services in this jurisdiction. A lawyer may be subject to the disciplinary authority of both this jurisdiction and another jurisdiction for the same conduct.

(b) Choice of Law. In any exercise of the disciplinary authority of this jurisdiction, the rules of professional conduct to be applied shall be as follows:

(1) for conduct in connection with a matter pending before a tribunal, the rules of the jurisdiction in which the tribunal sits, unless the rules of the tribunal provide otherwise; and

(2) for any other conduct, the rules of the jurisdiction in which the lawyer's conduct occurred, or, if the predominant effect of the conduct is in a different jurisdiction, the rules of that jurisdiction shall be applied to the conduct. A lawyer shall not be subject to discipline if the lawyer's conduct conforms to the rules of a jurisdiction in which the lawyer reasonably believes the predominant effect of the lawyer's conduct will occur.

CURRENT THROUGH: February 16, 2010.

Index

ACTIVISM
Confidentiality, **3:3**

ADMINISTRATION OF JUSTICE
Misconduct, **1:5**

ADVERTISING
Generally, **5:1 to 5:16**
Application of rule to advertising, **5:9**
Awareness of statements about you that are made by others, **5:12, 5:13**
Blogs, **5:5**
Conformance, inability to force, **5:14**
Controlling statements about you that are made by others, **5:11 to 5:14**
Copies of advertisements, **5:15**
Defined, **5:4, 5:5**
Disclaimers, **5:14**
Future of advertising, **5:16**
Lawyer rating sites, **5:13**
Other technicalities, **5:10**
Profiles, **5:4**
Reasons for advertising, **5:2**
Rules regarding advertising, generally, **5:3**
Text messages, **5:7**
Touchy trend - problems with posts, **5:8**
Trends regarding other advertisements, **5:6**

ADVISORY OPINIONS
Generally, **1:2, 1:3**

ANTICIPATION
Emerging affirmative duty to understand, anticipate and act, **8:7**

ASSISTANTS
Confidentiality, **3:5**

ATTORNEY-CLIENT RELATIONSHIP
Inadvertent establishment, **7:3**

BLOGS
Advertising, **5:5**
Confidentiality, **3:3**
Moderating comments, **5:11**

BUSINESS CARDS
Advertising, **5:6**

CHALLENGES
Generally, **1:3**

CLIENT INSTRUCTIONS
Future guidance, **9:9**

CLOUD COMPUTING
Generally, **8:1 to 8:10**
Consent of client, **8:8 to 8:10**
Emerging affirmative duty to understand, anticipate and act, **8:7**
Express instructions, consent of client, **8:10**
Fiduciary duty, **8:4**
Inadvertent vs. unauthorized disclosures, **8:6**
Questions to ask, **8:11**
Reasonable care standard, **8:3**
Sensitive information, consent of client, **8:10**
Storage of information, generally, **8:1**
Supervision, duty of, **8:5**

COMPETENCE
Generally, **2:2**

Index-1

CONFIDENTIALITY
Generally, **3:1 to 3:5**
Assistants and their duty to keep quiet, **3:5**
Cloud Computing, this index
Duties are not changed, **3:3**
Inadvertent disclosure, **8:6, 9:7**
Metadata, **8:13**
Postings never die, **3:4**
Two facets, **8:6**
Unauthorized disclosures, **8:6**
Wireless networks, **8:15**

COPIES
Advertisements, **5:15**

CRIMINAL CONDUCT
Misconduct, **1:5**

CRIMINAL DEFENSE
Advertising, blogs, **5:5**

DAILY-DEAL WEBSITES
Solicitations, **6:5**

DECEIT
Fraud, this index

DECORUM
Investigations, limits in jury situations, **4:3**

DEFRIENDING
Duty, **7:6**

DELAWARE RULES OF PROFESSIONAL CONDUCT
Text, **Appx A**

DILIGENCE
Generally, **2:3**

DIMINISHED CAPACITY
Solicitations, **6:1**

DIRECT MESSAGES
Solicitations, **6:3**

DISCLAIMERS
Advertising, **5:14**

DISCLAIMERS—Cont'd
Solicitations, **6:1, 6:2, 6:4, 6:7, 6:8**

DISCOVERY
Investigations, limits of lawyer's ability to obtain social media information, **4:2**

DOG BITES
Blogs, confidentiality, **3:3**

E-MAIL
Generally, **8:2**

ENCRYPTION
E-mails, **8:2**

ENDORSEMENTS
Advertising, **5:10**

ESCROW SERVICES
Generally, **7:7**

EX PARTE COMMUNICATIONS
Investigations, limits in jury situations, **4:3**

FEE SHARING
Solicitations, **6:5**

FIDUCIARY DUTY
Cloud computing, **8:4**

FIELDS OF PRACTICE
Advertising, **5:10**

FILING
Advertisements and solicitations, **5:3, 5:15**

FLASH DRIVES
Generally, **8:1**

FRAUD
Advertising, **5:9**
Investigations, limits of lawyer's ability to obtain social media information, **4:2**
Misconduct, **1:5**

INDEX

FUNDAMENTAL DUTIES
Generally, **2:1 to 2:5**
Check the chatter, **2:3**
Competence, **2:2**
Diligence, **2:3**
Professionalism, **2:5**
Supervision, **2:4**

FUTURE GUIDANCE
Generally, **9:1 to 9:10**
Client instructions and circumstances, **9:9**
Degree of sensitivity of information, **9:6**
Privileged or confidential information or work product, inadvertent disclosure of, **9:7**
Security afforded by technology, ability to assess level of, **9:2 to 9:4**
Technology permissibility factors, **9:10**
Third parties, legal ramifications regarding interception of information, **9:5**
Urgency of situation, **9:8**

HACKING
Investigations, limits of lawyer's ability to obtain social media information, **4:2**
Wireless networks, **8:15**

HELPFULNESS
Generally, **7:1 to 7:7**
Duty to defriend, **7:6**
Ignoring of not-so-hidden, hazardous realities of Internet, **7:7**
Jurisdiction, practicing outside of, **7:4**
Lawyer-client relationship, inadvertent establishment of, **7:3**
Unauthorized practice of law, **7:5**

HONESTY
Misconduct, **1:5**

HYPERLINK DISCLAIMERS
Solicitations, **6:7**

ICEROCKET
Confidentiality, postings never die, **3:4**

IMPARTIALITY
Investigations, limits in jury situations, **4:3**

INVESTIGATIONS
Generally, **4:1 to 4:3**
Jury situations, limits on investigations in, **4:3**
Limits of lawyer's ability to obtain social media information, **4:2**

IPADS
Generally, **8:16**

JURISDICTION
Practicing outside of jurisdiction, **7:4**

LAG TIME
Diligence, **2:3**

LAWYER-CLIENT RELATIONSHIP
Inadvertent establishment, **7:3**

LAWYER RATING SITES
Advertising, **5:13**

LIBRARY OF CONGRESS
Confidentiality, postings never die, **3:4**

MANIPULATION
Investigations, limits of lawyer's ability to obtain social media information, **4:2**

MATERIALITY
Advertising, **5:9, 5:10**

METADATA
Generally, **8:13**

MISCONDUCT
Generally, **1:5**

MISREPRESENTATION
Fraud, this index

Index-3

MOBILE STORAGE DEVICES
Generally, **8:1**

MULTIJURISDICTIONAL PRACTICE OF LAW
Generally, **7:4**

NON-LAWYER ASSISTANTS
Professionalism, **2:5**
Supervision, **2:4**

PAYMASTER SERVICES
Generally, **7:7**

POSTS
Advertising, **5:8, 5:9**

PRIVILEGED INFORMATION
Generally, **3:6**
Inadvertent disclosure, **9:7**

PROFANITY
Professionalism, **2:5**

PROFESSIONALISM
Generally, **2:5**

PROFILES
Advertising, **5:4**

RATING SITES
Advertising, **5:13**

REAL-TIME ELECTRONIC CONTACT
Solicitations, **6:9**

SENSITIVITY OF INFORMATION
Degree of sensitivity, **9:6**

SMART PHONES
Generally, **8:16**

SNOWDEN, EDWARD
Confidentiality, postings never die, **3:4**

SOLICITATIONS
Generally, **6:1 to 6:9**
Changes in technology, **6:6**
Daily-deal websites, **6:5**
Direct messages, **6:3**

SOLICITATIONS—Cont'd
Disclaimers, **6:1, 6:2, 6:4, 6:7, 6:8**
Hyperlink disclaimers, **6:7**
Real-time electronic contact, **6:9**
Rule regarding solicitations, generally, **6:1, 6:2**
Specific words of disclaimers, **6:8**
Text messages, **6:4, 6:6, 6:7**
Theory of rule, **6:1**

SOURCES OF GUIDANCE
Generally, **1:2**

SPECIALIZATION
Advertising, **5:10**

STATE OF AWARENESS
Heightened state, **1:4**

SUPERVISION
Generally, **2:4**
Extension of duty, **8:5**

SYSTEMATIC AND CONTINUOUS PRESENCE
Unauthorized practice of law, **7:5**

TESTIMONIALS
Advertising, **5:10**

TEXT MESSAGES
Generally, **8:12**
Advertising, **5:7**
Solicitations, **6:4, 6:6, 6:7**

THERAPY
Blogs, confidentiality, **3:3**

THIRD PARTIES
Legal ramifications regarding interception of information, **9:5**

TRICKERY
Investigations, limits of lawyer's ability to obtain social media information, **4:2**

UNAUTHORIZED PRACTICE OF LAW
Generally, **7:5**

UNDERSTANDING
 Emerging affirmative duty to understand, anticipate and act, **8:7**

URGENCY
 Future guidance, **9:8**

VIDEOS
 Advertising, **5:16**

VIGILANTES
 Confidentiality, **3:3**

VIRTUAL OFFICES
 Generally, **8:14**
 Solicitations, hyperlink disclaimers, **6:7**

VIRTUAL OFFICES—Cont'd
 Unauthorized practice of law, **7:5**

VOICE-TEXTING
 Solicitations, **6:6**

VULNERABILITY
 Solicitations, **6:1**

WAIVER
 Privileged or confidential information or work product, inadvertent disclosure of, **9:7**

WIRELESS NETWORKS
 Generally, **8:15, 8:16**

WORK PRODUCT
 Inadvertent disclosure, **9:7**